W9-ASD-433

Contents

FROM THE EDITOR

Yogi Berra is credited with saying, "When you come to a fork in the road, take it." This year the *Profession* staff and Advisory Committee came to just such a fork and decided that the journal should have a new design. *Profession 1996* is therefore longer than previous issues have been, partly because of the change in format and partly because the journal includes a substantial MLA commission report. The essays in this issue identify other, more important forks in the road, all involving choices that MLA members should consider. Topics include changes in the funding of higher education, a poor job market, promising developments in interdisciplinary studies, the proposed diminished role of literature in the secondary school curriculum, and the difficulties of teachers and students who wish to express religious views in their classes or to study subjects some members of the profession do not value.

Because shifts in the financial support of higher education are central to many articles in *Profession 1996*, some background information may be helpful. After much speculation and debate about who or what is responsible for the recent decline in funding for higher education, we now have a study that identifies a key cause of the depressed academic job market that is affecting the sciences as well as the humanities. Writing for the Center for the Study of the States at the Nelson A. Rockefeller Institute of Government, Steven D. Gold and Sarah Ritchie report that "significant changes occurred in state spending patterns during the first four years of this decade" ("How State Spending Patterns Have Been Changing," *State Fiscal Brief* 31 [Dec. 1995] 1). From 1990 through 1994, state spending for medicaid and corrections increased, while funds for higher education declined, along with support for other state programs, including transportation, economic development, housing, the environment, and parks and recreation. Gold and Ritchie caution against concluding that these shifts necessarily reflect changing priorities. To determine priorities, they say, one would have to analyze the "factors that influence spending," assessing, for example, the effects of federal aid and mandates. Even so, on one point their report is painfully clear: higher

1

education "was the big loser in the battle for state resources" in the first years in this decade (2).

Gold and Ritchie suggest that the trends they have discerned will persist. Medicaid costs are difficult to project, but they are not likely to decrease. Similarly, spending for corrections is likely to continue to rise, both because citizens appear "increasingly willing to spend public funds on building jails and housing prisoners" and because the prison population is expected to grow "more than 30% between 1995 and 2000" (3). Gold and Ritchie also argue that "since tuition and fee increases can compensate for part of state budget reductions, state colleges and universities will probably receive a less than proportional share of budget increases" (3, 6). Vying for state funds in the years ahead will be medicaid, corrections, elementary and secondary education, higher education, other state programs, and new needs imposed by welfare reform (6). In short, the competition for state funds promises to be more, not less, severe. The situation in the United States is not unique. Meeting this summer, the members of the International Association of University Presidents considered funding as their major challenge ("Around the World, A Myriad of Issues Confront Colleges," *Chronicle of Higher Education* [2 Aug. 1996] A32).

The first set of essays in *Profession 1996* examines the effects of the decline in public support and proposes ways of responding to it. J. Hillis Miller points to transnational corporations as a new source of funding for research universities and asks what effects such support will have on the college curriculum and on higher education's traditional commitment to carry out research that may not have immediate practical uses. He urges us to consider these questions and to reflect on how we can justify not only the study and teaching of languages and literature but also what Miller calls our "product of value": "new readings, new ideas." Like Miller, Leroy F. Searle asserts the value of faculty work and intellectual freedom and argues that his generation's style of debate and assumptions about institutions are no longer effective. He proposes a new approach to local "political" action.

Claire Gaudiani and Linda Ray Pratt focus on human relations in a period of financial stress. Gaudiani asks faculty members to protect academic values so that higher education does not become "just another modern machine grinding at the human soul," but she warns that the interests of particular academic departments may not match the changing needs of particular institutions. Hard times, she suggests, will doubtless require difficult decisions. Pratt discusses proposed changes in institutional management that encourage shared decision making; even these promising models, she says, will not eliminate the need for faculty members and administrators to negotiate differences in constructive ways. Cary Nelson proposes that the MLA undertake an aggressive lobbying effort in behalf of higher education at both state and federal levels. This goal can be achieved, Nelson says, by redefining aspects of the MLA's mission, governance, and activities. The final essay in this section of *Profession* puts the problems we face in a strikingly different perspective: Christopher Jon Delogu describes recent pressures on French universities.

The second cluster of essays concerns employment, both outside and within the academy. Mark A. Johnson writes enthusiastically about his experience in a software company, and Alison T. Smith describes the advantages of teaching in a private high school. Nona Fienberg gives advice to job seekers who want to teach in departments that focus on undergraduate programs, and the academic officers of a group of colleges and universities (the Commonwealth Partnership) outline what they look for in new faculty members. In "Queer Studies and the Job Market" Jon Harned brings together three brief essays. Gregory W. Bredbeck considers the decisions facing job seekers who specialize in gay and lesbian studies, María C. González discusses "comfort zones" and expectations about comraderie in academic departments, and Shelton Waldrep proposes questions that members of search committees should ask themselves about departmental support for faculty members who work "at the margins." In the last essay in this section, John Guillory provides an important context for viewing the job market and for assessing several related—and what may ultimately be self-defeating—professional practices.

Faculty work is the subject of the third group of *Profession* articles. Catharine R. Stimpson takes up a topic that many MLA members discussed this year: public intellectuals and the obligations of faculty members to the public. Michael Holquist describes promising new intellectual partnerships between humanists and social scientists, as scholars outside our field increasingly recognize the importance of understanding culture and therefore the importance of literary scholarship and language study. He concludes that we have much to learn from working across disciplines and professions. The next three essays respond to preliminary drafts of the content standards for the teaching of English in the public schools prepared by the National Council of Teachers of English and the International Reading Association. Concerned because the draft standards give little—and very limited—attention to the study of literature in the secondary school curriculum, Sandra M. Gilbert, then MLA's first vice president, organized a session at the 1995 NCTE convention at which these papers were presented. Charles Muscatine considers former and current connections between advanced work in literary study and what is taught in the schools. Noting that multiculturalism "is deeply congenial to widely held ideas about education's role in a democracy," he also observes that other developments in the field are less appropriate for the school curriculum and may have led to the elimination—in both the draft and the final document—of a "careful, disciplined reading of literature." Martha Banta demonstrates through an account of her own classroom practices that she is a "firm believer in the need for students to acquire a solid grasp of . . . how literature works." Borrowing several of E. D. Hirsch's terms and concepts, Gilbert proposes a new term—"literary literacy"—that she believes goes beyond cultural literacy and can lead to a "true education" in literature.

Emphasizing the ongoing importance of the humanities and an "open-ended" approach to education, Joseph R. Urgo, who chairs the department of English and humanities at a business college, reports that the American Assembly of Collegiate Schools of Business has adopted new accreditation standards that will require undergraduates to take more credits in the liberal arts and fewer in business courses. This change has made his department a partner in the redevelopment of the college's general education program. M. D. Walhout discusses a very different topic. Noting that the secularization of higher education in the United States has led to the elimination of religious perspectives from the college classroom, he joins other scholars in asking for "the freedom to express religious viewpoints while observing the procedural rules of academic discourse." Walhout shows how Gerald Graff's program for teaching the conflicts can be used to introduce religious viewpoints. In a response to Walhout's proposal, Graff recognizes the special problems the secularization of higher education poses for church-based institutions and the difficulties associated with the expression of religious views and indicates his preference for open discussion of the issue. Finally, Beverly Lyon Clark asks us to consider a common professional prejudice about the study of children's literature as she describes the evolution of an unexpected shift in her career and scholarly interests.

Profession 1996 concludes with two committee reports on subjects that concern many MLA members. The first, "Making Faculty Work Visible: Reinterpreting Professional Service, Teaching, and Research in the Fields of Language and Literature," was developed by the Commission on Professional Service, which hopes to initiate discussions within the field and in departments about the nature of faculty work and our long-standing assumptions about its value. Because of the length of the report, the MLA Executive Council asked that an executive summary appear with the document. The second, "Guidelines for Evaluating Computer-Related Work in the Modern Languages," was prepared by the MLA Committee on Computers and Emerging Technologies in Teaching and Research for departments to use in hiring and assessing faculty achievements in these areas.

This issue of *Profession* poses tough questions for scholars and teachers, the field, and the MLA. Financial and other pressures from society, from colleges and universities, and from students call for a rethinking of professional practices that may no longer serve us very well. Determining and maintaining key principles and values as we engage in creative problem solving seems the order of the day. Fortunately, these are the very traits that a liberal arts education encourages. I thank the members of the Advisory Committee (Michael Bérubé,

Joan Ferrante, Marianne Hirsch, and John Kronik) and my colleagues on staff (David Laurence and Elizabeth Welles) for their thoughtful evaluations of the articles we received for *Profession 1996*. Because committee members judged more essays worthy of publication than even an expanded journal could accommodate, I take responsibility for making the final decisions about what to include in this year's publication. We all, however, welcome your responses to these articles and your essays for *Profession 1997*.

Phyllis Franklin

Literary Study in the Transnational University

J. HILLIS MILLER

The title of the Modern Language Association of America panel for which this statement was prepared asked a question: Do We Understand How Our Universities Should Be Governed? Presumably this includes such questions as the proper role of nontenured faculty members in decision making, the relation of department chairs to deans and other administrators, and so on. I ask a different question. Who does now govern our universities? By "now" I mean not only the time when new communication technologies—computers, e-mail, faxes, VCRs, videos, CD-ROMs, hypertexts, and "surfing on the Internet"— are fundamentally changing the ways humanistic scholars interact and do their work. I mean also the time when the cold war has ended, when the power and integrity of nation-states are weakening, when economic and cultural systems are being globalized, and when the university's mission is as a consequence being transformed. This change in the university is irreversible. It affects all branches and departments of the United States research university, but in different ways. Its effect on the teaching of national literatures is especially strong. Those who teach and do research in departments of national literatures have hardly begun to be aware of the way these changes alter their work, though a growing number of books and essays are addressing this task from many different perspectives.[1]

The lack of a unified national culture in the United States has made it especially easy to shift with the global decline in the nation-state's importance to a

The author is Distinguished Professor of English and Comparative Literature at the University of California, Irvine. A version of this paper was presented at the 1995 MLA convention in Chicago.

university modeled on the bureaucratic corporation. The answer to the question Who now governs our universities? is that universities are more and more coming to be governed, however invisibly or indirectly, by corporations. This major change will have incalculable effects on university teaching and research. Money is power, in this area as in others. As federal and state sources of funding are drastically reduced, both public and private universities are turning to corporations for funding. At my own university, the University of California at Irvine, corporate support means seeking money from pharmaceutical companies, computer companies, medical technology companies, parts of the so-called financial industry, media companies, and the like. These companies may be owned by Japanese, English, French, German, Korean, or Taiwanese corporations, or they may do much of their manufacturing or much of their sales outside the United States. In any case, they do not owe primary allegiance to a single nation-state. Moreover, they are not just any kind of corporation. They are companies that are participating in the worldwide transformation that we call the coming of the information age or, more negatively, the age when everything is turned into spectacle. Today, money is information, passed around like other bytes on the Internet, just as information is money. An unbroken continuum binds pharmaceutical companies that deal in medical prostheses controlled by computer chips or that depend on genetic research to computer companies that invent the hardware and software making it possible to store and circulate information, for example in genetic research, to banking and investment companies that exchange the sort of information we call money, to media companies that turn everything into spectacle in film, television, and video, controlling thereby what people think, what they buy, and how they vote.

So what's the difference? As long as we get the funding can we not go on about our business of teaching and research in more or less the same old way? Do the faculty and the administration not still govern the university, determine its curricula and its research priorities? Are we not skilled in taking the money and doing more or less what we want with it? Have not humanists always benefited from the affluence of scientific colleagues? To some degree the answer to all these questions is yes. Nevertheless, the shift from state and federal funding to transnational corporate funding is altering the research university and its governance more radically than many people yet recognize. The university is changing from being an educational state apparatus, in Althusser's term, or, more benignly, a place of critical and innovative thinking, into being one site among many others, perhaps an increasingly less important site, for the production and transfer of globally exchanged information.

If the secrecy demanded by university military research during the cold war was deplorable, a new kind of secrecy is invading our universities, the secrecy demanded by corporations as a quid pro quo for their support of research. The measure of research accomplishment will be more and more not the acquisition of new knowledge but productivity as defined by the corporations to whom the university is accountable. These corporations more and more will govern the university in the sense of setting its priorities. They will govern the university because they will own a bigger and bigger piece of it.

What will be the role of the humanities, more particularly language and literature study, in the new transnational university? Our role in the research university directly in the service of the nation was clear enough. The study of Western literature has traditionally been organized in our universities as a number of discrete departments, each devoted to the separate study of a single national literature. The dominant literature in each country is the one representing that nation's language and literary tradition. Does this paradigm still hold? What is happening today with the study of national literatures?

The Western research university in its modern form originated with the founding in the early nineteenth century of the University of Berlin. It was established according to the plan devised by Wilhelm von Humboldt. Such universities had as their primary role service to the nation-state, still nascent of course at that time in Germany. The nation-state was conceived as an organically unified culture with a single set of ideals and values enshrined in a unified philosophical tradition and national literature (or in a certain way of appropriating Greek and Latin literature). The university was to serve the nation-state in two ways: (1) as the place of critical thinking and research, finding out the truth about everything, giving everything its rationality, according to the Leibnizian formula that says nothing is without its reason; (2) as the place of education, formation, or *Bildung* where male citizens (they were all male then in the university) are inculcated, one might almost say "inoculated," with the basic values of a unified national culture. It was the business of the university to produce subjects of the state, in both senses of the word *subject*: as subjectivities and as citizens accountable to state power and capable of promulgating it. For Humboldt and his colleagues, following Kant, the basis of *Bildung* was the study of philosophy. Thus people with higher degrees are still, for the most part, called "doctors of philosophy," whatever the discipline in which they received the degree. This practice is something of an absurdity these days, since philosophy proper does not, to say the least, still have the role it did in German universities in the days of Kant, Fichte, and Hegel, while most PhDs in other fields know little or nothing about philosophy.

With some support from Schiller's *Letters on Aesthetic Education*, Anglo-Saxon countries in the mid-nineteenth century, first England and then the United States, deflected this paradigm in an important way by substituting literature for philosophy as the center of cultural indoctrination. Grounds for this shift already existed in the centrality granted to literary education by many German theorists: the Schlegels, Schelling, and Hegel, for example. The shift occurred in England and the United States to a considerable degree under the aegis of Matthew Arnold's formulations about culture and anarchy, about the study of poetry, and about the function of criticism. The modern United States research university has inherited the double mission of the Humboldtian university. This continuity was evident in the founding of the Johns Hopkins University in Baltimore in 1876. Johns Hopkins was based explicitly and self-consciously on the German university rather than on the English university model, though Thomas Henry Huxley, as an advocate for the new scientific English university, spoke at the inauguration of Johns Hopkins. The admirable proliferation of both public and private research universities in the United States followed soon after or was already taking place.

The Humboldtian concept of the university and of the place of national literature departments within the university lasted until quite recently, at least as an ideal, in the United States. It is now rapidly coming to an end. We are entering or have already entered an era in which new paradigms for the university will have to be found. The nation-state's existence as a unified entity is weakening through one form or another of globalization and the consequent eroding of its boundaries. It will be harder and harder to tell where France ends and Germany begins, even where the United States ends and Mexico begins. We shall all come to feel ourselves living on some margin, fringe, or borderland, at the periphery. At the same time the integrity of the nation-state is weakening in another way. The United States is a striking example. In spite of energetic attempts by conservative politicians and educationists to impose a single language and a single literary curriculum, United States cultural life is made up of diverse interpenetrating cultural communities speaking and writing in many different languages. These communities cannot easily be reconciled. Their sites are the loci of mutually incompatible goods. These values would be impossible to unify by some overarching idea of universal human "culture." Nor does any individual belong unequivocally to any one of these communities. In a few more years more than half the citizens of California will have English as a second language. A poll taken recently of kindergarten classes in Irvine, California, an upper-middle-class and homogeneous-looking city,[2] found that over twenty different languages were spoken in the homes of these children. They will grow up, like most Chicanos and Chicanas, or like most Asian Americans, divided within by participation in at least two incompatible cultures. The frequently used figure of "hybridity" to describe this situation is misleading. It implies that the hybrid individual participates in a mixed culture that is made by mating stable genes from the two sources. In fact the original cultures that are hybridized were by no means as stable or unified as an animal or plant species is. In any case, the melting pot is no longer hot enough or capacious enough to melt all this difference down. Each self is inhabited by its other or by an indeterminate number of "others," in plural swarming. No Habermasian dialogue, conversation, or communicative discourse could or should bring all this diversity back to consensus. The traditional single set of values transmitted by aesthetic education is now seen as what it always was: an ideological fabrication made to serve primarily the power of educated white middle- or upper-class heterosexual males.

What possible role can literary study have in the new technological transnational university? In the United States and in one degree or another in many other Western nations those responsible for funding higher education no longer believe that their nation needs the university in the way it once did. The primary evidence has been the cutting off of funds, almost always justified by budget constraints, as has happened in the past few years at the University of California. That university was until recently arguably the greatest research university in the world. Now it has been weakened by budget cuts and through early retirements made for many professors irresistibly attractive by "golden handshake" offers of retirement benefits. About two thousand professors have taken early retirement. This procedure is borrowed from the corporate world. Those who pay for the university no longer have the same confidence in the need for basic research as something directly funded by the nation (that is, the federal government) or by its subdivisions, the separate states of the United States. Basic research was in any case always largely supported as ancillary to the military buildup. With the end of the cold war came the end of the apparent need for many kinds of basic research. It is difficult for most humanities professors to accept that their prosperity in the 1960s, 1970s, and 1980s was as much a result of the cold war as was the prosperity of aircraft and weapons manufacturers or as was the space race that put men on the moon. Nevertheless, we were part of the military-industrial complex. The expensive development of humanities programs was an ancillary part of our need to be best at everything in order to defeat the Soviet Union in the cold war. This goal was made explicit in the legislation establishing the National Endowment for the Humanities. Now that the cold war is over, humanities programs are being "downsized" along with scientific parts of university research and teaching. The NEH survives today with greatly reduced funding and is threatened with extinction. The job situation for newly trained physicists is nearly as bad as it is for new PhDs in English. For the latter it is extremely bad.[3] What those in charge (legislators, trustees, granting agencies, university administrators, foundation officers, and corporation executives) need, or think they need, and therefore demand, is immediately applicable technology. The weakening of our space program and the killing of the superconducting supercollider project are salient demonstrations of this. Much applied research can be done just as well or better by computer or pharmaceutical companies and the like. These have been increasingly funding applied research inside the university, co-opting the university's scientific skills and laboratory facilities (often originally paid for by federal money) for research that is oriented toward the discovery of patentable procedures that will make the companies rich. The university in response to these radical changes is becoming more and more like a bureaucratic corporation itself, for example by being run by a corps of proliferating administrators whose bottom-line business, as in any bureaucracy, is to perpetuate themselves efficiently, even if this sometimes means large-scale "administrative cutbacks." Almost the first thing the new president of the University of California, Richard C. Atkinson, did when he took office in 1995 was to hire consultants from the corporate world to advise him on how to make the central administration more "productive." It is easy to see that the president's having applied the business-world model of productivity to his own bailiwick will justify his subsequently applying it also to the teaching and research activities that are the university's reason for being.

In a concomitant change, "society" (in the concrete form of legislators and corporations that give money to public universities and of trustees who manage and corporations that support private ones) also no longer needs the university in the old way to transmit national cultural values, however much such authorities may still pay lip service to this traditional role of humanities departments. The work of ideological indoctrination and training in consumerism, it is tacitly understood, can be done much more effectively by the media, by newspapers and magazines, by television and cinema. Moreover, these academic bureaucrats and legislators are not stupid. After what has happened in humanities departments from the 1960s on, they now no longer trust professors of literature to do what they used to do or even, the bureaucrats might claim, what they are hired to do. The cat is out of the bag. Whatever the protestations of those running the universities about the eternal values embodied in the Western canon, the news has got through to them that the actual culture of the United States is multifarious and multilingual. Moreover, they know now that you can no longer trust professors to teach Chaucer, Shakespeare, Milton, and the rest in the old ways. New ways of reading them have shown that these authors, read from a certain angle, as professors seem perversely inclined to do and to teach their students to do, are what some governing the university consider to be dynamite that might blow up the social edifice. So the more or less unconscious strategy is to welcome the self-destruction of the traditional literature departments as they shift to cultural studies and then gradually cut off the money. In public universities this is done in the name of financial stringency and the need to build more prisons and fund welfare programs. In private universities the attempt to control what is taught in the humanities is sometimes more direct and blatant. An example is the twenty-million-dollar gift to the humanities at Yale by Lee Bass, a member of a wealthy Texas oil family. He thought his gift would entail the right to choose the professors his money would endow and the curriculum they would teach. What is most sinister about this dark episode, from which Yale admirably extricated itself by ultimately returning the gift, is the possibility that Bass's naïveté was not in assuming that his money would give him some right to govern the university but in being so up-front about it. Most such control is exercised in more tactful, subtle, and indirect ways. In a related change, professors have less and less importance as public affairs experts, no doubt because the media that allow those authorities to speak no longer have confidence that the ones from within the university will say what they want to hear, just as Bass did not trust Yale to make appointments of which he would approve. The experts on public radio panels, for example, are more and more drawn from conservatively funded think tanks rather than from universities.

What should we do in this new situation? First, we should take stock of these changes and try to understand them. Second, we must begin to think out ways to justify what we do in the humanities to this new constituency. This task will not be at all easy, especially since corporation executives and officials have probably had their ideas about the humanities formed by the attacks on theory, "political correctness," women's studies, and multiculturalism in the media. We often start out with two strikes against us. Moreover, many of these funding sources as well as the university bureaucrats who govern for them may have a predisposition to think that the humanities are primarily of use to teach "communication skills." In the new research university rapidly coming into being it will be extremely difficult to justify what we do in the old way, that is, as the production of new knowledge, the *Wissenschaft* appropriate in the humanities, as new knowledge about living things is appropriate in biology. New knowledge about *Beowulf*, Shakespeare, Racine, Hugo, or even Emerson, William Carlos Williams, and Toni Morrison is not useful in the same way new knowledge about genes is when it leads to the making of a marketable medicine. Those corporation officers who will more and more control the university are likely to say they admire the production of new knowledge in the humanities. Their general unwillingness to give money to support such research indicates that they do not really mean it.

The product of value we make in the humanities is discourse of a particular kind: new readings, new ideas. Nicholas Negroponte argues this concept forcefully for the research university in general in a recent essay in *Wired*.[4] Such ideas inaugurate something new, something unheard of before. Another way to put this is to say that the university is the place where what really counts is the ungoverned, the ungovernable. The ungovernable does not occur all that often. Most of what goes on in the university is all too easily governed. In fact it is self-governing, as when we say a machine has a "governor" that keeps it from running too fast. It just turns round at a moderate speed and keeps repeating the same. Nevertheless, the university has as its reason for being establishing conditions propitious to the creation of the ungovernable. Only if we can persuade the new corporate governors of the university that such creations have indispensable utility are we likely to flourish in the new conditions. Doing that will take much patient thought and rhetorical skill. Meanwhile we must go on as best we can with the work of reading, writing, and teaching.

NOTES

[1]See, for example, Weber; Bergonzi; Elbow; Derrida; Graff, *Professing Literature* and *Beyond the Culture Wars*; Pelikan; Borrero Cabal; Judy; Easthope; Wilshire. Many of these are discussed by Readings.

[2]It is not really a city in the traditional sense: it has no center.

[3]According to Huber, only 45.9% of those who received a PhD in English in 1993–94 got a tenure-track job (48). See also Nelson's essays on the job wars. The essays by Bérubé and Watt, from the same issue of *Academe*, also discuss the current job market and the conditions of graduate study. For the job outlook for new PhDs in the physical sciences, see, in the same issue of *Academe*, Brill and Larson.

[4]Negroponte claims that research universities will have a crucial role in the new situation where companies rather than governmental agencies increasingly support universities. The companies will need the universities as the place where new ideas in all fields are developed. Quite correctly he sees that process as expensive in the sense that not all new ideas pan out, but, according to him, the pedagogical mission of the university (producing educated students) will carry that crucial innovative role along: ". . . companies have realized that they cannot afford to do basic research. What better place to outsource that research than to a qualified university and its mix of different people? This is a wake-up call to companies that have ignored universities—sometimes in their own backyards—as assets. Don't just look for 'well-managed' programs. Look for those populated with young people, preferably from different backgrounds, who love to spin off crazy ideas—of which only one or two out of a hundred may be winners. A university can afford such a ridiculous ratio of failure to success, since it has another more important product: its graduates." What Negroponte says is as true for the humanities as it is for the sciences. The challenge is to persuade those in charge of the value of new ideas in the humanities.

WORKS CITED

Althusser, Louis. "Ideology and Ideological State Apparatuses." *"Lenin and Philosophy" and Other Essays*. Trans. Ben Brewster. New York: Monthly Review, 1972. 127–86.

Bergonzi, Bernard. *Exploding English: Criticism, Theory, Culture*. Oxford: Oxford UP, 1990.

Bérubé, Michael. "Standard Deviation: Skyrocketing Job Requirements Inflame Political Tensions." *Academe* 81.6 (1995): 26–29.

Borrero Cabal, Alfonso. *The University as an Institution Today*. Paris: UNESCO, Intl. Development Research Center, 1993.

Brill, Arthur S., and Daniel J. Larson. "Are We Training Our Students for Real Jobs?" *Academe* 81.6 (1995): 36–38.

Derrida, Jacques. *Du droit à la philosophie*. Paris: Galilée, 1990.

Easthope, Anthony. *Literary into Cultural Studies*. London: Routledge, 1991.

Elbow, Peter. *What Is English?* New York: MLA; Urbana: NCTE, 1990.

Graff, Gerald. *Beyond the Culture Wars: How Teaching the Conflicts Can Revitalize American Education*. New York: Norton, 1992.

————. *Professing Literature: An Institutional History*. Chicago: U of Chicago P, 1987.

Huber, Bettina J. "The MLA's 1993–94 Survey of PhD Placement: The Latest English Findings and Trends through Time." *ADE Bulletin* 112 (1995): 40–51.

Judy, Ronald A. T. *(Dis)Forming the American Canon: African-Arabic Slave Narratives and the Vernacular*. Minneapolis: U of Minnesota P, 1993.

Negroponte, Nicholas. Column. *Wired* Jan. 1996: 204.

Nelson, Cary. "Lessons from the Job Wars: Late Capitalism Arrives on Campus." *Social Text* 13.3 (1995): 119–34.

————. "Lessons from the Job Wars: What Is to Be Done?" *Academe* 81.6 (1995): 18–25.

Pelikan, Jaroslav. *The Idea of the University: A Reexamination*. New Haven: Yale UP, 1992.

Readings, Bill. *The University in Ruins*. Cambridge: Harvard UP, 1996.

Watt, Stephen. "The Human Costs of Graduate Education; or, The Need to Get Practical." *Academe* 81.6 (1995): 30–35.

Weber, Samuel. *Institution and Interpretation*. Minneapolis: U of Minnesota P, 1987.

Wilshire [Wiltshire], Bruce. *The Moral Collapse of the University: Professionalism, Purity, and Alienation*. Albany: State U of New York P, 1990.

Institutions and Intellectuals: A Modest Proposal

LEROY F. SEARLE

Not long ago, after the awards ceremony at the annual dean's dinner at the University of Washington, I overheard a woman about my age, lingering in her seat, say to her companion, "I just want to sit here for a while. It's been a long time since I sat in a lecture hall, and it feels good." Though the remark was simple, it seemed to encapsulate a mythology and folklore about universities that are intimately connected to public support for higher education. Here was a woman, obviously a friend of the institution, indulging a mild and pleasant nostalgia for college as she remembered it, though I suspect that she knew very little about the university as it is today or about how much trouble is in store for it.

Having never left the lecture halls, I still remember the feeling, though it is increasingly crowded out by the bureaucratic complexities of academic work and contemporary worries precisely over the question of public support. How we respond to institutions is a large part of what shapes them; and in these days of frontal assaults on universities, there may be no more complicated problem than remembering how to defend them—a far different thing than just attacking the attackers. Remembering the pleasure of sitting in a lecture hall doesn't cut it.

While I was preparing this discourse, trying to find the right ironic tone, amusing but with an edge, my own university was just concluding a budget reduction, nothing on the order of the 12% we lost in the early 1980s or the 7% lost over the last several years: a mere 2.4%, required in order to meet the strictures of a referendum passed by the taxpayers to limit the growth of state

The author is Associate Professor of English and Comparative Literature and Director of the Center for the Humanities at the University of Washington.

spending. The cumulative effect was that seven entire programs were reviewed for elimination (four in the humanities). This 2.4% broke more than the camel's back. The damage of those reviews, to say nothing of the four programs eliminated and the others slashed to the bone, will take perhaps a decade to heal, even if things go well in budgetary terms. And no one expects that.

While there is nothing amusing in this, there is irony abounding, a political irony, compounded by the stunning failure of the generation to which I belong (which has always thought of itself as political above all) to attend effectively to the political sphere in which we actually live and work. In the 1960s, almost everyone learned the style of attack, confrontation, demand, a style that makes backing down, when it is time to back down, exceptionally hard to do. The rough drafts of my speech that kept filling the wastebasket, for example, all seemed to turn into Jeremiads, sometimes veering toward Patmos and the juicy rhetoric of the apocalypse.

Universities need defending more than they ever have, but the language for doing it has not only fallen into disuse, it has been so thoroughly deconstructed that it now seems just an empty pack of signifiers. Part of the problem is the mythology that depicts colleges sentimentally, as places where young people experiment and stir things up before going off to lives where the nostalgia for an artificial freedom intensifies as grown-up constraints of the real world multiply. Irony is essential, therefore, to melt away some of the illusions, so that we can keep in sight the real freedom that intellectual work requires—and the real constraints that affect the large and bumbling institutions where it is mainly carried out. The privilege of intellectual freedom depends on remembering that the university is in every way a part of the real world, which gets incomparably worse when universities and colleges decline.

For a dozen years or so, I have occupied a series of low- to midlevel administrative jobs, affording the maximum degree of power with the minimum degree of responsibility, but at the cost of taking up an ungodly amount of time and energy in the midst of a fairly full teaching schedule. In other words, I have successfully avoided serving as a department chair, though I have succumbed to being the director of a number of programs. It is partly for this reason, and partly to remind myself of the peculiarity of intellectual institutions, that I keep close at hand the last book I know of to achieve that light, ironic touch on such matters, Hazard Adams's *The Academic Tribes*. Adams explains first that universities are liable to be compared to "businesses or some mode of civil service," whereas the apposite analogy is to "political organizations, microscopic nations of a very special sort" (2). In the mode of ironic sociology, Adams goes on to explain the academy, giving accounts of administration, stereotypical views of academic life (e.g., the Good Life, the Detached Life, the Absurd Life, the Nonlife), academic style, and the rhythm of the academic year, all punctuated with eminently quotable aphorisms and memorable phrases. I have even tried my hand at formulating an aphorism or two, bearing a vague family resemblance to Adams's "Principles of Faculty-Administration Polity" or the "Antinomies of Pure Administration."

There is, for example, my *Axiom of Academic Hierarchy*, asserting that for every step up the academic ladder, you lose power,[1] or the *Lemma of Administrative Innocence*, to which I am especially partial, describing the forgiving attitude one should take toward a brand-new administrator who does not yet know that her main job is not to Do Good but to prevent awful things from happening. These two, after some years of dialectical interaction, produced the *First Scholium on Administrative Corruption*, which lays out the essential quality required for administrative survival: the ability to "double-track" one's colleagues. That is, never forget that some persons you may respect, admire, even love don't have a lick of practical sense and must be (ever so gently) prevented from demonstrating it, to the detriment of the department and their own hurt. The *Scholium* goes on to explain why double-tracking almost inevitably backfires on the administrator who is practicing it, to produce rampant symptoms of cynicism (if not downright schizophrenia) and inevitable self-loathing: the administrator who double-tracks his colleagues commonly gets double-tracked himself.

None of my aphorisms, however, came close to the charm of Adams's description of rituals of the tribe: the job search—"*Trial by Fire*"; the convention interview—"*Trial by Ice*"; the campus visit—"*Trial by Sword and Stone*"; and the tenure review—"*Trial by Innuendo*" (78–91). So I leave the field of Ironic Sociology and Academic Stereotypics to him, with gratitude and best wishes. Even so, the problem is still there: how to carry out a defense of the university without being merely defensive and how to make clear that the issue is, through and through, too urgent politically for the familiar partisan bickering. This much is clear: one has to start by acknowledging the monumental ineptitude of these large and usually bovine institutions, admitting with as much good humor as current budget negotiations will allow how often the principle of intellectual freedom protects crackpots and cranks or permits really stupid ideas to gain the temporary assent of a lot of good people.

While the limit of irony may be a state of immediate and practical urgency (just as the prospect of execution tends to concentrate the mind), we need a sense of irony all the more when we are faced with problems of judgment but do not agree on the criteria for making them. Our universities are in trouble, inside and out, at the very moment when there is no clear picture of what they are and no consensus about what they are for. During the period of unprecedented growth starting in the late 1950s and early 1960s, which greatly expanded state universities, offering access to education for a burgeoning middle-class population brought great pressure to shape the universities as vocational schools; but the far greater and more successful pressure was to treat the universities as places for research and advanced study. (The former pressure emerged naturally from the desire of individuals to get on in the world; the latter from the megaversion of that desire among universities to get famous and among corporations to get rich.) Federal and private money for research, especially applied research, has so dramatically changed the structure of large universities that it is difficult, for many reasons, just to offer the general courses that are required of all students.[2]

The particular irony I want to address, however, is that such problems are more political than financial. Despite predictable increases in the population that needs access to higher education, the construction of new universities has all but stopped and budgets are being cut everywhere—just when the production of wealth in the United States is at an all-time high, creating not only obscene personal fortunes but equally obscene poverty and privation in what is coming to look like a permanent underclass. People in the middle are doing, more or less, OK. But we all find ourselves saddled with a profoundly stupid notion of what it means to be political, a notion that pervasively deflects analysis and corrupts political discourse all across the spectrum. I mean the tactics of opposition and the denunciatory strategies of making stridently self-righteous critiques of The System as if it were everywhere and always in the wrong. These strategies and tactics, improvised and perfected in our last great uprising of outrage, the 1960s, took on The System with all the fervor of the Puritans, who knew (to paraphrase George Santayana) not merely that evil exists; it is also good for evil to exist in order that it might be properly punished. In structural terms, politics as protest incorporates a still more vitiating illusion (making the very notion of being co-opted redundant), since the protester, opposing the bad guys, has already conceptually relinquished power to the opponent by assuming that there is some person, some corporate or institutional body, or perhaps just some evil cabal out there that already has the power to satisfy the demands of the righteous.

For my generation, it was institutional racism, neocolonial wars, corporate and environmental rapacity, and the suppression of women that showed the shape of evil, confirmed for us by the powerful idea that evil arises when people are not left free to pursue their own destinies. But our contest against wickedness produced the staged event, the protest as a form of street theater, the sit-in, which are all scriptable happenings that have no inherent tie to any particular notion of the good. For middle-class liberals who contracted the habit of thinking of themselves as radicals, it is hard to recognize these forms of action as the triumph of the idea of liberation when they return in the hands of religious fundamentalists, neo-Nazis, ethnic purists, and reactionaries of all sorts. The current versions of Nietzsche's *Übermensch* seem to be "right to life" activists blowing up women's health clinics, neoconservative members of Congress intent on dismantling the federal infrastructure of social welfare and environmental protection, and really scary groups that have taken up terror where the Weather Underground and the Yippies left off, with hijackings, assassinations, fertilizer bombs, and apocalyptic shoot-outs in virtually every corner of the world. But nowhere has terror produced one iota more justice than there was before.

We are witnessing a remarkable moment that demands reflection, under conditions alarming and violent enough to almost preclude reflection. On both sides of polarized confrontations, the common conviction is that our institutions—our systems or establishments—are rotten and deserve to be taken apart. It is no mere swing of the pendulum that the complaints and tactics mobilized worldwide by young people in the 1960s on behalf of liberty are now deployed out of fear and racial and ethnic hatred to protect the perceived interests of limited groups or classes. It is a symptom of a harder intellectual problem that bears in the most fundamental way on the idea of politics itself: political action can be taken only by individuals, but all political events are institutional. Events may be inflected by but are not governed by individual convictions.

I do not mean that politics has nothing to do with morality, but the moralizing of politics since the 1960s has only shown us the wide and destructive range of actions that are possible when people believe in the impeccable virtue of their own positions. Universities as political institutions are unusually susceptible to damage, not merely because they evolve and change over cycles about equal to a generation, barely perceived by the people who stay for intervals of four or five years. Universities can be hurt precisely because they do have a moral function in people's experience, but they exist in a fragile relation to the other established institutions of society, a relation that depends fundamentally on collective trust and mutual goodwill. Universities are meant to make us free—at the least, free of the moral dogmatism that seems to be the natural state of the seventeen-year-old. Events have shown that people don't automatically grow out of that state unless the adequacy of their ideas and convictions is put to an intellectual and practical test.

People of my generation went to college with a charmingly literal belief in university folklore and mythology. Universities were supposed to be beacons of light in a dark world and by that fact alone should be able to prevent folly, ameliorate suffering, or otherwise directly affect the world of practical events for the better. The all but universal discovery that things don't work that way quickly transformed a loss of innocence into a search for guilt: What is the university doing on behalf of social justice and against wickedness in high places? The general absence of a convincing answer suggested that the university was no different from other social institutions. In other words, it was amoral if not deeply corrupt, and furthermore it was already co-opted by a larger and more sinister economic geopolitical system. The large abstractions common to such judgments are more malleable than local realities, in no small part because they permit us to congratulate ourselves for being insightful without having to think very hard about immediate problems.

This is a fundamental dilemma that attends all efforts to think historically. At the moment of an apparently decisive event, we do not see the historical lag or wrinkle in the sheet of temporality, where institutions (unlike persons) are affected not by what happened yesterday or last year but by actions a generation old. Thirty years ago, administrators in consternation over student uprisings invoked such euphemisms as "unrest" or treated riots as mere symptoms of postadolescent rebellion void of political or historical meaning.[3] Everyone was too busy looking ahead: new campuses were opening across the country as the direct consequence of the public commitment and political will of the previous generation but reflecting the paradoxical moral optimism of the United States as a world leader during the cold war era, when even good actions were undertaken in the name of fear.[4] But at that very time, dealing with disturbances (usually by repressive means) provoked more disturbances and tended to interrupt the process of careful, specific planning for the next generation. The next generation is here, and we are simply not ready for it.

Everyone recognizes that universities are today in a very real and immediate crisis, given the decline of public funding and support (both national and local) just when the need for quality education is deep and urgent. Alas, people within the universities have contributed to the collapse of public support, not just by endorsing a critical rhetoric that treats the university as some kind of enemy (it is, after all, part of "The System") but also by ignoring the details of local institutional histories in the pursuit of radical critiques of power. In the imaginative equivalent of Gresham's law, bad stories drive out good, and the chief characteristic of good stories, in this context, is their capacity to explain why our institutions are as they are and how they got that way. Ironically, on the left and the right, the one story we have been dead set on telling propagates preposterous analyses of historico-political institutions as fundamentally, irretrievably, and cynically corrupt. Even Newt Gingrich proclaims himself a revolutionary in his own assault on the system, perhaps not realizing that he merely parodies the rhetoric of the old New Left. Examples like this offer a sobering reflection of what it means when such language is adopted by reactionaries a good deal less sedentary and even farther to the right than Congressman Gingrich. Isn't it time for us to develop a better way to think about politics?

I suggest that universities add a new graduation requirement, an explicitly political requirement, for all our undergraduates. It would, of course, be wonderful if we could first require all faculty members to meet it too, but that would render my suggestion not so much political as wildly utopian. The requirement is simply that students study, in detail, the history of the institution where they pursue a degree. They need to know how it is funded and how it is governed. They need to know the story of the place, with enough narrative particularity to recognize that what surrounds them was built step by step and is not part of some Transcendental Fiat that merely called it forth.

A proximate historical legacy (and curse) of our time is that a significant fraction among the teaching faculty already believe they have imposed a political requirement, such that the classroom, always a scene of moral suasion, becomes an explicit place for training the troops in whatever war of position the faculty member believes himself or herself to be waging.[5] Among my colleagues at the University of Washington and elsewhere there are any number who could offer elegant and incisive accounts of the effects, for example, of global capitalism on the teaching of language and literature (it's bad) but haven't a clue about where the money for the Xerox machine comes from or what happens to the leave recapture money when they take a sabbatical.

The point of my political requirement is suggested by another slogan from the 1960s, "Think globally but act locally." The problem is that thinking globally is so easy and exciting to do that it never trickles down to the local level. In practice, my new requirement would be more like "Think locally before you act at all." For a number of years I have taken the liberty, when there is some disturbance on campus to which many students feel called (as I myself felt called), to offer students the option of going out to join the demonstration, confrontation, march, or what have you or devoting the class period to talking about the issues apparently at stake. So far, the students have overwhelmingly opted to stay and talk, and almost always, the discussion turns to very local matters.

What I have learned from this exercise is alarming and I think very revealing. It turns out that most of my students believe that the State of Washington collects an income tax (there is none) and that their tuition pays from half to two-thirds of the costs of their education (it's about 11% of the budget). In the most recent in-class forum, to my astonishment, ninety-eight of one hundred students were not aware that the second most important tax in the State of Washington (after the sales tax) is the Business and Occupations tax—indeed, only three students had ever heard of this tax, which is levied on the gross dollar volume of business transactions (so that Boeing or Microsoft pay roughly the same rate as the Mom and Pop grocery store on the corner). Only one student (he had run his own business) even knew what it was. Thus there was no way for them to know that state funding, under such a scheme, makes the general fund (from which university budgets derive) go up and down like a yo-yo according to patterns of consumer spending and levels of business activity, so that it is almost impossible for any state office or agency to do sensible fiscal planning. My students also had no clear picture of how the university is organized into colleges, no idea about who makes personnel decisions, and no understanding at all of the legal agreements and covenants under which the university operates.

In short, my very bright and most engaging undergraduates are, in local terms, political know-nothings. They don't know where they are. They don't understand the conditions that enable them to be where they are. Neither their public school teachers nor their parents (the same parents who voted for the tax-limiting initiative, no doubt) have bothered to tell them anything practical about the political conditions that shape their lives immediately and will indirectly influence their capacity to make reasonable political judgments about issues that may not register in the dialectical scales of world history but will affect the ability of schools and universities to even keep their doors open. When I reflect on what my colleagues appear to know, most of whom have been ever so much more insulated from administrative drudgery than I have, deep gloom descends upon me.

Intellectuals of my generation, shocked into criticism by a swarm of disasters, have invested so much in sweeping theories that the localities in which we work virtually disappear. I return therefore to the paradoxical principle of academic hierarchy, that the farther up the ladder you go, the more power you lose. Following our diverse puritanical dogmas, we have sought to liberate or empower our students by teaching them to distrust and detest the very institutions in which and through which they are being taught, protected, and nurtured. It ought not to surprise us that we are now in a large crisis, largely of our own making: for a generation, our students have learned the lesson of distrust too well. We have not recognized that our students already have power; what they lack is the understanding, information, and experience by which to connect their minds and imaginations to the mundane, everyday circumstances they confront both as students and as citizens.

One of the few politically meaningful things we can do right now is teach students about the structure and funding of the university they attend, not in the hyped-up and morally incendiary terms of current theory, but in terms of the very simple historical and fiscal facts by which modest but actual power flows in and through the system that currently affects their daily lives. We in the intellectual professions have in manifold ways undercut our own credibility by supposing that the only locus for theory is, if not transcendental, at least elsewhere: in the past, in the Third World, in the mysterious seats of power, always in the form of something ominous or dramatic. Following the new puritanism of the left, we court a fashionable theoretical difficulty: Master this vocabulary and these analytical moves, and you will feel empowered to indict wickedness in high places as if you were really there. The new puritanism of the right contemns these abstract niceties in favor of moral toughness and theoretical reductiveness: Face up to the fact that government is evil and that you yourself can act to dismantle it—and make history without even having to think about it. Both these dramas end in catastrophe: the abstract morality play of the left renounces any possible way to take meaningful political action, while the reductive and concrete moralism of the right renounces any nuanced understanding of political reality by taking direct action on one's moral convictions. This only brings on bloody tragedies that subvert the rule of law by encouraging true believers to take the law into their own hands.

Choosing the middle way, I am arguing for a kind of political education that almost certainly would not be perceived, in the present climate, to be such: to focus, with care and patience, on how things happen, in fact, right where you are. We need to study, with our students, in unglamorous and empirical terms how the institutions we partly claim as our own got to be the way they are. We do not need prior recourse to grand abstractions like Labor, Capital, Identity, Race, Religion, Gender, or Class, because those abstractions will emerge on their own, though not necessarily in the form of any of the grand synoptic narratives that we have been telling ourselves in postmodern fashion have all collapsed anyway. In all the cases where I have sought them, the local stories turn out to be more comic than otherwise; they preserve, in their own hearts of darkness, possibilities not at all remote; they offer real access to power—most immediately, the power of our students, who already work, vote, run for office, and will send their children to college.

The job seems to be fairly simple: let them know, from the first day they appear on campus, that the story of the place is going to be, in a significant and immediate way, their story too. Let them know that if they want something from the place, it is worth the effort to find out how it really works; let them know this without recourse to general moral and political principles that invite students to judge social institutions prematurely. If they find, on examination, that the present way of doing things is flawed, deficient, cumbersome, or wrong, they are fully competent to recognize that institutions are put together by real people who are not perfect, adequate, graceful, and right on all occasions and in all modes. They can learn in the same way that institutions are open to being changed by people who try to do better.

If we opt for the high rhetorical way, we may please ourselves as theory makers and perpetuate the folklore and mythology of the university as a place so austere, removed, and spiritual that people later feel nostalgia for the lecture hall instead of feeling a real commitment to the health and well-being of an actual and changing institution. But if we take that way—certainly, it is the way my generation took—we should not be that surprised to discover, too late, perhaps just one or two budget cuts away, that we have been deeply and foolishly complicit—on high principles, of course—in running with our students over the edge of the cliff, leaving behind colleges that will not have anything particularly valuable to offer anyone. Though it makes me suspicious, given my training, to conclude on this note, the alternative seems to me not gloomy at all. If we undertake to theorize our universities and colleges, our own departments and programs, my guess is that we will find, amidst the wreckage, a still hardy commitment to the intellectual good, to the value of thought in specific relation to immediate lives that has always made the feeling of sitting in a lecture hall not just nostalgia but the recognition and recovery of something good.

NOTES

An earlier version of this paper was delivered as a lecture 6 May 1995 at the University of Washington, for the Honor Society parents' weekend.

[1] This principle, related to Adams's dictum that an administrator's power begins to decay from the point of the first administrative decision, has so great a feeling of paradox about it that it appeals, perhaps, to the formalist ghosts of my ancestors. Surely, one thinks, *that must be wrong*. But wait: taken literally, my axiom indicates that students, at the ostensible bottom, are the most powerful—as indeed they are. Without them, the universities would cease to be educational institutions. But being students, normally both ignorant and inexperienced, they do not know how to use the power they do not know they have. The corollary is that if they *did* know how to use that power, nothing could stop them. About once a generation, a whiff of this great truth enters the population like a drug (as it did in the mid-1960s), inducing students to simply seize power. Being inexperienced and ignorant, however, they make a hash of it, leaving confusion in their wake for about thirty years, until the next wave is due. I'm expecting one any month now.

[2] The problem is not merely that faculty positions have generally followed the money, to the disadvantage of teaching faculties in the humanities and social sciences. It is also that the very notion of what ought to be required is in disarray, while ideas about what should be expected of faculty members who might be plausible candidates to teach what ought to be required is almost totally disconnected from the prevailing structure of rewards. The general adoption of a research model, for example, puts enormous pressure on faculty members to publish even those things no one expects anyone else to ever read once they are in print. There is a corresponding pressure on administrators to defer judgment concerning how published books and articles actually advance understanding or even make sense. Those hard questions are left up to specialists in the field, who typically talk only to one another. These are just a few of the complexities that make it unusually awkward to answer the most strident contemporary critics of the universities, those from the far right, who conveniently take incoherence as the sure sign of wrongdoing.

[3] Even Adams, in his discussion of the "spring riot" as a cyclical event, verges on using this device. See *Tribes* 105–07.

[4] To note but one obvious oddity, the students who in the late 1960s were in revolt over Vietnam were, in significant numbers, supported by fellowships, grants, and loans made possible by that odd successor to the GI Bill of Rights, the National Defense Education Act— I among them.

[5] See, for example, Watkins 47–76. The notion of the "war of position" is derived from Antonio Gramsci's *Prison Notebooks*.

WORKS CITED

Adams, Hazard. *The Academic Tribes*. 2nd ed. Urbana: U of Illinois P, 1988.

Gramsci, Antonio. *Selections from* Prison Notebooks. Ed. and trans. Quintin Hoare and Geoffrey Nowell Smith. London: Lawrence, 1971.

Santayana, George. "The Genteel Tradition in American Philosophy." *Selected Critical Writings of George Santayana*. Vol. 2. London: Cambridge UP, 1968. 85–107.

Watkins, Evan. *Work Time: English Departments and the Circulation of Cultural Value*. Stanford: Stanford UP, 1989.

The Soul in the Machine or the Machine in the Soul?

CLAIRE GAUDIANI

All the way to the horizon in the last light, the sea was just degrees of gray, rolling and froth, on the surface. From the cockpit of a small white sloop—she was 35 ft. long—the waves looked like hills coming up from behind, and most of the crew preferred not to glance at them. There were no other boats in sight. . . . Then it got dark. Running under shortened sails in front of the northeaster, the boat rocked one way, gave a thump, then it rolled the other. The pots and pans in the galley clanged. . . . Sometime late that night, one of the crew raised a voice against the wind, asking "what are we trying to prove?"
—Tracy Kidder, *The Soul of a New Machine*

Higher education and individual colleges and universities are small white sloops in a nor'easter at night. Intelligent, trusting teamwork between captains and sailors is fundamental to a safe journey through the storm, and the storm is all around us as it has always been. Pushing toward the future, universities struggle through the processes of thinking, interpreting, searching, finding, inventing the modern, but also pulling back, conserving, resisting, rethinking, preserving tradition. They are the place where the *querelle des anciens et des modernes*, where reflection and action are the business of the day every day. Universities have for a thousand years nurtured the aspiring soul of human development in the machine of modernism in the West—until recently.

With changes in age-old relationships in and outside the university and deep financial pressures, internal governance and trust are so disordered in

The author is President of Connecticut College. A version of this paper was presented at the 1995 MLA convention in Chicago.

many institutions that higher education is in danger of becoming just another modern machine grinding at the human soul. The sloop, with no captain (or all captains), no maps or agreed-on destination, and no star to steer her by, is in danger, with her whole crew and the society that awaits her cargo. What *are* we trying to prove while the storm rages around us gathering intensity?

On many campuses, the faculty, president, and board of trustees cannot work well together because they are all caught in an invisible web spun by the forces of modernism in conflict with the forces of tradition. This conflict is also destabilizing families, communities, health care, and other sectors in contemporary life. Since the Enlightenment, the forces of modernism have spread rational analysis and efficiency-optimizing, systematic processes into institutions whose bureaucratic structures operate with clear rules and regulations, explicit rights and contracts, processes for evaluation and strategic planning. We live better and longer than our great-grandparents did, but for many people modernism has not brought more satisfying personal or community relationships, despite the more materially comfortable, efficient, consumer-oriented daily experience. Many people now look back romantically at the rich relationships and sense of common values and shared purpose that their older relatives speak about—where families knew each other for generations, where deals were struck by a handshake, where trust was extended on the basis of familial and group bonds tested over decades. Where risks were assessed not by data analysis but by personal knowledge of a name and a reputation, life is sometimes described by the term *premodern*. Premodern life sounds appealing, of course, until the racial, gender, and ethnic exclusions of those eras play themselves back from our memory banks. Ultimately, like efficient, systematic modernism, premodern life has both advantages and disadvantages.

Some synergy between the advantages of both would be ideal, but our contemporary institutions have mostly lost their premodern structures—not higher education, though. Academic institutions have preserved millennia-old traditions. Witness academic robes and processions. Witness the guildlike structures that bring young people through faithful relationships—from apprenticeships with their graduate school faculty members to journeymen and master status under the guidance of senior faculty members, as the processes of tenure and promotion unfold. Witness the tradition of guaranteed lifetime security that is tenure. Witness the traditional commitment of faculty members to work for social and moral rewards instead of focusing on pay. Colleges and universities preserve the tradition of shared governance and lifelong professional and social relationships. No wonder faculty members feel uncomfortable with a lot of the planning structures, the rules and contracts, and the imposition of choices made on economic bases that are a part of modern academic life.

Campuses have also learned, however, to use modern systematic organizational structures to some significant advantage. Higher education is able to show many examples of how to incorporate the best of modern laws and regulations and economic and technological innovation. Working in centers of research and practice, both developing and using scientific methods and data-driven quantitative analyses, academics are clearly not Luddites who refuse modernism in the polite pursuit of faithful relationships. But as financial issues press harder each year for greater efficiencies and better optimization, economic rationality and modern management are imposing themselves vigorously in many institutions, altering basic relationships and assumptions.

On many campuses, deteriorating relationships suggest that many academic institutions have been living off and depleting their fund of social capital, James Colman's term for "the ability to work together for common purposes in groups and organizations" (95). The most serious obstacles facing us as we struggle in this web are relentless waves of broken relationships and financial pressures. Both work against our ability to govern together. If boards, presidents, faculties, and staffs could explore these issues and understand the potential, colleges and universities could build synergy between the premodern and the modern and create on campuses laboratory models of life in a modern democratic civil society.

We would begin by understanding much more about the bonds that shape (and distort) our relationships and the sources of the authority that shape (and distort) our institutions. Max Weber's discussion of the differences between status and purposive contracts best describes the tension embedded in academic relationships and other enterprises in American society (*Economy* 668–81). In status contracts, people pledge themselves to each other in relationships defined by long-standing practices and expectations handed down from generation to generation, much like the relationships among masters, journeymen, and apprentices or graduate students, untenured, and tenured faculty members. Status contracts describe the unwritten faithful relationships that are a feature of premodern social structures. In purposive contracts, individuals enter into specific focused and time-limited obligations for a specific economic interaction. Weber identifies the proliferation of purposive contracts as one of the key features of the rise of modernism (*Economy* 669). On campuses in the United States today, the traditional, softer status contracts that faculty members are used to confront the sharp edges of purposive contracts with merit pay and signing perks. Presidents are in the crucible of this conflict. Who are we to each other? And how can we govern together if we no longer understand the answer to this question? The high turnover and rapid burnout among presidents bear witness to the struggle presidents feel.

Conflicting definitions of contracts are compounded by conflicting ideas about authority. Some say most faculty members tend to reject any authority. Others say presidents fail to exercise authority appropriately, either overconsulting and failing to make tough decisions or underconsulting with faculty and

staff members and overgoverning. But Weber defines three sources of authority that help explain this problem (*Essays* 245). Handed-down tradition or direct inheritance identifies some authority, such as that of the pope or Queen
Elizabeth. People with charismatic or God-given authority, such as Gandhi and
Martin Luther King, Jr., hold power as a unique and personal gift. Bureaucratic
authority is the outcome of a committee. The bureaucratic leader is identified
by a selection committee operating with rules, representative membership,
and a contract to offer (*Essays* 196). In the framework of modernism, college
and university presidents fall into this third category, but this has not always
been the case. Presidents in earlier times were part traditional and part charismatic leaders. They used to be former faculty members or community leaders
who had earned the trust and respect of colleague faculty members, trustees,
and students over decades. They knew the institution's history, its mission and
values. As presidents they both exemplified and transmitted the school's most
precious traditions. In *Universities and the Future of America*, Derek Bok describes the long tradition of college presidents' teaching all seniors their final
course, which was in moral philosophy and education for citizenship (65).
These presidents held authority as the acknowledged gift of the long-standing
relationships that had nurtured and prepared them to exercise it. When and
how often is this true now? How do faculty members and trustees want presidents to lead? How deeply connected are today's presidents to their own institutions? Can their different views of authority be reconciled?

The relationships between senior and junior faculty members have also suffered as modernism has arrived on campus. Some blame the different standards
expected for tenure and promotion. Others blame the gradual shift in faculty
loyalty from institutions to disciplines, and, like star athletes, many faculty
members are willing to move to the team that offers the best contract or negotiate signing contracts that include an array of special perks. Still others blame
administrative attempts to connect the quality and quantity of faculty work with
merit salary increases for the fact that faculty members pull back into their own
work and away from common effort with their colleagues and their students.

Some weakening in relationships results from changes most of us see as true
progress. Many professors experience increased demands on their discretionary
time, for instance because many more of them are involved in dual-career families. Faculties are also more diverse than ever, with higher numbers of women
and people of color and those from widely varying economic backgrounds and
areas of academic specialization at work. On most campuses, consequently, it is
more challenging for faculty members to feel deeply connected to each other
and to share norms and values that they are willing to place above their personal and individual interests.

Relationships with off-campus constituencies have changed, too. Many
nonacademics feel less supportive of faculty members and administrators, and

books like *Profscam* and authors like Dinesh D'Souza are only one sign of the change. Years ago the unionization of faculty members changed the relationship between them and students and their families, risking the kind of alienation baseball players are feeling from their fans. More recently, confidence has dropped because of the allegations of personal and financial malfeasance by administrators. Allegations of exploitative amorous relations between faculty members and students have also done damage.

Citizens lose respect for higher education every time racial or sexual harassment incidents hit the public press. Higher education seems quite incompetent at making the point that, since the end of the draft, campuses are the only place where large numbers of America's highly diverse young people are randomly sorted into residential settings and asked to live and work together in harmony day in and day out.

Citizens' relationships to faculty members have suffered from alienation as many workers, particularly college-educated white-collar employees, are subjected to massive layoffs while faculty members sustain the long-term security of tenure. People express greater frustration over sabbaticals, summer release from course teaching, and other structures in academic life that look like perks to nonacademics.

In addition to altering relationships, financial pressures deteriorate trust and teamwork on many campuses, creating competing interest groups among academic departments and individual faculty members, as well as among staff members, students, the president, and the board. In the public system, state support has dropped substantially below fifty percent of annual budgets in almost all institutions and below twenty percent in a significant number, including such flagship institutions as the University of Virginia. The cost-price squeeze in the private sector is reducing the enrollment of students from middle-class families, whose incomes, flat for more than a decade, do not qualify their children for aid but are not sufficient to permit them to pay the full cost either. The Justice Department has exacerbated these problems by forcing these colleges to bid competitively for scholarship students. This process has replaced the single aid offer that highly selective schools once made to cover financial need without injecting merit dollars. In addition, financial counseling magazines now advise well-off parents on how to hide their substantial assets and apply for and receive need-based financial aid dollars that colleges mean to distribute to low- and middle-income matriculants.

In the midst of these conflicting and weakening relationships and financial stresses, many boards of trustees, faculties, and presidents are grinding each other up, rather than working together. Most boards and presidents have been pushing modernism into higher education to address financial pressures and have largely ignored the threat to relationships from lost social capital on campus. Many boards have made their presidents managers of systematizing bureaucracies, not leaders of academic communities. Many presidents consult less with faculty and staff members and students but more and more with "experts" in marketing, public relations, planning, and financial management, and they are rewarded for making no enemies, taking no risks, and asserting no positions. The press of time on the bottom line makes them poor listeners, and, consequently, people stop telling them what they need to know. A systematic, efficient deployment of resources is what often assures both public and private sector boards that the president is doing the right job. Short-term gains and long-term pains result on many campuses. Merit pay may be a sound concept in a purposive contract, but it needs special tending not to destabilize relationships defined by status contracts. In some settings, legislators and boards are trying to prescribe how many hours faculty members should be at their desks on campus with students or in the classroom, changing a guild-trained master scholar to a clock-punching hourly worker. Incongruously, many trustees want faculty members to spend time shaping students' writing skills, refining their critical judgments, and supporting their integration of the knowledge available to them in the curriculum—a Mr. Chips–style relationship. Boards often do not see how infrequently the system around a faculty member suggests that this time is well spent, because teaching and advising are still often poorly assessed and lightly valued.

Faculty members have mostly pushed modernism back and fought against the tactics imported into academe to address external and financial pressures. They have fought to sustain relationships and premodern structures, including faculty hegemony over when, what, and where they teach and who gets hired and tenured. They often, however, refuse to see the short- and long-range negative effects of myopic and self-absorbed choices on the future well-being of their whole institution. They want to decide issues in their own or their department's self-interest, overlooking how deeply both are linked to the college's best interests as a whole entity. Many want shared governance until it means taking responsibility for hard academic judgments, particularly about colleagues and programs. Then they want the president and the board to make the tough choices. They often also reject requests to build appropriate ways to measure student learning outcomes even when these are not imposed from the outside.

This tug-of-war is not unlike those invading hospitals and corporations. Everywhere it has eroded trust. In his recent book *Trust*, Francis Fukuyama says, "Law, contract, and economic rationality provide a necessary but not sufficient basis for both the stability and prosperity of post-industrial societies: they must be leavened with reciprocity, moral obligation, duty toward community, and trust, which are based in habit rather than rational calculation. The latter are not anachronisms in a modern society but rather the sine qua non of the former's success" (11). Both modern economic rationality and premodern leavening are essential. Both must be sustained. Maybe faculties, presidents, and boards have each been right in a certain way.

Colleges and universities have the tools to integrate both modern and pre-modern structures. They value progress because they are that enterprise just as powerfully as they are the processes of socialization and tradition making and minding. The campus community is as powerfully invested in its history and traditions, confirmed annually in cycles of ceremonies from convocations to graduations, as it is invested in intellectual inquiry, exploration, and discovery and the pursuit of truth and the good. How would an academic institution pro-ceed if it were to decide to become a laboratory where contemporary society could integrate the best of modernism and premodernism as organizing princi-ples to rebuild academic governance and help strengthen other institutions in our democratic civil society? With eight years in office, this college president would advise each constituency as follows.

To the board of trustees   Evaluate carefully the balance of knowledge candi-dates for your presidency bring. There is wisdom in engaging presidents who are experienced with academic life. To play the role they need to play now, pres-idents must know deeply and intuitively both the premodern, loyal traditional relationships of the academic world and the rational, efficiency-optimizing structures of modernism often learned outside universities. It is easier to learn the latter than to learn the former. Ask the presidential candidate for a vision that respects the institution's traditions and strengthens its use of its own re-sources as well as engages imaginatively with the external environment.

Watch candidates for signs of loyalty to ideals, to people, and to traditions as well as signs of strategic planning and decision making. Presidents either will push their institutions farther away from the trust-sustaining relationships that are the cardiovascular system of the academic body politic or will build trust and with it the muscles of self-discipline that the faculty, students, and staff will use to optimize their resources for the health of the school. The president's ability to build trust can free faculty members to improve teaching and learn-ing, the curriculum, and their own scholarship and service. It can raise their willingness to face data and make courageous and generous decisions for the greater good of the college. Conversely, the president's commitment to rules and regulations or arbitrary overgovernance can focus faculty members on self-defense or moving up in the hierarchy, on bargaining and negotiating for their material security and well-being.

Boards need to ask how most faculty members are being inspired to spend their time and then patiently support their president whose personal values support the synergy between the premodern and the modern. Decide whether the president can develop charismatic authority to go with the bureaucratic au-thority conferred by the board.

In recent years boards increasingly seek managers limited to bureaucratic authority. Can we imagine a campus voting in its president if it had a choice and knew the other candidates? It is understandable that boards feel they need this kind of leader—someone to oversee the acquisition of funds from legislators, foundations, and individuals; someone to oversee the defense of the institution from the contracts obligating it to its work staff, its faculty, and even lately its students, parents, and alums. But the bureaucratic president gets hired to manage an entity that does need management but actually wants charismatic and traditional leadership. In the academic community, trust, pride, and respect are as crucial to a strong future as a balanced budget, better salaries, lower tuition, better facilities, and more technology.

Ask the president to teach, write, and know the people on campus as well as wealthy prospects and legislators. Some presidents have no time to feel connected, absorb the traditions, learn the profiles of the institution's earlier leaders. Presidents are often resented for making statements on intellectual or moral matters (Why is he or she not out fund-raising?) and resented as well for not making them (Why can't the president take a stand on this? Does anything of deep value matter to her or him? That bureaucrat.).

Be patient; not all avenues taken in academic life are direct and efficient in the short term. Like good evolutionary biology, higher education tends to work toward long-term survival and flourishing.

To presidents   Resist bureaucratization. Know that faculty members have hopes for premodern values but have a lot of personal experience with the relentless forces of systematizing, efficiency-optimizing, modern bureaucracies. They will require years of experience with a new style to begin to consider trusting you, even if you make no mistakes—an unlikely event.

You show your values one person at a time. Strive for excellence with a compassionate heart. Education values people as individuals in long-term, faithful relationships sharing intellectual honesty, rigorous inquiry, and commitment to emotional investments in each other.

Show up for brisses, baptisms, weddings, and funerals that define the lives of faculty and staff members. The president has to model the premodern values, the personal relationships, because personal relationships, not job descriptions, define what we mean to each other and what we do in higher education. In the long run the hours you invest in caring about people come back to the institution many times over in the form of hours people spend caring for each other, their students, and their responsibilities to the common good.

Plan with data and strategies but with everyone at the table. Even the least-paid staff members have important contributions to make to the pursuit of excellence, cost saving, and restructuring. Devise a continuous process for planning and implementation of plans that includes wide participation from all members of the community, and it will reap deep commitment and high achievement for much less cost, over a long time.

Manage tasks, lead people, and be sure supervisors know that their staff members should spend time and energy to advance the institution's goals, but let supervisors know as well that they are responsible for ensuring that no one suffers an expense of spirit—that no one goes home dispirited from a day's work because of the quality of work life.

Relationships at work are as important as achievements at work and are deeply linked. Improve the former and the latter will improve, most often faster than they would with direct focus on achievements without effort expended on working relationships.

To faculty members You are right to insist that the academic traditions be preserved. They cannot be replaced, but they will not be preserved unless they actually co-opt the systematizing bureaucracies that define modernism. The forces of trust, imagination, generosity, and integrity that are fundamental to academic life are the most powerful assets you can bring to temper and humanize modernism as it is having its effect in a wide array of other contemporary institutions in America. These forces reduce costs and increase choices, both high values in modern life.

The bureaucratic systems and controls needed in low-trust settings drive up the cost of doing business no matter what the enterprise, including education. Most enterprises need to operate with more trust and simply do not know how. We used to know how, and we must remember again.

Imagine how together faculty members and administrators could *graft* the advantages of our premodern tradition of relationships and expectations to the advantages of systematic organizational structures so that common sense and common values could make tough decisions possible, reducing internally self-destructive activities, changing the incentive structures to reward both teaching and scholarship. Work with your president and administrators to understand the problems you face as an institution, and discipline yourself and your colleagues to make courageous decisions together in real time—before crisis management robs you of a set of options. Be as tough on yourself and your colleagues as you are on the president, the administrators, and the board. In the academy, if we work well together we can avoid getting swept into the slow (clock-stopping), bureaucratic (rule-bound), expensive (lots of players and specialized teams) game of football when our ability to use the best of premodern and modern structures makes us natural world-class soccer players.

Imagine that your president means the best for you personally and for the faculty as a whole, and then do not let the president get isolated. Invite your president to dinner or lunch with colleagues or students or to a department party. Write or call when something *good* happens.

Spend time with each other in and outside your department. Coteach and consider integrated volunteer service courses to connect the world to the classroom your own way. Test your readiness to serve society as a public intellectual. More faculty members need to be heard outside the campus.

Spend time with students—the one gift they need when even their parents are less available to them—time revising papers, time discussing *their* future.

To students, parents, and all the constituencies of higher education   Academic institutions have the best chance to refine and then model synergy between the modern and the premodern, a synergy that could be adapted in other settings in American life. The prototype of modern, diverse, democratic civil society could emerge from these communities, but it will take a conscious commitment from all constituents to yield success in this social experiment that could redefine the role of higher education in American society. This effort would also support necessary changes in other institutions in modern America and would help to remake American society by avoiding an impossible choice between two goods: the good of modern technology and progress and the good of high-trust social interactions among people. Higher education is in a unique position to point toward synergy, and it needs your encouragement to take up this challenge energetically.

At the end of the cold war, Americans can be proud of higher education. It deserves significant credit for staggering achievements across all fields. With fourteen million Americans in higher education, no country has ever educated a larger percentage of a more diverse population than we are educating in the United States in the 1990s. The last twenty years have seen an astonishing growth of the upper-middle- and upper-income groups. In some sense education promised all of us a better life and has helped bring better material life largely by extending the power of the scientific method beyond the sciences to health, business, law, finance, social systems analysis, and education itself, among other fields.

You can encourage higher education's faculty members, presidents, and trustees to rethink the strength of its modern and premodern governance structure, even in the current storm. You can raise expectations that colleges and universities will rebalance their cargo and retrain the captain and crew, reexamine the maps and refine the technology of navigation so that both higher education and other sectors in contemporary American life can improve work relationships as well as their financial strength and productivity. Higher education can integrate the soul and the machine, the premodern and the modern, both on our campuses and eventually in society. We ought to use our dual strengths to prove that this integration is possible and that, in fact, our success in arriving at this synergy will define the future of sustainable human communities.

WORKS CITED

Bok, Derek. *Universities and the Future of America*. Durham: Duke UP, 1990.

Colman, James. "Social Capital in the Creation of Human Capital." *American Journal of Sociology* 94 (1988): S59–S120.

Fukuyama, Francis. *Trust: The Social Virtues and the Creation of Prosperity*. New York: Free, 1995.

Kidder, Tracy. *The Soul of a New Machine*. Boston: Little, 1981.

Weber, Max. *Economy and Society: An Outline of Interpretive Sociology*. Vol. 2. Berkeley: U of California P, 1978.

———. *From Max Weber: Essays in Sociology*. New York: Oxford UP, 1946.

Negotiating Agendas?
Academic Management for
Quality and Control

LINDA RAY PRATT

The stalest jokes in the academy are the ones faculty members tell about administrators. These jokes typically compensate professors with superior qualities to offset the administration's superior powers and reinforce adversarial tensions between the two. In many institutions, however, forces are at work to change these attitudes. Current management trends embracing cooperation and negotiation in the workplace have taken deep root in the academy in this time of funding crises and external demands for accountability. For most faculty members, this change is most obvious at the level of the college when deans and the faculty together fight to maintain their collective authority to control the direction of the college. Though the change in faculty-administrative relations may be more of degree than kind, and more from necessity than desire, the pressures driving this change are complex and sustained. To many faculty members, however, the causes seem remote and almost invisible.

At least four major developments underlie efforts to alter administrative-faculty relations. One is the growth of large public university systems dependent on public funding and accountable to government. A second is the decline of support for higher education that has left both the faculty and the administration worried about future funding. A third is a widespread movement in labor-management relations away from confrontational models to cooperative ones in an effort to be competitive. And the fourth is the influence of "total quality management" (TQM) or its derivatives in the contemporary workplace.

The author is Professor of English and Chair of the Department of English at the University of Nebraska, Lincoln. A version of this paper was presented at the 1995 MLA convention in Chicago.

These four trends have often resulted in closer alliances between faculty members and deans and within the college unit; above the level of the college, however, they have frequently resulted in greater differences between the work of the faculty and the administration. These changes are both encouraging and disturbing for the faculty's role in governance.

THE GROWTH OF PUBLIC UNIVERSITIES

The GI bill at the end of World War II altered the status of possessing a college degree from being mainly a privilege for the few to being a democratic possibility for the masses. College enrollments accelerated in the 1950s and 1960s as the economy expanded and the number of technical, professional, and semi-professional occupations increased. In 1940 total enrollment in United States colleges was 1.5 million, but by 1980 it was 12.1 million (Kerr 143). To accommodate the pressure for accessible higher education, state governments invested heavily in expanding university systems. In such populous states as California, New York, Texas, Pennsylvania, Michigan, and Illinois, as many as twenty-five or thirty separate public campuses have come into being since 1945, many of them since 1965. State university systems such as those in California and New York (SUNY) expanded rapidly in the 1960s. Today approximately 75% of all full-time faculty members work in publicly funded institutions.[1] The demographic forecast is that enrollments will increase another 20% in the next twenty years (Kerr 175). Some small private colleges have collapsed, and the proliferation of branch campuses of the major state universities has ended. The rise of numerous community colleges, however, means not only that higher education's dependence on the tax dollar is likely to increase in the next twenty years but also that funding will shift away from universities to the less expensive two-year campuses.

THE DECLINE OF PUBLIC FUNDING

During the expansion of the 1950s and 1960s, public funding was rarely openly linked to public approval of academic life. During the Vietnam War, however, campus disorders angered the public and government officials. The legislative fallout taught administrators that they needed to control dissident faculty members in order to manage the university's public image. Between 1984 and 1994, funding pressure intensified as a stalled economy and a conservative turn in government resulted in a transfer of the cost of federally mandated programs back to the states. State appropriations for higher education took a nosedive. Between 1991–92 and 1993–94, state appropriations for higher education averaged out to a –4%; only seventeen states increased their appropriations. The highest increases (10% and 12%) were in states like Mississippi, Georgia, and

Tennessee, whose lagging economic growth had historically held down funding for higher education. Many states took 4% to 9% cuts; California topped the list with an incredible –29% change (Kerr 172; Lively).[2] Some states were investing more heavily in their prison systems than in their public universities.

One effect of the funding crisis in public universities was to unite faculty members and administrators behind a common agenda. Cooperative efforts developed over such issues of common concern as budget cuts that eliminated programs or failed to raise salaries. In recent years the alliance between faculties and administrations has been strengthened by their concern with the presence of state postsecondary education coordinating and review commissions. These commissions, set up to protect the state government's interests, often regulate such basic academic matters as program approval. Although the influence of these commissions has already diminished, many of them still have the power to overrule campus administrators on program issues.

In an environment in which administrative control is subject to intensive outside regulation and influence, deans and other administrators have a diminished autonomy to control directions within the college. Facing tough competition for budget and program control, both chairs and deans must produce data about the quality of the programs, plans to meet enrollment demands, an increasing number of credit hours and external grants, and more and better undergraduate instruction. Confronted with similar demands beyond the college, deans and chairs are more likely to negotiate agendas that result in similar goals for quality and productivity. When they do not cooperate, they undermine each other's authority within the larger structure of powers beyond their control. External regulation of institutions and the litigious climate in our society have also enhanced the attractiveness of shared decision making. Agencies outside the institutions regulate everything from hiring to interviewing live research subjects, and the "bloated" administration that many have noted is in part the result of external reporting demands (see Bergmann).

CHANGING LABOR-MANAGEMENT RELATIONS

Although the academy does not usually locate itself within the larger pattern of worker-management relations, today's cooperative or collaborative models in university administration reflect current trends in labor management generally. In 1993 the movement toward cooperative worker-management relations was formalized for possible amendment of the National Labor Relations Act. At President Clinton's initiative, the United States Department of Labor under Robert Reich created the Commission on the Future of Worker-Management Relations. Known widely as the Dunlop Commission after the name of its chair, former Secretary of Labor John T. Dunlop, the commission was charged to respond to three major questions. They were as follows:

1. What (if any) new methods or institutions should be encouraged, or required, to enhance work-place productivity through labor-management cooperation and employee participation?
2. What (if any) changes should be made in the present legal framework and practices of collective bargaining to enhance cooperative behavior, improve productivity, and reduce conflict and delay?
3. What (if anything) should be done to increase the extent to which workplace problems are directly resolved by the parties themselves, rather than through recourse to state and federal courts and government regulatory bodies? ("Fact Finding Report" 1)

Traditional unionists feared that the Dunlop Commission would open the door for "company unions"; the American Federation of Teachers (AFT) and the American Association of University Professors (AAUP) saw an opportunity to amend the National Labor Relations Act so as to supersede the 1980 Supreme Court decision *NLRB v. Yeshiva University*, which took away the right of faculty members in private institutions to collective bargaining.[3] Others saw it as a broad effort to define a more democratic model for workplace relations that reflected the change from the industrial union to the high-tech and multirace and gender demographics of a more educated and professionalized workforce of white-collar employees. The new model stresses employee participation as a means to enhance productivity and resolve disputes through cooperative structures that include both labor and management.

Little came of the Dunlop Commission's recommendations after Democrats lost control of the House and Senate in 1994, but the workplace philosophy behind the commission's existence moves forward in other ways. The Teamwork for Employees and Managers Act of 1995, which Clinton vetoed in July after both the House and Senate passed it by narrow margins, sought to amend section 8(a)(2) of the National Labor Relations Act to allow employers to establish organizations of management and workers to address matters of quality, productivity, and efficiency. This amendment would eliminate the prohibition against employer-dominated "company unions." The "Findings and Purposes" of the TEAM Act specifically link it "to enhancing the productivity and competitiveness of American businesses" in the manner that "foreign competitors have successfully utilized" (sec. 2 [a][4] and [5]).

Because about 75% of all faculty members are employed in four-year public institutions, higher education is increasingly affected by labor-management practices in public sector employment. The parallel between labor-management relations in the nonacademic public sector and faculty-administration relations is largely a subject for silence or denial in the academy. Yet administrators have widely adopted the quality management system that "foreign competitors have successfully utilized" (TQM), and the employment conditions of faculty members in public institutions are increasingly influenced by practices set up by policies and contract arrangements originating in other divisions of the public sector. Some still think of the labor movement as the industrial and craft unions in the original AFL-CIO. Labor organizing today, however, is focused on state, county, and municipal employees, many of whom are professionals. Only about a third of higher educaton is unionized, but that third includes major university systems in California, Connecticut, Florida, Michigan, New Jersey, and New York. Other large states such as Illinois, Ohio, and Minnesota have significant numbers of unionized faculties. Yet other states have large organizations of educators that are not unions but that function in a similar way. The National Education Association (NEA), which defines itself as a professional association and is not a member of the AFL-CIO, is both a union and a professional organization. The NEA and the AFT are in the midst of merger talks that, if successful, will create the largest union in the world, with a membership of over 3 million. While AFL-CIO membership dwindles to only about 15% of the total workforce, the professional and technical workforce has increased by 283% in the last forty years and includes about 20 million people, more than a quarter of whom are represented in collective bargaining (Shanker). Such large organizations of public employees, whether union or nonunion, influence a range of employment conditions in the public sector.

QUALITY MANAGEMENT IN THE UNIVERSITY

The issues before the Dunlop Commission and the TEAM Act may seem remote to faculty members, but college administrators have embraced the same management strategies for several years now. "Quality" workshops and training seminars urge administrators to involve faculty and staff members in the pursuit of productivity, evaluation, and budget reduction. In these forums the utility of part-time faculty members and the need to eliminate tenure are frequently discussed as necessary for good management. The adaptation of quality management systems to higher education is part of the corporate and institutional strategy to minimize disruption and inefficiency in order to compete better in a sterner world of limited resources, external pressures, and sharply conflicting interests.

Quality management in higher education derives from TQM—total quality management—the factory system that began in the Toyota factories of postwar Japan. Invented by the American Charles Deming, who became an international guru on management after the success of Japan's economy was a business legend, TQM strives for "continuous improvement." Its original mechanism was the "quality circle," a workplace structure in which labor and management collaborate to attain the continuous improvement that yields productivity and profit. In the United States TQM was adopted by the agencies and departments of the federal government, most particularly the military, before it became widespread in business. Quality management has been especially attractive to management in workplaces that traditionally provide continuous employment based on seniority and status, such as in civil service, unionized industries, the volunteer military, and higher education. Until recently academicians rarely spoke of education as a "product" or students as "customers," but the techniques of quality management in a time of "downsizing" were easily adapted because faculties and administrations were already accustomed to shared governance. Faculty members expected to have a say in such matters as hiring, promotion, tenure, curriculum, and policy making through the processes of faculty governance. The distinction between serving on a college committee and participating in a workplace circle can be more a matter of rhetoric than of substance. Faculty members are now asked to focus on collaborative efforts to improve teaching through "teaching circles," for example, and the peer review of classroom performance as part of evaluation delegates to the faculty a form of surveillance and advising once considered an intrusion on academic freedom when done by administrators.

Shared decision making and collaboration for quality and productivity hold the possibility of greater wisdom and empowering through participation. When separated from authentic empowerment, however, they can also disperse responsibility, co-opt dissent, and increase work pressures. In the traditional workplace, quality circles may offer workers who have little say about their jobs an opportunity to participate in their design. In the aging industrial world where both unions and markets are declining, some believe that cooperative models may allow both the union and the company to survive, while others believe that they will result only in co-opting workers in plans for their own dismissal. Similarly, in higher education, quality management systems may undermine the role of faculty governance in institutions where the faculty senate and committee bylaws give real authority to faculty decisions, or it may enhance participation in areas where the faculty has little power or control. In general, faculty governance is at its weakest when addressing budget and planning issues.[4] But in institutions faced with declining support, allocation of resources and priorities in planning are the critical issues to influence. For faculty members, the choice is a complicated one: do we participate in managing our decline, or do we hold out for agendas that cannot be realized? The clear trend in administration is to encourage more participation at lower levels, such as the college, but to invest greater authority for final decisions at the higher levels of provosts and presidents. At the upper levels of administration, decisions about budget priorities are often openly political and designed to appease or inspire state, federal, and business interests. Whether the faculty and the administration can forge effective alliances at the college level to promote the academic agenda at the upper levels of administration is not yet clear. The shift from tenure-track to part-time faculty members creates a workforce more vulnerable to administrative control. The fact that many faculty members will not invest their time in faculty governance or concern themselves with matters outside the discipline further threatens faculty power within the institution.

.The pressures on higher education driving these changes are likely to increase as conflicting social agendas sharpen demands on public funding. In many states budget decisions will come down to a rhetorical choice between welfare for the poor or pay raises for government employees, medicaid for the elderly or education for the young. The growing pressures from the business community will not ease as long as business faces tougher international competition, and the public's demand for accountability will not be silenced as long as college costs continue to rise. In our classes, the number of enrollments will most likely continue to go up, and the number of tenure-track faculty members will go down. The pessimists believe that funding for higher education may be cut by as much as a third in the next decade, and the optimists believe it may be only half that bad. Faculty members and administrators face the same future. Whether we can indeed negotiate our sometimes conflicting agendas for the common good will determine how much reality we can give to the concept of democratizing cooperation and collaboration in our academic workplace.

NOTES

[1]Based on data for 1993 made available to the American Association of University Professors by the National Center for Education Statistics, Department of Education, April 1996.

[2]Amounts adjusted for rate of inflation in Kerr. See Lively for 1993 figures.

[3]Both organizations presented written and spoken testimony to the Dunlop Commission about *Yeshiva*.

[4]The experience and, hence, the strength of faculty governance have most often been in academic areas of curriculum, degree requirements, and grading policies or in due process issues such as procedures for tenure, promotion, and grievance. Faculty governance traditionally has had little role in budget planning or oversight.

WORKS CITED

Bergmann, Barbara. "Bloated Administration, Blighted Campuses." *Academe* 77 (1991): 12–16.
"Fact Finding Report: Executive Summary. Commission on the Future of Worker-Management Relations." US Depts. of Labor and Commerce. May 1994.
Kerr, Clark. *The Uses of the University*. 4th ed. Cambridge: Harvard UP, 1995.
Lively, Kit. "State Support for Public Colleges Up 2% This Year." *Chronicle of Higher Education* 27 Oct. 1993: A29.
Shanker, Albert. Written statement submitted to the Dunlop Commission. 29 Apr. 1994.

How to Reform the MLA: An Opening Proposal

CARY NELSON

For a number of decades the MLA has been essentially a neutral structure designed to showcase research in literature and provide career opportunities for its members. Those career opportunities range from interviewing for jobs to presenting convention papers to publishing articles in books and journals. So long as the profession was either expanding or fully replacing its members on retirement, that utilitarian, content-free structure served us rather well. Its last major overhaul, nearly thirty years ago, came when a narrowly focused annual convention resistant to newer methodologies was replaced with a much broader and more representative one. The Delegate Assembly was also introduced, and it has successfully given the membership somewhat more influence over the association's policies and given the association a more critical and energetic national presence.

Unfortunately, over the same period we have also seen the size of many large department faculties gradually shrink, while the number of undergraduate students served, which declined from the early 1970s through the mid-1980s, has now returned to its 1970 level.[1] More recently, political support for higher education has declined in the wake of the cold war's conclusion. Meanwhile, a long-term job crisis that leaves many new PhDs either unemployed or marginally employed in part-time jobs has become semipermanent. Tenure is not so much under assault as it is being whittled away by a slow but inexorable shift to part-time employees. Academic freedom may begin to be undermined as fewer and fewer faculty members have any meaningful job security; people

---

The author is Professor of English at the University of Illinois, Urbana.

---

vulnerable to immediate termination are less likely to speak freely. The profession as a whole is now highly dependent on low-paid apprentices who have little prospect for permanent employment. Contrary to the cheerful reassurances some MLA members have offered, many informed commentators on higher education expect these trends to continue (see Benjamin); some expect a shakeout and a reduction in the number of full-scale research universities over the next decade. No rational observers expect the job market to improve to the point where the unemployed PhDs of the last twenty-five years could find full-time tenure-track jobs.

Of course, we do not know how many PhDs from the 1970s, 1980s, and 1990s are still seeking full-time tenure-track jobs. We could find out, but we have not tried. My own knowledge is anecdotal, based on correspondence with individual PhDs and on conversations with department heads. What I do know from both these kinds of sources is that some people have eked out near poverty-level careers on the margins of the profession for fifteen to twenty years. I have vitae for people who've pieced together part-time academic employment, often at multiple institutions, while continuing to read and publish, for as long as two decades and who still hope for permanent jobs. One department head who employs them calls them "our discards." Another department head said, "We have people who've been teaching part-time for us for fifteen years. They still think they'll get a full-time job. I tell them, 'Don't count on it.'" We need to document these employment patterns more fully. Indeed, we need to recover the whole forgotten social, economic, and human history of the discipline, a history long ignored because we believed the discipline's intellectual history was all that mattered. Thus we often talk about the job market without having a full sense of what its human consequences have been.

In this environment a Modern Language Association devoted primarily to enabling its members to add lines to their vitae does not serve our most urgent needs. The MLA should lobby far more widely and aggressively on behalf of higher education and train its members to do the same. Its officers should be highly visible, readily identifiable spokespersons outside the profession, participating in public policy debates at both state and national levels. The organization should explore new kinds of MA programs designed to channel graduates into alternative careers. It should take an active role in limiting the size of PhD programs. It should encourage more-enlightened faculty retirement programs. It should study the human costs of doctoral training far more thoroughly and deeply. It should monitor how changes in technology and the slow collapse of the academic book market will affect requirements for tenure. It should set ethical standards for graduate study, the job market, and the probationary period for new faculty members in times of economic crisis. It should organize and encourage discussion, debate, and research among its members on all these issues and communicate the results widely.

To do all these things effectively, I believe, will require the MLA to redirect its financial resources. The publishing program, for example, may need to be curtailed. One wonders what its real costs are when staff time and overhead are added to the costs of typesetting and printing. How well do many of these books sell? How much income do book sales produce? Is this the best focus for the organization? There are other publishers, but there is no other comparable national organization representing teachers of modern languages and literatures.

We will also need new ways to elect officers and perhaps new ways of running the organization. Here some blunt language is warranted. Notoriously efficient at running the annual convention and editing manuscripts, the members of the permanent staff consistently do their jobs well. On many issues the staff is neutral. That is entirely appropriate for an academic organization. It is inappropriate to look to the staff members for more-polemical advocacy or for leading positions on issues where the membership might disagree. Even an executive director is necessarily limited in the kinds of public positions he or she can take.

It is therefore often the organization's elected officials, most notably the MLA president, who should provide active leadership around the social, political, institutional, cultural, and policy issues directly affecting literature and language departments, especially when the issues are controversial. This is not, I should emphasize, a matter of taking positions on Vietnam or Bosnia. It is a matter of assisting and, if necessary, confronting politicians, journalists, faculty members, and administrators, as well as members of the general public, whenever the funding or interpretation of research and teaching in higher education is at stake. The MLA almost appears *designed* to be politically ineffective or invisible, a dismissible or irrelevant player in the public sphere. The organization sometimes seems like a factory assembly line serviced (but uninfluenced) by its staff and officers. Two points seem obvious. First, we elect an MLA president on the basis of a bibliography and a sound bite. The statements of purpose are so brief as to be little more than empty generalities. So a member must predict candidates' conduct in office by examining their scholarly work. But there is no necessary connection between how one interprets literary texts and how one responds, say, to the job crisis. The members have tended to elect scholars doing progressive work, but progressive scholarship unfortunately guarantees nothing about a person's views on other professional issues and nothing about a person's administrative ability. Second, a one-year presidential term provides insufficient time to master the organization, influence its operation, and build a reputation as a national spokesperson for higher education. The MLA tries to compensate for that problem by having future presidents serve initially as first and second vice president. While that procedure no doubt helps educate them about the office, it does not turn them into national leaders, and the eventual officeholder is still too transient to establish a national presence.

The MLA presidency has largely been an honorary office, the chief curriculum vitae enhancement the organization offers. Scholars can accept the job without fear that their research will be seriously interrupted. When the profession was in relative boom times, no damage was done. But we now face an era when politicians will propose unimaginative and often destructive solutions to our fiscal problems. We can do better ourselves, especially if we work together. But for that we need MLA presidents who are devoted to working on these problems and who can deal effectively with policy issues outside their areas of literary expertise. For the association needs to be far more involved in a broad range of issues affecting our future. Many departments have neither the resources nor the expertise to come up with creative solutions to this multilevel crisis. They need the pooled resources and imagination of the profession as a whole. The president should be at the forefront of that effort.

There is an array of practical issues debated at the state or national level with a special inflection for the disciplines represented in the MLA. Consider the heavy use of graduate teaching assistants. We are among the disciplines that use them most heavily and effectively, yet the public argument over this subject often centers on aspects ludicrously irrelevant to us, like TAs' language ability. Class size and teaching loads are other obvious examples where our interests do not always match those of other disciplines. The much more intractable topics of our day—from the use and exploitation of part-time employees to expectations for tenure—also require organized input from the MLA.

But one-year presidents and presidents uninformed about or uninterested in these and other problems cannot lead such an effort. I would recommend three changes in our method of governance. First, candidates for the MLA presidency should write a platform statement of perhaps a thousand words that includes specific proposals for action. Drafts should be submitted to the Nominating Committee for review before a final group of candidates is selected, and the full statements should be distributed to the membership with the ballots. Second, the MLA president should have a three-year term, and presidents should be eligible to succeed themselves by election to one additional term. Third, new presidents should have a significant budget reserve to initiate new programs.

Candidates for election to the Executive Council should produce statements of about five hundred words, in which they could identify the presidential proposals they agree or disagree with and offer proposals of their own. Alternatively, candidates for the presidency and the Executive Council could stand together as a slate. In any case, an MLA member must be able to vote for candidates committed to specific actions and must know that the elected officers will have the resources to make good on their promises. No one can be certain that the membership would make the best choices in these matters, but it is time to have an association that can identify and respond to trends that threaten us rather than one that simply promotes individual careers.

At the same time, the Delegate Assembly needs to revise its methods of operation. As it currently functions, over a hundred academics gather together on one crowded afternoon to decide a host of often complicated proposals. Sometimes the motions merit extended discussion over weeks; questions arise that require consultation with people not present. The delegates have little opportunity, if any, to debate proposals before the meeting where everything is to be decided. The general membership mostly has no detailed advance information about motions. It is no surprise that the assembly is much better able to deal with large moral questions focused elsewhere than with issues bearing directly on daily academic life.

Ideally, the Delegate Assembly would meet on at least two occasions a year, including a weekend not connected with the convention. But that schedule would almost certainly be too expensive. One alternative might be a forum for delegate discussion on the Internet, in which delegates committed themselves to participating for at least an hour each week throughout the academic year. In any case, the delegates need a way to work through motions and resolutions together before the meeting where decisions are made.

Whether any of these proposals is adopted in exactly the form described is, of course, less important than the necessity for MLA members to begin discussing what sort of organization can deal effectively with a less hospitable political and economic climate. The association has often played the fool in reporters' accounts of the annual convention. That is partly because we have too often left a vacuum where we should have aggressively established a public presence. The organization needs to be a political force to reckon with if it expects to do anything other than preside over a diminished professoriat during the next decade.

The American Association of University Professors (AAUP) provides a model of a professional faculty organization more focused on public policy issues. It has seminars to train its members how to lobby legislators; there is no reason the MLA could not do the same. Unfortunately, most faculty members belong only to disciplinary organizations, not to the AAUP as well. That is because academics imagine they have no common interests; they see disciplinary organizations as appropriately focused on the only thing that matters, enhancing individuals' careers. That perception has to change. Meanwhile, disciplinary organizations must broaden and intensify their political profile, in part because without them there aren't a sufficient number of organized faculty members to have a political impact and in part because there are interests and perspectives that only disciplinary organizations can represent. We will never return to the boom times of higher education, but we can successfully resist many efforts to undermine our teaching and research, and we can devise alternative practices that even improve higher education. Certainly no one else will do so. We are a wonderful and underutilized resource—thousands of professors with adaptable language skills. We and the organization that represents us, the MLA, need to be part of the solution to the problems we face. The association cannot be so if it does not change.

NOTE

[1]One rough measure of enrollment is the number of degrees granted. About 56,000 bachelor's degrees were awarded by English departments in 1970 and again in 1993, although the 1993 figures represent a lower percentage of the total number of undergraduate degrees. From 1978 through 1987 we awarded fewer than 37,000 per year. As Phyllis Franklin points out, degrees awarded in the humanities, social sciences, and physical sciences declined between 1974–75 and 1984–85, while degrees in business, computer science, and engineering increased. As Bettina J. Huber notes, "among English departments in Research I institutions, average faculty size declined steadily during the 1980–94 period." Some departments gained back a portion of these losses in the 1990s, but many remain significantly under their faculty strength of twenty years ago. The English department at the University of Illinois, Urbana, has 30% fewer faculty members; Indiana University has 10% fewer. The precise numbers and the timing of these changes often reflect local or state circumstances. Thus California lost many faculty members to its special early retirement programs over the last decade. Overall, as a profession we are now doing much more teaching with graduate students, adjunct, or part-time faculty (Benjamin). That *structural* change is a national phenomenon, and it is important not to let local differences obscure it.

WORKS CITED

Benjamin, Ernst. "A Faculty Response to the Fiscal Crisis: From Defense to Offense." *Higher Education under Fire: Politics, Economics, and the Crisis of the Humanities*. Ed. Michael Bérubé and Cary Nelson. New York: Routledge, 1995. 52–72.

Franklin, Phyllis. "From the Editor." *MLA Newsletter* 20.4 (1988): 2–6.

Huber, Bettina J. "Highlights of the MLA's Survey of PhD-Granting Modern Language Departments: Changes in Faculty Size from 1990 to 1994." *ADE Bulletin* 109 (1994): 46–47.

Crisis and Chance in Higher Education: The View from Here

CHRISTOPHER JON DELOGU

L'histoire des peuples, comme l'histoire des institutions, comme l'histoire de la langue, se compose de crises, partielles ou totales, et d'états changés par ces crises, c'est l'abc de tout.

The history of human societies, like the history of institutions and the history of language, is composed of crises, partial or total, and states changed by these crises, it's the abc of everything.

—Ferdinand de Saussure

Cette crise peut donc être une chance si nous savons répondre à la hauteur des attentes exprimées.

This crisis may therefore be an opportunity if we are able to rise to the level of the expectations that have been expressed.

—François Bayrou

After ten years of higher education in America (a BA in philosophy at Dartmouth, 1985; a PhD in comparative literature at Yale, 1991) and one year teaching French in a nonrenewable slot at Connecticut College, I was on the verge of leaving the profession, when I was offered a teaching job in France. I have been a *maître de conférences* at large state universities (in Aix-en-Provence and now Toulouse) for the last four years. I teach English literature (Chaucer

---

The author is Maître de conférences in the English studies program at the Université de Toulouse, Le Mirail, in France.

---

to Janet Frame), American history, and translation. People back in the States regularly ask me what it's like here, and for some time I have wanted to write an informative essay about the French National Education system with special reference to higher education. I even thought of a title: "*L'éducation nationale aujourd'hui: Un drôle de drame.*" The subtitle was a playful allusion to the film by Marcel Carné and Jacques Prévert, *Drôle de drame* (1937). By pure coincidence, the film was recently rereleased. After seeing it for the first time one idle afternoon (a six-week strike interrupted most classes at my university from mid-November up to Christmas break), I decided to get started on my essay, but with a different title and a more critical focus.

I had often heard about this film and its famous dinner scene where the words *bizarre bizarre* are exchanged back and forth between two gentlemen. Many things about the film are indeed bizarre. For example, this French classic takes place in London! Also, a number of bizarre scenes depict crowds of people wildly moving about the city. Near the end, a mob storms into a house; but catastrophe is narrowly averted, as in the dinner scene, by means of a sophisticated cover-up. The mob charges back into the street to help the police (also depicted as a kind of mob) pursue the murderer, who has a vaguely German name—bizarre—William Kramps. As the word *Fin* appears on the screen, one sees a small child abandoned in the middle of the empty street. A man goes back and grabs him by the hand, presumably to rejoin the mob.

Afterward, I stood on the sidewalk with friends, recalling favorite scenes and bits of witty dialogue. But I also could not help thinking of those final images of the mob. In a word, I felt bizarre. Later I read a description of the film in the program guide, hoping, I suppose, for an explanation:

> Taken from an English detective novel, *Drôle de drame* is an explosive mixture of typically British humour and the poetic madness particular to Prévert. It creates a fantastically charming but without a doubt quite disturbing atmosphere: this would explain the film's total lack of critical and popular success at the moment of its release before the war. It would be necessary to wait for a succession of revivals in order for *Drôle de drame* to take its true place within the warm interior of our cinematic memories. (my trans.)

One can well imagine that in 1937 the French found the film's atmosphere more disturbing than charming. The terror of the mob and much of the film's plot, which revolves around censorship, random violence, and social upheaval, are likely to have hit a little too close to home for French audiences from 1937 to 1945. Neither the trick of setting the action outside France nor the strategy of saying to oneself, "It's only a movie" or "It's all a joke," seem to have been able to lighten the chilly early reception of the film. After the war, the interpretation of *Drôle de drame* gradually shifts such that today *drôle* far outweighs *drame* in the public's very warm reception of the film. Today the film's status as cultural icon seems to depend on the incessant repetition in the public sphere of the words *bizarre bizarre*. These words and their droll-dramatic recital—the quintessence of Prévert's poetic madness—appear to be one of the many spells or prayers by means of which, in the French cultural imaginary, forces of good will battle forces of evil and forces of order will see to it that nothing too dramatic disturbs France's exceptional and charming cultural routines. Clearly, the history of the reception of the film is as much a *drôle de drame* as the film itself.

As in 1937, a typically British sense of humor may be in short supply today, in France and elsewhere. At the end of 1995, there is a widespread perception in France that the nation is in crisis. Prolonged strikes of the postal service, transportation systems, garbage collectors, and even students and professors— it looks, sounds, and smells serious. People far away may not understand what is going on ("Students striking?" "You must be joking!" "Those silly French!" etc.). Here is an explanation that the *International Herald Tribune* offered to its readers: "Philippe Martinez, a 40-year-old postal worker who walked off his job in solidarity with the train drivers, said: 'We all realize this strike is about saving the social benefits that make life in France so special. It's also to show our disgust with a government that has lost touch with the people'" (Drozdiak). Many people would agree with Philippe Martinez that France is special; it has arguably the highest standard of living and quality of life in the world. But there are indications (reported fragility in the banking sector and the possible future bumping of France from the G7, for example) that the wealth of the nation is decreasing. If this is true, then France must decide to make do with less, or else find ways to increase its wealth. One might interject that if *wealth* could come to mean something other than the production and accumulation of commodities—something like vitality or well-being—this either-or decision might be transformed into a richer state of both-and. But that would take time, and there is a growing feeling that time is running out, a perception of urgency commonly translated by the term *crisis*.

First, the recent university unrest, student-led strikes throughout the nation, stems largely from problems specific to the institutional history and function of the various campuses. Overcrowding was the initial complaint, but this was quickly fanned into a general protest about the present condition and the future uncertainty of university life. Currently a nominal annual enrollment fee gives a "student" access not only to classes but also to low-cost health insurance, meal plans, housing subsidies, and other benefits that go along with this *statut social*. Within the university, students, professors, and administrative personnel are distinct groups with different agendas, and the university group is distinct from railroad workers and other laborers in what is known as the public service sector. However, at times these distinctions can be overlooked. When you see a mob in the streets where usually there is mostly orderly if noxious traffic, your immediate impulse is to make it go away. There was hardly such a bizarre cover-up as in *Drôle de drame*, but it took the French government six weeks, some vague promises, and the soothing effect of Christmas to get things back to normal.

Second, the public university system today is *not* one of the things that make life in France "so special" in the way I believe Martinez intends that phrase. The system suffers from a chronic lack of specialness. The exceptions—pockets of distinction, creativity, and positive energy—merely set off the truth of this gloomy verdict. The history of the rapid but sometimes halfhearted expansion of the public university system during what the French refer to as "the thirty glorious years" (roughly 1950 to 1980) resembles in some ways the history of the French version of subsidized housing known by the letters HLM (*Habitation à loyer modéré*). French initiatives in both areas, while often well-intentioned, have a reputation of being imposed from the top down, along a complex chain of command that can be wasteful, corrupt, insensitive, and demoralizing. The harmful consequences play themselves out daily in the lives and minds of those concerned. In the case of the HLM, these have now and then captured the public's fleeting attention; but in the universities the scandal has been more carefully hidden, often with the conscious or unconscious complicity of those who are arguably its worst victims. One senses that there is a great deal of pain and shame involved. During the strike, in a small informal gathering of teachers and students, a colleague of mine—by accident? a woman—compared the university situation to wife beating. There was instant laughter. Her *drôle* remark had evidently hit a nerve close to the *drame*. What I think she meant was that the university system suffers (and inflicts) a lot of abuse, but which, like wife beating, is difficult to explain or resolve rationally.

What seems clear is that French higher education *en lettres*, a term that roughly corresponds to *in the humanities*, is confronting its own version of the general European and North American education crisis over the identity and mission of these institutions, albeit from a somewhat different direction. Recent calls for a renewal of the social contract known as *civisme* do resemble America's recent "family values" campaign. Its proponents want to solve the problem of delinquency by pumping a new and improved brand of humanism or *culture générale* into the unruly masses of French youth at the university level, in the belief that teaching *Romeo and Juliet* or the history of the Peloponnesian War or the lessons of Matthew Arnold will bring about the proper civilizing effect. Others (in France and elsewhere in Europe) propose burying the humanities curriculum instead of praising it. They want universities to focus on the development of guidance counseling, marketable skills, and apprenticeships in the real world—in French, *la vie active*. These tendencies are often referred to as the *secondarisation de l'enseignement supérieur*—that is, a conversion of the French *faculté des lettres* into additional providers of the vocational training cum health and human services that constitutes the current double duty of most secondary schools. The observation that secondary school teachers and their institutions often suffer under the weight of numerous social responsibilities, however, has led many in the universities to be dubious about taking on additional tasks. (The country took notice this year when teachers at several French high schools went on strike to protest unsafe working conditions; that is, student violence.) University professors claim that teaching and conducting the research projects necessary for the renewal and extension of knowledge in their various fields is difficult enough. "And besides, look at all those burnt-out high school teachers, that's no way to live!" A reasonable attitude? Perhaps, but then these cautious souls may be singled out for shirking their duty and loudly accused of elitism. (Curiously, the inquisition rarely goes all the way to the top to indict the French equivalents of Harvard, Yale, and the other name schools of the Western world. The elitism of a select group of French state schools—ENS, ENA, X, and other "*grandes écoles*," all with cryptic names and stringent entrance exams—is rarely if ever questioned. Whether one ought to regret or feel thankful for this omission is a legitimate question.) By far the favorite target today—like picking on the fat, brainy kid—is France's public university system. With or without its consent, various parties—including government officials, students, parents, and the media—have chosen it to serve as a kind of shield, buffer, or punching bag that separates elite and mass, haves and have-nots. The cushioning effect comes by means of bizarre acts of misrepresentation and miscalculation of the system's mission that often stymie effective action.

What makes these acts bizarre—and thus capable of provoking laughter or rage, depending on one's position—are the gaps that exist between expectation and reality, intention and action. The French public universities—and I mean the *facultés des lettres*, since the *facultés des sciences* and the *facultés de droit* have mostly already gone over to the technobureaucratic tail that is currently wagging the dog of Western civilization—find themselves in a tense situation of contradictions and mixed messages. Public opinion often aligns "*la fac*" right next to other client-driven state institutions, such as the post office and the National Employment Agency, yet many of those institutions' workers believe that the *facultés des lettres* should be less client-driven and have a mission more like that of the École normale supérieure (ENS) or the Centre national de la recherche scientifique (CNRS), where other purposes are allowed to come into play. Institutions of higher education are special places where, in theory at least, the links between the use values and exchange values of their activities may loosen. Under relatively controlled conditions and in relatively free and ordered spaces (laboratories, seminar rooms, learned publications), there is the intention of actually provoking crisis, taking risks, and trying something new—acts and accidents without which the honest teacher-researcher knows there is no chance to do more than make endless calculations and reproductions of the same thing. Efforts to move constructively within this difference of opinion about the principal mission of the public universities—should people be free explorers, designers, and producers of new knowledge or well-trained consumers and reproducers of technical know-how?—have thus far met with little satisfaction. The result is a lot of going along to get along (*"C'est comme ça"*), interrupted by occasional grumpy outbursts (*"Mais où va-t-on?"*), strong accusations (*"Les facs sont des décharges"*), and pessimism (*"On va passer à la trappe!"*).

To summarize the above description of the situation, we may borrow Jimmy Carter's memorable expression and say that France's *facultés des lettres* are experiencing a crisis of confidence. What, then, can be done? What ought to be done? The first thing I would say is, Don't panic. Take a deep breath. Recall that crisis, insofar as it is a species of change more or less voluntary, is, as Ferdinand de Saussure once said, the ABC of everything. It would therefore be pure folly to imagine overcoming crisis or putting an end to crisis. The end of crisis is not an option.

Next, in view of almost everyone's private doubts about the French public university system, it may be worth asking publicly if the system can or ought to continue to be nationwide. This may seem unimportant to Americans, who readily accept that geography is destiny and know full well that Paris, Texas, is not Paris, Maine. The French, however, and especially Parisians whose department name suggestively means "Island of France," see things differently. For one thing, they take synecdoche seriously: in education the national diplomas, exams, recruitment, policy making, and budget are designed so that Paris III, Paris XIII, Pau, and all the other schools will form one egalitarian community. That fewer of my students have been to England than the students of English in Lille means nothing, because their diplomas will be identical. But many universities seem simply too big (28,000 humanities students in Toulouse, 3,000 of them taking English) and the admissions criteria too few (a high school diploma plus lots of waiting in line and you can become a "student") to allow one to speak convincingly of community. The students in the humanities faculties come from a variety of backgrounds and will go off to live their own lives. They spend an average of four years at a university, and for most of them their stay is a rather fragmentary, poorly defined, and provisional association with teachers, classrooms, course materials, and other students. It would be a naive and cruel charade to pretend otherwise, and yet it happens.

The strikes temporarily brought together the frustrated, the disillusioned, and the disoriented in a fitfully organized simulacrum of community to denounce injustice and hypocrisy. But events have shown that such a negative community, founded on a lamentation over the lack of true community and common ground, while it may to a certain extent be punctually efficacious, is difficult (or even dangerous) to sustain. This volatility does not itself invalidate such efforts, but one may want to ask how to get from such a fragile community of denunciation to a perhaps more stable, lasting community of affirmation, and this without falling back into degenerate fantasylands and other totalizing (not to say totalitarian) visions of community. The policy in recent years to develop smaller and more autonomous suburban and regional campuses (e.g., Albi, Montauban, and Rodez within the academy of Toulouse) may be one such positive step. With good local leadership and with mutual respect among Paris, the institution, and the host community, these smaller university sites have the chance to be more responsible and responsive to the needs of faculty members, students, administrators, and the surrounding community. These sites may also take some of the pressure off the large urban campuses, especially when it comes to dealing with the large numbers of first- and second-year students.

François Bayrou said, "C'est la réforme de fond qui nous permettra de répondre aux véritables questions posées" ("It's a reform from the ground up that will allow us to respond to the true questions that have been asked"). Although people from the minister of education down to the most inexperienced first-year university activist have called for a thorough examination and reform of the university system, it is curious how certain things can be left out of account. Where, for example, has been the debate about the French system of university career-exam competitions, or *concours*? The CAPES and Agrégation exams are the twin idols whose legitimacy no one appears willing to question. These *concours* are an essential part of the apparatus by which the institution of French National Education, and hence the French nation, reproduces itself. No small deal. How is it, then, that asking about the structure and function of these *concours* is not recognized as a legitimate question? Until the question is addressed, there may be no way—except perhaps by the wildest of accidents—of producing anything other than what has been produced and reproduced for the last two hundred years. Surprisingly, few people seem troubled by this prospect of nothing new.

Even at Toulouse, supposedly one of the most militant campuses during the strikes, there was little if any open resistance to the business-as-usual functioning of the CAPES and Agrégation cram courses that prepare students to execute predetermined mental exercises on preselected texts and subjects. All regular courses were interrupted, but arguably the most objectionable were allowed to go on with everyone's blessing. How could that be? As I marched along in demonstrations and listened to impassioned speeches at general assemblies, I recalled my colleague's remark comparing university behavior to wife beating—hardly a comforting thought.

It is remarkable, moreover, how the pros and cons of introducing some admissions selection procedure can be debated without anyone's looking up to notice that the present system is nothing but one giant selection apparatus from first year to last. Anyone who by chance has noticed this realizes that the whole system is driven not by the client or by some ideal of academic freedom but by the inhuman operation of an institutional machinery that seeks to reproduce itself as efficiently as possible through the substitution of identical new parts for the old worn-out ones. In the eyes of the National Education system, all courses, no matter what the year or subject area, will be conducted, openly or secretly, to prepare students for *concours*. There is no point discussing curricula, because the system has predecided and preprogrammed both the form and the content of all courses. There is no point discussing teaching methods, because the conceit is that everyone will teach the same way, the way that most efficiently prepares students for their exams, exams that are all stages on the race to *the* exam, the *concours*, which, if they are among the chosen, the elect, the elite, will instantly convert their accumulated cultural capital into material capital, in the form of a life-time contract of employment in the National Education system. It's essentially a pyramid scheme, a type of confidence game, and, like all confidence games, it depends on several factors including high levels of nearly anonymous participation, arcane rules, and an atmosphere of urgency. If one or more of these factors is lacking, confidence may falter, and the potential for a small or large crisis arises. For better or worse, this may be what is happening now.

Even though discussions of such delicate subjects as *concours* and the mediation between education and nation were mostly drowned out by the safer, conventional pleas for money and jobs, the strikes did demand a more serious scrutiny of higher education than has ever occurred in the history of these institutions. In comparison, the much ballyhooed unrest of May 1968 now looks more like a positive physical checkup during a period of growing pains. In the fall of 1995, the patient seems to have been in more critical condition, and people have been forced to take notice. In that way Bayrou is right: crisis has given those concerned an unexpected chance—an opportunity to examine the situation, ask tough questions, formulate expectations, make decisions, and take new steps instead of simply continuing to apply the standard procedures and life-support systems.

When it comes to these tough questions and decisions, professors of the humanities, and especially literature professors, may have something valuable to offer, a small good thing. After all, literature professors know about crises of loss and absence. They do not need the news media to inform them of "the death of literature" because they have been caring for the "sick rose" all along. They have experienced the panic that comes with the realization that those scribbles of ink and sculpted typefaces on the page mean absolutely nothing, are quite useless, until someone or something has a chance to set about making organizational decisions and careful investments of time and attention—in effect, a chance to work. Literature professors remember that *poet* means "maker" and that the poets were the first inventors and builders. Literature professors also know much about those buildings. And therefore it may be that we—women and men who care about the future of France's humanities faculties and about humanity in general—will want to look (forward) today to the poets and the professors of poetry, prose, and plays, to the record of their vast experience and their lessons, in order to ask, How shall we build now? With what? For whom? and Why?

Those who have been selling the humanities short in recent years, especially poetry and the teaching of poetry, may be surprised by the rebound that could be preparing itself even now, unforeseen and unbidden. For my part, I am bullish on poetry, but my bull resembles less the mascot of Merrill Lynch Securities and more the bull named Ferdinand in a wonderful children's story I remember from long ago. Ferdinand the bull is more a lover than a fighter; on one occasion, however, he is mistaken for a fierce bull, captured, and expected to be useful in the economy of the bullring with its ritualized conflicts, division of labor, winners, losers, prestige, and speculation. But Ferdinand is not concerned with the horns of a dilemma among exchange values and use values; he is aware of another economy alongside the market economy of the bullring. On the big day, to everyone's surprise and consternation, this other economy is glimpsed by the general public when, instead of behaving like other bulls—*crisis*—Ferdinand sits in the middle of the ring and smells the flowers in the hair of the lovely ladies. He wins—not the bullfight but a suspension, displacement, and reinvention of everything and everyone involved in bullfighting. In that instant, the reader, along with the men and lovely ladies, discovers that Ferdinand is at heart a poet and that he moves in another economy, the gift economy of the work of art.

The story of Ferdinand and what could be called Ferdinand's strike should be kept in mind as we ask how higher education is to be reinvented. With some imagination, courage, and a little luck, France could come through the current crisis better and sooner than either England or the United States can. One reason is that the French government—unlike England and the United States, where budgets for education and the arts have been decreasing for years—continues to expand its financial support. To give some idea, its spending on education and the arts is fifty percent greater than its military budget (22.6% vs. 14.1% in 1995). Today, along with hundreds of state-supported museums, libraries, and parks—gifts that are the pride of the country—France has this ragtag collection of public universities. However, despite bureaucratic horror stories about lines and paperwork, these schools are some of the most democratic and accessible institutions of higher education in the world. "Ils ont le mérite d'exister," as they say.

So where's the problem? The problem is deciding what the public universities are for. What is their raison d'être? The French get worked up about this, perhaps because no version of the Romantic Anglo-American ideology of liberal arts education and general, mind-expanding studies has ever taken hold in French universities. There has been no Shelley to defend a different kind of (poetic) education that "acts in another and diviner manner, [that] awakens and enlarges the mind itself by rendering it the receptacle of a thousand unapprehended combinations of thought" (487). Since Charlemagne and on through the eras of Henry IV and Napoleon, most French schools have been classically didactic places where very specific programs of study are pursued for narrowly utilitarian purposes; in other words, career training. Of course Romanticism did rub off in other areas of French society, notably in politics (think of the heroine Marianne, *the* stamp of the French Republic, and Delacroix's *La Liberté guidant le peuple*, the Romantic emblem of revolutionary politics) and in economics (think of France's café culture, its ardent defense of workers' rights, and the quasi-religious significance of *vacances*). The French combination of classical education and Romantic political economy may seem odd, and it can cause some strange twists. In libraries, museums, and parks, for example, the French allow for considerable freedom among the users; this permissiveness is the source of the French notion of free time or *loisirs*. In these areas, they would not dream, I don't think, of imposing a normative scheme to determine what constitutes a successful or failed visit; however, many educators, true to their classical training, can become wildly obsessed with *formations* (training), *filières* (tracking), and *contrôles de connaissances* (testing and ranking).

It will be a tragedy worthy of representation by some future poet, if France decides, out of some crazy impulse to measure everything by the same yardstick of technical excellence and efficient useful performance, to retreat from its long-standing social commitment to easy access and equal opportunity (*égalité des chances*) in higher education. The nation will bring dishonor and blight on itself if it decides to take back with one hand what was so generously given by the other. Of course, some form of competition and other methods of evaluation and judgment must exist. Capable women and men of goodwill must be encouraged to enter and enrich all professions with their ideas and leadership; but, at the same time, the thousands of students who simply attend and who may never even complete an advanced degree must not be bulldozed under like so much landfill. I hope that France has the courage to resist, to continue to be the cultural exception, and to carry on into its public universities the bullish Romantic thinking that has inspired so many of its more felicitous actions in the development of public parks, museums, and the arts in general. If it does, France will have shown itself to be all the more special.

WORKS CITED

Bayrou, François. Fax to French university presidents and personnel. 4 Dec. 1995.

Drozdiak, William. "Juppé Names Mediator in Attempt to End Upheaval." *International Herald Tribune* 8 Dec. 1995, Toulouse ed.: 8.

Program guide. *La gazette: Utopia cinémas*. Dec. 1995. No. 20, 5.

Saussure, Ferdinand de. *Cours de linguistique générale*. Ed. R. Engler. Vol. 4. Wiesbaden: Harrassowitz, 1967. 23.

Shelley, Percy Bysshe. "A Defence of Poetry." *Shelley's Poetry and Prose*. Ed. Donald H. Reiman and Sharon B. Powers. New York: Norton, 1977. 480–508.

Professions beyond the Academy

MARK A. JOHNSON

After I earned my English PhD in January 1995, rather than resign myself to life as a PhD-carrying Tom Joad, itinerant and at the mercy of what one writer calls "a kind of academic Great Depression" (Curren 59), I looked for work beyond the MLA *Job Information List*. There I found a place that's hungry for young, ambitious humanities PhDs; a month after I graduated from Boston University, the California-based software company Intuit hired me as a technical writer. Once I stopped seeing myself as just another unemployable literature PhD and cast my job net beyond the university, I discovered that nonacademic professions for PhDs are numerous and rewarding—a fact that may surprise anyone who hangs around literature departments or who keeps up with the gloomy job-market articles in publications such as *Profession*, the *Chronicle of Higher Education*, and *Academe*.

What follows are strategies I used to land a challenging job outside the academy—a job that draws on the research, thinking, writing, and teaching skills I honed while earning a PhD. Along with identifying steps graduate students can take to tailor their skills to jobs outside the academy, I suggest ways to challenge received wisdom about what literature PhDs should do with their skills and about what life is like in a nonacademic profession.

Be catholic, not insular.

The university is not the only life-support system the world has to offer PhDs. Especially in the humanities, PhDs new and old tend to be ignorant and often

---

The author is a Documentation Lead at Intuit Corporation.

---

disdainful of job opportunities beyond the academy.[1] Such a limited vision is understandable. Ten or more years of higher education steeps us in a culture of research, high art, student mentoring, and humanist values. By the time graduate students snag their PhDs, Steinbeck, Dickens, and Rebecca Harding Davis have taught them to be suspicious of the world beyond the academy. And because graduate departments and advisers are "clone factories" (Gies 6) that prepare students for careers as teachers and literary critics in elite graduate programs, it's difficult to imagine that a PhD can be useful, let alone survive, outside the university.

In *Profession 95* Seth Katz suggests that departments and job seekers broaden their definition of their profession when he reminds graduate students that jobs exist outside top-ranking research institutions—those who broaden the job search will find that community colleges and small private schools offer plenty of opportunities for satisfying careers (64). Also in *Profession 95*, David Gies encourages the professoriat to offer instruction in "things beyond the traditional focus of graduate-level literature studies" (6), namely, practical secondary school teaching skills. Both writers wisely challenge the attitude that literature and language PhDs are worthy of working only with other educational elites, yet I don't agree that literature and language departments should offer more practical training.

Beyond the world of higher education is a sea of corporations that live and die by their ability to serve up facts, ideas, and new knowledge to a voracious, computer-savvy public. The phenomenon called the information revolution is real, and a big portion of today's business world clamors to hire employees equipped with the intelligence, creativity, research skills, and drive of a PhD. To take advantage of these job opportunities, graduate students must reassess their goals and identify the practical skills wrapped in the mantle of today's rarified, theorized, and superspecialized graduate programs.

Ask yourself, Do I really want to teach?

Before despairing at the supposedly nonexistent job market for humanities PhDs, examine your values. As I got closer to my dissertation defense, I asked myself hard questions about what was important to me. I admitted that I was unwilling to sacrifice my first love—surfing—for a temporary teaching position anywhere at any salary. So I moved to San Diego and opened myself to any career that would call on my literacy and my ability to navigate a library. I also opened the classified ads and found 350 San Diego software firms employing 15,000 people and growing at an annual rate of fifteen percent (Hawkins). Getting interviews was relatively easy; my PhD gave me instant cachet with high-tech firms and University of California spin-off companies, and my interviewers seemed impressed by the effort that went into my degree.

Data from the Society for Technical Communication's San Diego chapter suggest that there are many positions open to applicants with extensive training in writing and teaching: 196 companies in San Diego alone employ technical communicators (*San Diego*). And this demand for literate employees is nation-wide—for instance, the technology reporter Laurence Zuckerman notes that in Seattle, Microsoft is expanding the range of topics covered by its CD-ROMs and is therefore busily "hiring people with editorial skills who can research and package information in new and innovative ways."

Unfortunately, neither society at large nor the academy itself readily imagines a literature PhD doing anything but teaching at Harvard, so it's difficult for graduate students to picture themselves working outside the classroom. Graduate students must also hurdle the stigma attached to corporate vocations. When an English PhD who graduated a couple of years before me tired of teaching four sections of freshman English for little money and few benefits, she moved to California for a position in the software industry with a good salary and full benefits. Told of her career advancement, her graduate adviser remarked, "That's too bad." Because my colleague put her professional interests above some tacit blood tie to universities, she was seen as betraying a higher calling. Graduate students and new PhDs would do well to question the belief that the corporate world is categorically venal and utterly beneath a literature PhD.

Reject the notion that there are too many PhDs.

In a letter to the editor of the *Chronicle of Higher Education*, Richard Sax voices received wisdom when he writes that "there are simply too many people with PhDs, especially in the humanities and social sciences." There may be too many PhDs for the country's literature and language departments, but my experience in the software industry tells me that the world at large can never have too many literate critical thinkers. Beyond the university, PhDs are a rarity, a human resource whose skills information-driven corporations need and are willing to pay for. A case in point: in my department of eighteen writers, editors, translators, graphic artists, and multimedia producers, there are two PhDs besides me: one in psychology and one in philosophy. Both are graduates of the University of California, San Diego. My boss has a master's degree in creative writing from the University of California, Irvine.

Be practical, but not too practical.

To create PhDs employable in private industry, literature and language departments do not have to become corporate America's vocational schools. In the software industry at least, people who can theorize and teach are cherished. As Marian Barchilon and Donald G. Kelly write in the journal *Technical Communication*, today's industries value employees who are able to combine information from multiple disciplines, to apply new knowledge in context and with an awareness of how information affects larger socioeconomic events, to do research and develop expertise in a field, and to set aside personal prejudices and work smoothly with people from other cultures (591–93). Because bad decisions—those not based on expert research and consideration of theoretical implications—cost money, industry values those who can derive what William James might call cash value from their theoretical and practical research skills.[2] As Michon Scott writes, in technical communication, "our business is to help others learn: learn new software, learn new procedures, even learn new concepts. In short, our business is sharing knowledge" (85).

Because a substantial chunk of corporate America makes money by providing the public with information and with the means to manage that information, graduate departments and students should continue exploring undiscovered literary and cultural countries, no matter how rarified the results. While some disparage literary criticism's tendency to view art as a result of social and historical power struggles, the critically trained mind that understands how disparate forces affect present and future realities is crucial to corporate success. Today's PhDs are trained in the art of thinking contextually. They can doggedly track down information and recognize relations among apparently incoherent parts of a culture or a history. And as Barchilon and Kelley observe, industry lives or dies by analytical minds that can "go beyond the individual facts and be able to see the broad picture when solving an industry problem" (593).

Be creative.

The ability to imagine and create is more important outside the academy than inside. At Intuit, technical writers work alongside software engineers and marketers when designing and improving tax software. I cannot imagine a greater creative challenge than turning the nightmarish snarl of the US tax code into something elegant, straightforward, and user-friendly. Along with my colleagues, I'm constantly pressed to imagine ways to improve our products. Furthermore, envisioning the needs of the other is a critical component of my job. In my case, the other is a customer who lives in a world apart from software development and tax law. Thinkers who can shed prejudices and assumptions and put themselves in someone else's shoes distinguish themselves in the software industry.

Companies that value creativity offer stimulating work environments. Marc Andreessen, the University of Illinois graduate who created the browser software that made the World Wide Web accessible, confirms the value of a humanist background and echoes my belief that the intellectual life exists outside the university. "Most of the interesting things are happening in companies, not at universities," says Andreessen, who at twenty-four is already worth some $157 million (Zuckerman). While I don't quite pull in Andreessen's salary, I also find the software industry to be a refreshingly intellectual place. At Intuit, as at many other major software firms, continuing education is an important part of the corporate culture. Classes on subjects as diverse as Web-page construction, software architecture, and leadership skills are often taught in the workplace, usually at no charge to employees. (In fact, I teach writing courses for Intuit employees.) It's not by chance that many of today's high-tech firms have sprawling campuses and that their employees dress as casually as college students.

My colleagues are universally intelligent, quick-thinking, and well-read; they know what I'm talking about when I allude to Casaubon's unfinished encyclopedia. But creating software products inspires an intensely collaborative atmosphere that's far different from the personality-driven world of the university. Unlike academics, who rise or fall according to what they've published on their own, my coworkers and I are engaged in a communal endeavor. Indeed, when a group of minds assembles to brainstorm on ways to improve a product feature, the energy is palpable—it's like being in a seminar again, only the results of the session have practical consequences that directly affect our sense of self-worth and our financial well-being. The company, our stock options, and our collective state of mind depend on our creativity, our willingness to work hard, and the Intuit report cards that appear as business articles in the *Wall Street Journal* and *New York Times*. This corporate communalism, while insanely demanding at times, is 180 degrees from the university, a juggernaut that plows on with indifference to the fate of its individual crew members.

Remember, the Industrial Revolution is over.

During the Industrial Revolution, workers survived by virtue of muscle and resistance to pain; managers advanced by virtue of their ability to drive bodies to exhaustion. Today's high-tech industries do not need the sort of worker drone that powered the Industrial Revolution. A company that relies solely on its top executives for creative thinking is doomed, because unlike its forward-thinking competitors, it is not taking advantage of its collective intellectual resources. Companies need managers and workers who can think, inspire, and collaborate. Employees who can drive themselves and their colleagues to new heights of creativity stand apart. PhDs come preloaded with these skills, and as Eric Johnson notes, "Increasingly, smart personnel officers of computing corporations will prefer to hire those with a liberal education" (410). More specifically, Johnson writes:

> The best assurance that technical writers have the indispensable imagination to write good computer documentation is their completion of a traditional liberal education in the arts and sciences. Enormous imaginative power can be developed by following the three-part inventions of J. S. Bach, by grasping

the ideas of Descartes or Pascal, and by conceiving the fictional worlds of novels by Austen, Dickens, and Faulkner. (410)

Because many companies are expanding abroad, the ability to understand other countries and languages is also in demand outside the academy. Localization, the adaptation of a product to fit the needs and idiosyncrasies of a foreign country, offers many opportunities for empathic, polyglot language PhDs. The tasks associated with localization—from translating a software manual into three languages to understanding a German's perspective on balancing a checkbook—constantly call on a language PhD's practical and theoretical skills.

View graduate school as an apprenticeship.

Instead of decrying the publish-or-perish environment of the university, recognize it as a less humane version of the corporate world. Elizabeth Langland suggests reforming the PhD process so that students do not founder in "the expansive, uncharted meadow of qualifying exams and dissertation writing" (30). While it's a good idea for departments to offer ABDs more guidance, getting from prospectus to dissertation defense is excellent training for PhDs who go on to industry.

Just as public universities reduce staffs when taxpayers yank the purse strings, corporations do so at the drop of a Wall Street hat. In such an unpredictable environment, the people who thrive (and who don't get fired during downsizing season) are those who are so resourceful and self-directed that the company would do itself a financial disservice in firing them. For instance, Saul Carliner observes that corporate "professionals want to feel comfortable about their recommendations, and research can provide them with that measure of comfort" (550). However, it's expensive to hire outside research firms, and many corporate professionals are at a loss in today's libraries. Carliner describes a professor whose industrial colleagues call for information instead of going to the library, because even if they were to make it to the library, "they don't know where to begin looking" (551). By aggressively undertaking research projects that shed light on company decisions made with minimal background information, a PhD can establish a name for him- or herself. It is relatively easy for a PhD to become an expert, the person others come to for answers, research directions, or help extracting information from formal studies, yet such an undertaking can yield great professional dividends in a corporate environment.

Learn that society is willing to pay your salary.

Cary Nelson suggests that the country does not have a glut of PhDs but, rather, "lacks . . . the will to pay their salaries" (21). While our national parsimony may affect PhDs at the university, PhDs in industry are earning a decent wage. And having a PhD boosts your salary. For example, according to the Society for

Technical Communication's 1995 nationwide salary survey, the median salary for writers and editors with a PhD is $48,000; the top quartile earns $50,750 or more and the bottom quartile $40,250 or less. In contrast, for technical writers and editors with a bachelor's degree, the median salary is $40,000; the top quartile earns $48,000 or more and the bottom quartile $33,000 or less. These numbers reflect salaries in all industries; the survey points out that salaries in the computer industry tend to be $2,000 to $3,000 above average. This information refutes the argument that society is unwilling to pay PhDs for a good day's work.[3]

Search the World Wide Web.

While you're still in graduate school, take advantage of university-sponsored Internet connections. The World Wide Web is a far-reaching clearinghouse for jobs at companies all over the globe. When thinking about potential employers, start by considering products you like and use. Whether they be bicycle helmets or software programs, look up the manufacturers on the World Wide Web. Many post job listings and standard compensation packages online. Some encourage you to submit your résumé by e-mail directly from the Web page. If a company intrigues you but its Web page does not list a human resources contact, send an inquiry to the Webmaster (listed in italics at the bottom of the Web page), who will either forward your message to the appropriate person or send you a contact address.

Start taking deadlines seriously.

If you decide to find a job in industry, banish university time frames. Things get done fast in corporations. Extend a work project into a seven-year fiasco like the typical dissertation, and you're out the door. Especially in the fast-paced world of software, scheduling major projects and meeting deadlines—tasks often only as important as the individual makes them in a university—are not to be taken lightly.

Write, write, write.

During my first year in the private sector, I've interviewed quite a few job candidates for writing and editing positions. Knowing that many academics are experts at grinding out turgid prose, I ask candidates with academic backgrounds to prove that they can write clearly and at a level that's comprehensible to a nontechnical audience. When interviewing for a job, be prepared to meet this challenge. One tactic that is also a good way to get your résumé noticed is to enclose published writing clips. While in graduate school, I wrote articles for bicycling magazines and weekly alternative newspapers. I covered topics ranging from punk rock to forensic photography to velodrome bicycle racing, and

I'm convinced that these clips helped me get a job. Published, accessible articles prove that you can write clearly, that you can teach with words.

Remember, the sky does not have to fall.

Lamenting a world that fails to throw money, tenure, and a windowed office at every PhD, self-help articles I've run across often strike me as self-defeating and disingenuous. For example, Cary Nelson's *Academe* article "Lessons from the Job Wars: What Is to Be Done?" is peppered with weepy phrases that, in an effort to make the PhD haves feel guilty about the plight of the PhD have-nots, only erode a graduate student's self-respect and initiative: "PhD programs have only one economic rationale—they are a source of cheap instructional labor for universities"; "apprenticeship with no future is servitude" (18); "one of our PhDs lives with his wife in a tin cow shed on the Texas border"; "the long-term job seekers of the academy are like lepers in the acropolis" (20); and "the job market's blunt message: There is no future in the PhD" (21). Proposing a "twelve-step program for academia" (22), Nelson's article furthers the perception that PhDs are hapless victims of a bad environment. While his twelve steps to reform are valid, Nelson does not suggest that professors or their ABD charges look beyond the university for employment. In the guise of a forward-looking reform strategy, Nelson's article allows graduate students and professors ample opportunity to wallow in self-indulgent sorrow—in a tin cow shed, at that! Blueprints for action such as Nelson's are earnest, even strident—yet because they are insular, granting nary a nod of acknowledgment to the world of opportunities beyond the university, I don't find "lessons" like Nelson's much help at all.

In the world beyond the academy, a PhD puts you far ahead of job candidates who come equipped with only a BA. The PhD earns you more money, and it garners respect, even awe, from colleagues that is nonexistent in the university, where everybody has a PhD. Keep an open mind, reject ivory-tower arrogance toward the corporate world, and take the doomsayers with a grain of salt. For me, doing all those things led to a profession that is as rewarding as any I could expect from the academy.

NOTES

[1]See Gies for similar comments on ivory-tower myopia.

[2]For analysis of how information-based organizations value collective creativity and why they reject the hierarchical management structure typical during the Industrial Revolution, see Zuboff.

[3]For a discussion of how higher levels of education correlate with higher salaries and better job opportunities in various occupations, see Kletzer.

WORKS CITED

Barchilon, Marian G., and Donald G. Kelley. "A Flexible Technical Communication Education Model for the Year 2000." *Technical Communication* 42 (1995): 590–98.

Carliner, Saul. "Finding a Common Ground: What STC Is, and Should Be, Doing to Advance Education in Information Design and Development." *Technical Communication* 42 (1995): 546–54.

Curren, Erik D. "No Openings at This Time: Job Market Collapse and Graduate Education." *Profession 94.* New York: MLA, 1994. 57–61.

Gies, David T. "Responsibilities? Dream On!" *Profession 95.* New York: MLA, 1995. 5–9.

Hawkins, Robert J. "Job Seekers, Start Your Search Engines!" *San Diego Union-Tribune* 27 Feb. 1996, sec. ComputerLink: 12.

Johnson, Eric. "Computer Documentation: Writing about Technology." *Computers and the Humanities* 29.1 (1995): 409–11.

Katz, Seth R. "Graduate Programs and Job Training." *Profession 95.* New York: MLA, 1995. 62–67.

Kletzer, Lori G. "Young and Highly Educated in the 1990s: Job Prospects in the Professional Labor Market." *Profession 95.* New York: MLA, 1995. 51–55.

Langland, Elizabeth. "The Future of Graduate Education; or, Which Graduate Programs Have a Future?" *ADE Bulletin* 111 (1995): 28–32.

Nelson, Cary. "Lessons from the Job Wars: What Is to Be Done?" *Academe* Nov.-Dec. 1995: 18–25.

Sax, Richard. Letter. *Chronicle of Higher Education.* 23 Feb. 1996: B5.

Scott, Michon. "Technical Communicators as Managers in the Informated Workplace." *Technical Communication* 43 (1996): 83–87.

Society for Technical Communication. "1995 Technical Communicator Salary Survey." Online. World Wide Web. 15 Feb. 1996. Available http://www.clark.net/pub/stc/www/salary.html.

———. *San Diego Companies That Employ Technical Communicators.* Brochure. San Diego: Society for Technical Communication, 1996.

Zuboff, Shoshana. *In the Age of the Smart Machine: The Future of Work and Power.* New York: Basic, 1988.

Zuckerman, Laurence. "High-Tech Tycoons Tell How to Ride Wave of Future." *San Diego Union-Tribune* 27 Feb. 1996, sec. ComputerLink: 13.

Secondary Education:
Still an Ignored Market

ALISON T. SMITH

I confess that I read the last two issues of *Profession* from cover to cover, anxious to unearth some scrap of hope for my professional future. Instead the articles crushed my ambitions; my aspirations foundered on the dire predictions of the shrinking job market. The weeks immediately following the defense of my dissertation had been euphoric—the sky was the limit! Slowly reality set in when, after months of searching, I had not received a single call for an interview.

The problems were compounded by my calculations. Some people predicted that the job market would not turn around for another five to six years, which for a thirty-three-year-old meant the possibility of not landing that first tenure-track job until the age of thirty-eight or thirty-nine. Adding the five or six years required to get tenure (should I be so lucky), I realized that I would then be in my mid-forties. Staying in this profession would require tremendous personal sacrifice and offer slim prospects and few guarantees.

Despite the odds I resolved, with the naive hope that all the predictions did not really apply to me, to continue my job search. I consulted successive issues of the MLA *Job Information List*, read the *Chronicle of Higher Education*, and submitted résumés to all jobs for which I had a hope of qualifying. I was somewhat limited geographically, but several friends with similar qualifications did not share this limitation, and they had had no luck getting jobs either. A few people mentioned the possibility of teaching in high school. I was not receptive to that idea, although I had taught part-time in a private high school while completing my dissertation and that teaching assignment proved one of the most rewarding

The author teaches Spanish and English at the Hill Center in Durham, North Carolina.

I ever had. People had warned me, however, not to stay there too long lest I be labeled a high school teacher, which would forever destroy my prospects of getting a serious job at the college level.

By July 1995 my one-year replacement teaching appointment expired, and I still had no prospects for the following year. Financial necessity forced me to reconsider my options, and I began an all-out campaign to get any sort of teaching job. I called everyone I knew who might have information about employment. I consulted with a career counselor at my graduate institution, who assured me that with two languages (French and Spanish) I would certainly get a high school job and would probably have several to choose from. Within three weeks of intensive networking I had three offers: two from high schools and one from a university.

In the end I chose one of the high school jobs, for several reasons. The university job entailed teaching four sections of French at levels 1 and 2 (which I had been doing for ten years), offered no benefits, and paid an appallingly low salary: less money per course than I had made in my first year as a teaching assistant, when I was working on my master's degree. I have since discovered that these conditions are commonplace in both public and private institutions of higher education. It is particularly shocking that one of the private institutions that practices such exploitation has an outstanding academic reputation, is heavily endowed, and charges exorbitant tuition. The high schools, however, offered me benefits, reasonable salaries, and the opportunity to teach in new areas. My hesitations about secondary education were overcome.

Settling into my new job, I wondered why this market with such tremendous need for qualified teachers has been ignored. Although teaching at the secondary level has been endorsed officially in the *MLA Newsletter*, it has not been embraced as an appropriate career path by large numbers of MLA members. The prejudices are evident in remarks such as the one made by Daniel T. Kline in his letter endorsing teaching in the two-year college. In an attempt to dispel stereotypes, he actually perpetuates them: "Traditionally, the primary responsibility of two-year college faculty has been to teach and of university faculty to extend their teaching with research. This bifurcation for too long has fostered stereotypes damaging to both faculty groups: little more than glorified high school teachers, two-year faculty are unconcerned with research . . ." (100). A well-intentioned professor advised me that it would be better to tutor and do translations to survive than to accept a high school job because of how that would look on my résumé. With such attitudes it is hardly any wonder that 9.9% of PhDs in foreign language prefer to remain unemployed rather than join the ranks of the 3.2% that have chosen to teach in secondary and elementary education ("Survey" 2; table 1).

I would like to dispel some of the prejudices that block so many new PhDs from finding meaningful employment. I teach Spanish and English at a private school whose mission is to serve students with identified learning disabilities. My colleagues are highly trained, well-educated professionals who care deeply about helping students learn. I am in an environment where I have the opportunity to learn and to make positive contributions. Being an integral member of the faculty is an experience unlike that of being a non-tenure-track instructor at the university level. I participate in curriculum decisions, plan my courses, select textbooks and software, advise students, meet with parents, and participate on committees. I participate in professional conferences as both a teacher and a scholar, attend training workshops, and will have the opportunity to take a group of students abroad during the summer. All these experiences are contributing to my professional growth in ways that were not available to me as a university instructor. I am gaining valuable skills and training that are important for both secondary and postsecondary positions. I find my current position far more satisfactory than that of temporary professor, so accurately described by Lydia Belatèche in *Profession 94*. While I can speak only to the high school experience, I have friends who have left higher education to teach in elementary and middle schools and who have found those environments as well to be very satisfactory professionally.

Many changes must occur before significant numbers of new PhDs choose to seek employment in secondary education. Of primary importance is altering the attitude of university professors, and hence that of their graduate students, toward teaching at the high school level. High school teaching should be viewed as an appropriate step in a career and should in no way bar an individual from ultimately teaching at the college level. Professional associations such as the MLA should encourage the membership and support the continued scholarship of those who choose this path. On recently renewing my SAMLA membership, I was struck by the categories that simply relegated me to "other" because I was neither a professor nor a graduate student.

On the other side of the employment equation, obstacles that prevent PhDs from obtaining jobs in secondary education (such as stringent certification requirements) should be removed. The MLA could become an advocate for PhDs who wish to teach in high school; it could attempt to influence state boards of education to remove obstacles. Perhaps an acceptable alternative to certification would be a significant research project in the field of education. PhDs have demonstrated research skills that could be the source of new knowledge. But high schools must be willing to provide time and funds for such research.

Finally, endorsement of high school teaching as an appropriate career choice directly benefits university professors. With an expanded job market there will no longer be a need for the drastic cuts anticipated in graduate programs. If support for teaching assistants evaporates, perhaps arrangements could be made for part-time positions at local high schools. Preparation for high school teaching may require graduate programs to offer a more broadly based curriculum, but this is certainly a more palatable option than having pro-grams slashed. Another bonus is the ensuring of top-quality undergraduates for the future, because today's high school students are tomorrow's undergradu-ates. University professors will be reassured to know that a significant body of well-qualified PhDs are preparing high school students for the future.

The job I ultimately found is not the one I originally set my hopes on. How-ever, it is a good, stable position that has many rewards and that allows me to develop as a professional. The salary, benefits, and level of respect I receive from colleagues are better than what I found at the university level. I believe I am making a difference in the lives of my students, a far more satisfying feeling than that of just hurrying them through the language requirement, which was my experience so often at the college level. It is time for the MLA to take an ac-tive interest in improving education across all levels in our country by support-ing its members who choose to engage themselves personally in that endeavor.

WORKS CITED

Belatèche, Lydia. "Temp Prof: Practicing the Profession off the Tenure Track." *Profession 94.* New York: MLA, 1994. 64–66.

Kline, Daniel T. Letter to the editor. *Profession 95.* New York: MLA, 1995. 100–01.

"The MLA's 1993–94 Survey of PhD Placement: Major Findings." *MLA Newsletter* 27.4 (1995): 1–3.

"The Most of It": Hiring at a Nonelite College

NONA FIENBERG

In 1981, the same year that Iowa State University hired Jane Smiley, they hired me and my husband. After we had received our degrees from Berkeley in 1978, we first took a shared appointment for one year at Sewanee, the University of the South. It meant we could share also the care of our new baby. Next, Lorne and I endured two years of a commuter marriage, taking two two-year replacement positions. While I taught at Carleton College in Minnesota, he taught at Grinnell. Our son Daniel was two and three in those years. When Iowa State offered us each three-year adjunct appointments to teach composition and business writing courses, we saw it as a chance to consolidate our family, have our second son, Ori (Jane loaned me her maternity things), and still stay full-time in the profession. I started reading Jane's books with *Duplicate Keys*, went backward to *Barn Blind* and *At Paradise Gate*, and haven't missed one since. So it was natural that while I was reading *Moo*, I was also alert to the possibility that she might have something to say about hiring.

Cecelia Sanchez is in her first year at Moo U.

> Cecelia Sanchez, assistant professor of foreign languages and teacher of Spanish, . . . found the Midwest eerie, but it was not only the flatness that threw her. Each day of the past two weeks she would have picked a different source of dislocation. . . . (16)

The author is Professor of English and Coordinator of the English and Journalism Department at Keene State College. A version of this article appeared in the Winter 1995 issue of the ADE Bulletin.

All through high school, college, and graduate school, Cecelia's great belief about herself was that her heart was in research. In the midst of the passions, disappointments, conflicts, and noise of her family and her ex-husband, she had dropped her eggs one by one into a single basket, the life of the mind. . . .

At UCLA, she had treasured up her days in the library, first in a distant carrel far from any entrance, deep into the Hittite and Sumerian shelves, where no one ever went. Later, she'd gotten her own little windowless office and filled it with books and journals about medieval Catalan literature. . . .

At the beginning of the fall, she had confidently found herself another distant carrel, this time amidst the Icelandic and Greenlandic collection, no volumes of which had been checked out in seven years. . . .

The fact was, in spite of the cooler weather, her mind had no life. All medieval Catalan literature did for her was put her into a coma. . . . Nevertheless, she came to her carrel every day and sat down, opened her books and began. . . . Somewhere in them, it seemed, she would find the golden seed. She imagined herself eating it, and desire rooting and blossoming once again.

(116–17)

How did Cecelia get there, in Iowa, at Moo U., from L.A., or is it from Costa Rica? Dark-haired Cecelia in Nordic Iowa, where her latest dislocation crisis is a haircutting crisis; her haircutter had never seen hair like hers. Dropped there, alien, beautiful, refined, with an extraordinary history that is lost, indifferent to most, utterly exotic to any to whom it is not indifferent. How, in the times we academics have known, do we get any jobs at all? Then, somehow—and strangely, having never stopped wondering at our own dislocation—we become those who pick someone up from UCLA and drop her off at Moo U., where we must know and understand that what she, Cecelia, feels is "dislocated." We pick out our likely job candidates as if they were marvelous chess pieces and try to assemble them in our departments and college communities by the process we call hiring. We cannot wonder at the dislocation our new hires feel, who have been trained, like Cecelia Sanchez, to put all their eggs in one basket, the research basket, both in undergraduate programs and graduate programs, almost certainly at elite institutions.

In our English department of twelve full-time faculty members at Keene State College, a public undergraduate four-year college of about four thousand students in southwestern New Hampshire, we have in the last four years hired three full-time tenure-track faculty members. Last spring we had to adhere rigorously to our deadline for student registrations since our first-year class was early overenrolled. We are scrambling now to staff additional classes for the high number of students who will be entering this fall. It is an embarrassment of riches, and we expect it to continue. While we cannot hire as many faculty members as we ought to, neither do we expect to endure downsizing or the panic of underenrollment and fears of closure. When we do hire, we discuss our needs and our students' needs fully; then we determine how to define the position, and we word our ads clearly. "Four courses per semester, half of them teaching composition and first-year students. Some opportunity to teach in area of specialization. Experience in teaching crucial. Active scholarly interests too." If we could, in the ad, we would tell our story in more detail. We started as Keene Normal School in 1909. At the last spring convocation, about a third of our students graduated with associate degrees in arts or in science. Forty-six percent of our students come to us as first-generation college students, many of them hoping to be teachers. Some come wanting to be sports therapists, to gain degrees in sports medicine or industrial technology. Some have settled, for now, for an associate degree until they can finance the completion of the bachelor's. There is a substantial proportion of nontraditional students; about one in five is over twenty-five years old. In New Hampshire, we have a tiny percentage of students of color but a great deal of diversity in social class, ethnicity, age, and ability; we have a large foreign student population and many students in the Aspire Program, that is, students with documented disabilities. We have determined that our job ads need to use the word *teaching* four times to make the point about who we are at Keene State. When we talk with the nine or ten candidates we interview at the MLA convention, we try to engage them in a dialogue about what it means to teach nonmajors, since teaching nonmajors is the bulk of our responsibility. Of our seven hundred students who graduated with BAs in 1994, thirty-six were English majors.

What do we see when we interview? What do we experience when we hire? We see job candidates who fully expect that their careers will be played on the same chessboard that they have been making moves on for their undergraduate and graduate careers.

Candidate A's dissertation is on contemporary female American multicultural autobiographies. She is dynamic on Maxine Hong Kingston, on Maya Angelou, on Alice Walker. One of the interviewers asks if she has read widely outside her dissertation subject. How about Sara Suleri's *Meatless Days*? Does Anne Moody's *Coming of Age in Mississippi* teach well? Has she had success with John Edgar Wideman's *Brothers and Keepers*? How about autobiographical traditions: Ben Franklin? Montaigne? Rousseau? Harriet Jacobs? What challenges has she faced in teaching multicultural literature in her classes? Do her students respond well to this material? What different teaching approaches does she use in her classroom? When she is discussing her research, she is poised and confident; when she is asked about teaching challenges, she takes ten minutes to describe the progress of a semester-long confrontation between her and an African American man in her class who questioned her credentials as a white woman to teach the works of people of color.

We are interviewing Candidate B for a composition job. His range of experience outside the academic world sounds, in his letter, like it would have helped him develop a breadth of vision equipping him for the range of student challenges he would meet in our classrooms. He is articulate on the ways composition theory informs his experience in developing the comp curriculum at his graduate institution. He asks about where we go if we need a research library. Is course release time available for research projects? We ask him what works in his own composition classes. He hesitates, not able to draw on a classroom moment, an anecdote, a favorite assignment, a strategy.

Those we do hire find the transition from graduate school to a job at Keene State College in New Hampshire a difficult one. We decided on an idealist, a strong, dynamic teacher with a wealth of interests. The college imposes no boundaries on the enterprising faculty member. He has received generous faculty development grants that have encouraged his research, which he reports on in an informal faculty research forum. He has taught one of the few senior seminar courses we offer; he designed the course of his dreams, a course in which students were happily stretched and often achieved beyond expectation. When he asks, in department meetings, in college forums, whether a proposed move will lower standards, why a given process resulted in an ambiguous compromise, why our curriculum reform efforts have not yet resulted in a new program, I recognize the struggle to define one's place in an institution, to deal with the challenges of dislocation. At times, maybe late in the semester, when patience runs thin, questions can sound like accusations. "Will this decision mean that the education program now runs the college?" "Are we allowing the administration to weaken the faculty?" "Will this step deviate from our mission as a liberal arts institution?" As we work with our students, our colleagues, with the other programs at the college, even with the administration, some of our number work also to cultivate, both in ourselves and in our new colleagues, the ideals that brought us together.

In *Profession 94* Gordon Hutner, of the University of Wisconsin, Madison, considers what we talk about when we talk about hiring and wonders what would happen if we asked who hires our students and what do *they* need (78). Often the "we" who hire the graduates of the University of Wisconsin at Madison are so different from the "we" to whom he refers in his essay that only at academic conferences and conventions do we ever form a single "we" at all. When we at Keene State College talk about hiring, we don't use the words he quotes, although I know them; they speak of the privilege of elite institutions. We don't speak of "the most impressive mind," "a first-rate intellect," we don't talk about "major coups," "aggressive appointments," or even about "rising stars" (76). I think he is probably right about the "romance of resemblance," about the "dream of the nuclear family" (76), although a New England reticence would modify romance to acceptance. Our language is different. We talk about "a match." We talk about teaching English composition, about general education required courses, about contributing to our curriculum revision process, about adapting pedagogy to different learning styles, about group work, the writing process, contributing to grant proposals, working to train the best secondary school teachers we can.

Yet we see—from the University of Wisconsin at Madison, from Miami University in Ohio, from all over the country—job candidates who have learned exclusively and narrowly the monolithic discourse of the research institution. I was an undergraduate at the University of Toronto and a graduate student at Berkeley, but when Lorne and I took a shared one-year appointment at Sewanee, a person I counted as a friend and mentor exclaimed, "You could have done better!" Listen to the discourse: What is a good school? What is a good job? Is it the one that offers a range of teaching opportunities? that offers support to write successful grant applications to bring twenty secondary school teachers onto campus to work together on Shakespeare in Global Perspective? that offers regular sabbaticals? that offers a faculty member preparing a new course full funding to attend the School of Criticism and Theory at Dartmouth? We in the nonelite undergraduate institutions speak a different language. We too have a set of ideologies that we value. It includes research, writing, and publication but may not offer course release time for such things. It will, however, encourage faculty members to collaborate in the writing of an NEH grant to bring together thirteen colleagues from across the college for a six-week seminar on the cultural construction of race.

All academics need to learn about the diversity of academic cultures as well as of ethnic cultures.

In the end, no matter how adept graduate students may become in the arts of the contact zone, no matter how much we all come to understand the diverse cultures of the academic worlds we move in, the profession has not enough jobs for graduate students. By issuing a call for colleagues able to embrace the challenge of a diversity that includes nonelite institutions, I am proposing another standard that, even if they reach it, cannot help those who have earned the credentials of our profession but will not get jobs in higher education. So for some graduate students, I am speaking of the world beyond the academy. Having dedicated some ten years to the language of yearning and desire, they will have to learn a second language.

And those who, like me and my colleagues at Keene State College, find themselves in nonelite undergraduate institutions teaching mostly nonmajors will also be asked to learn a new language: the language of accommodation. It is the language of teaching, of pedagogy, of first-generation college students. Let me assure you that this is an essential tongue, one of economic, spiritual, and intellectual self-preservation. While I may be bilingual, while I know that those we at Keene State College hire will need to become bilingual or sink into embitterment, my first language remains the one that drove me into this profession and that has kept me in it since 1978. So despite my mastery of the second tongue, despite my belief in the mission of a college like Keene State, the voice of this chair of English at a nonelite institution is really a tangle of voices. One voice exhorts colleges and universities to prepare graduate students for diverse teaching opportunities in a range of academic communities. But another voice celebrates our nurturance of the love of research, the golden seed that Cecelia Sanchez, dislocated in the Midwest, imagines herself eating, her desire rooting and blossoming. In truth, when I speak in that voice in class, some of my students are frightened; but some respond.

A New Hampshire poet helps me explain what it is like to listen for those responses when, as sometimes happens in the press of a semester, I have, shall I say, thought I "kept the universe alone."

> For all the voice in answer he could wake
> Was but the mocking echo of his own. . . .
> He would cry out on life, that what it wants
> Is not its own love back in copy speech,
> But counter-love, original response.
>
> (Frost, "The Most of It")

Ears become tuned in the classroom, or in the company of reading student papers one listens for the surprise, for what seems dissonant but rings true. We know we're not going to get what we expect or what we hope for, mostly, but we may get something else quite marvelous: we may hear "counter-love, original response." My reconciliation is, it seems, Robert Frost's now old-fashioned modern one: I make the most of it. I hope that such an old-fashioned reconciliation is not without meaning for those postmodern graduate students who may meet us one day.

WORKS CITED

Frost, Robert. *Complete Poems of Robert Frost*. New York: Holt, 1964.
Hutner, Gordon. "What We Talk about When We Talk about Hiring." *Profession 94*. New York: MLA, 1994. 74–78.
Smiley, Jane. *Moo*. New York: Knopf, 1995.

What You Should Know: An Open Letter to New PhDs

THE COMMONWEALTH PARTNERSHIP

Recently there has been a great deal of discussion in the press about the state of higher education—much of it very critical. Some of the criticism is thoughtful and well deserved, some is foolish and ill-informed. It behooves all of us who teach and work in colleges and universities to listen carefully to our critics, and those of you who are currently preparing for a career of teaching and research must be especially attentive. It is to you that this letter is addressed, because the future of the institutions within the Commonwealth Partnership in Pennsylvania, and similar ones all over the United States, depends on you.

Our institutions, while differing in important ways, share a vision of the kind of education we want our undergraduate students to have and the sort of faculty members we must attract if we are to realize that vision. The purpose of this letter is to let those of you who have decided to pursue careers in higher education see that vision articulated by twelve college and university deans and provosts who hire, mentor, and assess the faculty members to whom thousands of parents entrust the education of their sons and daughters each year.

The teachers we want to attract are first and foremost committed to the advancement of learning. Combining serious commitment to teaching and to research is difficult, and, in our view, enabling faculty members to achieve a balance in which the two activities actually complement each other is one of

---

The Commonwealth Partnership is a consortium of twelve independent colleges and universities in Pennsylvania that works to advance and enrich curriculum and instruction by linking elementary and secondary faculty members with each other and with college faculty members through professional development programs.

---

the most important contributions we can make. In our institutions, faculty members do not devote themselves to research and creative activity that removes them from their students or detracts from their teaching. Rather, our faculty members are expected to involve students in their research, sometimes as collaborators and at other times by bringing new connections and their excitement about them into the classroom. We are looking for those among you who welcome the challenge of that combination of commitments.

To engage students, our faculty members' interests and aptitudes must extend beyond working in their disciplines to introducing undergraduates to those disciplines. Faculty members need the perspective to place a discipline in a larger intellectual context and the flexibility to cross disciplinary boundaries because, often, they will be teaching students with little or no disciplinary experience, who need help making connections to what they do know.

It is essential that our faculty members have strong communication skills and be willing to teach those skills along with the content of their disciplines. They must understand how students learn and be prepared to work with students who come to the classroom with a broad range of backgrounds, preparations, and aptitudes. Further, they must balance a willingness to adapt to different needs with a commitment to high standards for all students.

While academics are often portrayed as loners, the faculty members we seek should be prepared for a great deal of social involvement. As residential colleges, we are engaged in an effort to give students the opportunity to experience a democratic community. While the struggle to invite the participation of all our constituencies often makes us look inefficient, it is part of our educational mission to ask our students and faculty members to help build communities in which citizenship and service are taught by example. Our colleges and universities should be models of communities in which diversity, responsibility, and cooperation thrive. Our larger society needs leaders who have learned the requirements and rewards of citizenship. We have an unusual opportunity, and therefore a clear responsibility, to teach them.

Our faculty members shape students' educational experiences as much by who they are as by what they teach. They share an interest in the personal as well as intellectual development of young adults. At different times and with different students they must be nurturing and demanding, supportive and critical. The personal interaction between teachers and undergraduates is essential to the education we offer. While new and exciting uses of technology can enhance this interaction, they cannot replace it as the most effective means of helping young adults achieve a complex set of goals.

We want students who graduate from our programs to have the ability—and confidence—to think and work independently, as well as the skills needed to cooperate and collaborate. We try to inculcate in them a healthy skepticism that includes a respect for evidence and a tolerance for ambiguity. They should know how to assess the ever-increasing amount of information available to them. They should know how to express themselves clearly, forcefully, and effectively in both writing and speaking. While we cannot pretend that in four years they can begin even to sample all areas of knowledge, we can and do insist that they develop a range of competencies in different modes of inquiry, as well as a considerable depth of knowledge in at least one area. We hope to graduate individuals with integrity, a sense of social responsibility, and the ability to make ethical judgments.

Many of the attributes we seek to develop in our students are precisely those that are viewed as essential if democratic societies are to flourish in the next century. We see the impact of our institutions as far wider than the individual students we graduate. It is precisely our small size that gives us a unique opportunity to enable students and faculty members to work together in ways that can have the most profound and far-reaching effects. Our students should leave our institutions with a lifelong commitment to educating themselves and others. This commitment will be modeled on what they have seen in their own teachers. We seek those of you who are willing to be such teachers. Make no mistake—our work is demanding, time-consuming, and challenging. For the right person, this is a wonderful opportunity, and we invite you to consider it.

Bruce J. Smith, Dean of the College
Allegheny College

Robert Dostal, Provost
Bryn Mawr College

Eugenia P. Gerdes, Dean, College of Arts and Sciences
Bucknell University

Paul T. Christiano, Provost
Carnegie Mellon University

Anne Steele, Vice President for Academic Affairs
Chatham College

Lisa A. Rossbacher, Dean of the College
Dickinson College

P. Bruce Pipes, Dean of the College
Franklin & Marshall College

Daniel DeNicola, Provost
Gettysburg College

Elaine Hansen, Provost
Haverford College

June Schlueter, Provost
Lafayette College

Alan W. Pense, Provost
Lehigh University

Jennie Keith, Provost
Swarthmore College

Queer Studies and the Job Market:
Three Perspectives

========

EDITED BY JON HARNED

Queer studies now stands at the threshold of institutionalization as an academic discipline, but its full acceptance is by no means a foregone conclusion, an inevitability guaranteed by the brilliance of its accomplishments or by the forces of history. The uncertainty of its future exacts a particularly heavy toll at present on those at the lowest level of the profession, graduate students. One has only to sit on a search committee to become aware of their anxiety, for in my experience, at least, very few job candidates explicitly describe their dissertations as projects in queer studies or list queer studies among their areas of expertise. Many applicants submit what I would call closeted vitae and letters, presenting themselves as engaged in less controversial, often interdisciplinary fields and yet mentioning discreetly, here and there, significant engagement with a queer author or scholar. However theoretically justifiable such eclecticism might be, it also indicates, as I have found in talking with graduate students at a variety of universities, a pervasive fear that in an unusually tight job market, "out" applicants might very well be risking their professional careers. These job seekers have become classic illustrations of the closet as an apparatus of social regulation. Their vitae operate like an "open secret," the term coined by D. A. Miller to describe "the odd compromises [fictional] characters strike,

Jon Harned is Associate Professor of English at the University of Houston, Downtown. Gregory W. Bredbeck is Associate Professor of English at the University of California, Riverside. María C. González is Assistant Professor of Literature at the University of Houston, University Park. Shelton Waldrep is Assistant Professor of English at Georgia State University. Versions of these papers were presented at the 1995 MLA convention in Chicago.

like Freudian hysterics, between expression and repression" (205). Such rhetorical performances can encourage the academy to examine the political structures that define us all.

ADVISING ABOUT THE "QUEER" MARKET:
SOME NOTES FOR MENTORS

Gregory W. Bredbeck

In their introduction to *The Lesbian and Gay Studies Reader*, Henry Abelove, Michele Aina Barale, and David M. Halperin set forth a view of "gay and lesbian studies" that is symptomatic of the conditions I address here. The essays in this germinal volume "constitute . . . some of the best and most significant recent English-language work in the field of lesbian/gay studies." This field, however, quickly dissolves: "The essays collected here show [that] lesbian/gay studies is not limited to the study of lesbians, bisexuals, and gay men. Nor does it refer simply to studies undertaken by, or in the name of, lesbians, bisexuals, and gay men" (xv). These two sentences correlate with what Eve Sedgwick has termed minoritizing and universalizing viewpoints on homosexuality (1). The first statement assumes the presence of a determinable field easily labeled by the words "gay and lesbian," while the second assumes a core indeterminacy to that very field, a universalizing flux that traumatizes the definitional ability of the words "gay and lesbian."

The *Lesbian and Gay Studies Reader* demonstrates a point that is crucial for faculty members who are in the position to advise graduate students entering the job market in gay and lesbian studies: one cannot know for sure what it means to enter that market, not the least because one cannot know for sure what it means "to do" gay and lesbian studies. Some, like Sedgwick, would view this undecidability factor as a generative source of power, whereas others, like George Haggerty and Bonnie Zimmerman, would minimize its power and presence (4–5). But in either its central or marginal theorization, this contradiction becomes crucially stressed for graduate students in the job market, who must be able to present a coherent image of themselves as candidates.

It is worth looking momentarily at the exact parameters of this thing that I refer to as the market in gay and lesbian studies, parameters that do nothing to help this dilemma. Although gay, lesbian, and queer studies are now a visible presence in the market, they exist primarily conjunctively: ". . . *and* gay and lesbian studies." Nor does the euphemism "gender studies" offer much that is definite, for gender is the domain of normative heterosexuality as well as of radical feminism and queer theory. While there are now highly visible tenured gay, lesbian, and queer scholars, only a small number of them have *gained* that tenure by producing openly gay, lesbian, or queer work. And while many people have commented on the gay, lesbian, and queer publishing breakthrough, there is reason to view this also with some skepticism. People like Dennis Altman, Joan Nestle, Karla Jay, and Robert Martin, to name but a few, lived through the first such boom, only to see it collapse in the 1980s.

The points I am trying to make here are that while gay, lesbian, and queer studies are definitely a presence, they are not, institutionally speaking, a substance; and while "gay and lesbian studies" is a demonstrable phenomenon, it is certainly not a determinant field. I suspect that the most helpful strategy in advising graduate students entering the lesbian and gay studies job market is to *foreground* these facts. Any advising that refuses to admit them denies the reality of graduate students' experience. Such conditions create paranoia, and it is precisely to avoid this that I advise my graduate students who self-identify as participants in the "field" of "gay and lesbian studies" on the following points:

- *Identifying with this "field" will require a personal identification as well.* Although people of many sexualities, orientations, preferences, and desires produce work that deals with sexuality, homosexuality, and gay and lesbian textuality, someone is always going to wonder, Is s/he or isn't s/he? Placing this issue on the table at the outset keeps it from falling into the potentially dangerous realms of secrecy and gossip. It does not mean that candidates must publicly self-identify as gay, straight, bisexual, or something else; it does mean that they should have a coherent way of talking about the issue of personal identification. This may be neither right nor just, but it is inevitable.
- *Candidates must construct the field into which they will be hired.* Since, as I have already suggested, simply saying "gay and lesbian studies" is meaningless, successful candidates will have to educate their employers on the definition of the field and the ways in which their work is at its forefront. This does not mean that they must have figured out what the "field" is even though it is undefinable; what it does mean is that they must be able to make a persuasive case that what they are doing at least potentially can be viewed as "central."
- *Candidates must learn the importance of conjunctions.* Although the supplemental status of gay and lesbian studies in the academy is regrettable, it is real. Candidates are going to have to demonstrate conjunctions between their work in gay and lesbian studies and other fields—periods, theoretical discourses, other minority discourses. One benefit of this necessity is that it can add definition to the field of gay and lesbian studies by mapping it within the parameters of established discourses. It is easier, in other words, to speak of Marxist gay and lesbian studies or of queer studies in modernism than it is to speak of gay and lesbian studies in general. Again, this is not necessarily as it should be; it is simply as it is.
- *Candidates must define success.* This, finally, is the most important advice. Obviously anyone entering the market wants to get a job. But candidates must have a sense of what will constitute personal success beyond that specific goal. If they identify as gay or lesbian and also have politicized that identification, then one obvious route is

to value the process of being "out" on the market as its own goal. Contrastingly, if candidates cannot find value in anything other than getting an academic job, then it may be most responsible to advise them to consider fields in which the terrains are a little more knowable and more easily strategized.

Approaching the job market for gay, lesbian, or queer studies, students must systematically hierarchize and evaluate the multiple components of their own identifications if they are to survive the experience with any sense of self-esteem intact. This phenomenon is seldom pushed to such a conscious level, yet most gay, lesbian, and queer graduate students grasp it immediately. It is therefore something that should be openly acknowledged. Although I have been concerned here with what I perceive to be the specific needs of gay and lesbian graduate students, I also think that what I have outlined is, in fact, a set of issues that concern every person on the job market. The position of students marketing themselves in gay and lesbian studies provides a crucial case study in the complex identification politics of any field. As is so often the case, the experiences of the sexual margin, whether as a person or as a field, contain the displaced dynamics that move the whole, and a profession that fails to see this will be, to borrow one final time from Sedgwick, "not merely incomplete, but damaged in its central substance" (1).

THE QUEER PROFESSOR:
MEMBERSHIP IN THE ACADEMY

María C. González

Queer studies in the academy encompasses a broad band of experience—especially when the job market and the academic field are brought together. And as with most nascent fields, one ends up studying the anecdotal more than anything else to ground one's authority to speak on the subject. So my discussion attempts to understand how being in the job market, being out, and belonging to a cultural minority become part of the complex matrix that makes up our anxieties about becoming accepted in the academy. Those who do queer studies and identify as queer in the academy focus on the relation between the (for lack of a better word) stereotypical straight, white, male professor and the queer professor. If to the queer professor we add characteristics that are not those of the traditional professoriat, like ethnicity and gender, we begin to see the disruption and deconstruction of the traditional professoriat.

The academy is no longer—if it ever was—avowedly straight, white, and male. It is becoming more and more the domain of the other. But if certain other identities are now less of a threat to the academy, the resistance to otherness has not yet disappeared. We have seen that with the increasing number of women entering the profession (nationally, approximately 35%–38% of the professoriat), the threat of women professors to the stereotype has diminished. As ethnic minorities enter the profession in greater numbers (approximately 13% of the professoriat), that challenge is less obvious. Now we have the openly queer professor, and once again the stereotype is challenged. The queer still represents an obvious threat to the academy. While judicial precedent is on the side of women and ethnic minorities, sexuality still is not a protected class within the whole academy or the country. Hence the queer population remains vulnerable to exclusion from the ranks of the professoriat.

Using the model of the entrance into the academy of ethnic minorities, we can make some predictions at this stage about the acceptance of out queers. It is important to recognize that the doors are more open than ever before. However, entrance is still hazardous. Since the traditional professoriat is fundamentally homophobic, sexist, and racist, those who enter the field enter at their own risk. The professoriat is a community of scholars; faculty members garner authority and privilege by belonging to the group. To be a professor on the job market and an outsider of the traditionally identified faculty group is to be left vulnerable to the powers that resist change. This resistance can include not getting an invitation to interview, a frosty interview process, a campus visit that is sabotaged at some point, or eventually getting an appointment and being denied tenure. Throughout the whole process of being selected a member of the professoriat, the road is littered and lined with endless barricades to keep the other out. When I was on the job market in 1991, it was very clear and easy, from my vita, to see my ethnicity and my interest in the study of ethnicity. However, the committee reviewing my vita, unless they were familiar with Chicana lesbian writers, would never hazard to assume I was anything but straight. That is the fundamental assumption made by the academy—that everyone is straight. I came out to committees when I got the campus interviews. Now, when I send my vita out, I have presentations and publications in the field of lesbian studies and queer theory that indicate my growing interest in this new field. The academy will no longer make the assumption that I am straight. While I recognize the obvious risks of out publications and presentations, the issue of my sexuality is like the issue of my ethnicity; it is the work I do, enjoy doing, and expect to continue to do. The problems I now face are different from those I faced simply as an ethnically marked professor. As a lesbian and minority professor, I have removed myself even farther from the traditional identity of the professoriat.

I have had the opportunity to compare experiences with other Latina-Latino faculty members across the country. Consistently the issue of attempting to become a member of the faculty clique on our campuses has always been one of the underlying if not always voiced concerns of my Latina-Latino colleagues. As we swap stories about landing jobs and the tenuring process, one of the underlying tensions and anxieties expressed concerns whether or not we are "fitting into" the clublike atmosphere of the professoriat. The responses to otherness vary from campus to campus and from individual to individual. I do have hope that the academy is attempting to create a space that allows for the out professoriat. What it sometimes takes, however, is the personal experience of one privileged member to acknowledge what it feels like to lose that sense of privilege.

A colleague of mine, who was president of one of the Chicano studies organizations during the period that Colorado passed its discrimination amendment, did a great deal of work on discrimination. As part of his responsibilities, he helped work on and assisted in the writing of an amicus curiae brief supporting gay and lesbian rights. In the process he learned a great deal about discrimination against gays and lesbians in the academy. And, like most academicians, he began to speak on this information. As he came forward to speak, he discovered what it felt like to be discriminated against for being gay. He is actually straight. His experience gave him a whole new insight into the unspoken and unconscious level of homophobia in the academy, and today he speaks about the differences and similarities between racism and homophobia in the academy. I hope that more straight people learn to recognize their privileged status in the academy.

Comraderie, while not necessarily an obvious part of the responsibilities of the professoriat like research, teaching, and service, often represents the actual hidden agenda of group-member status. An ethnic minority or female candidate can and often does elicit the question of whether or not this person can become a colleague. The answer in the past was consistent until judicial and legal action forced the exclusive academy to open its doors. Yet even with legal challenges, one must have grounds on which to challenge. More and more colleges and universities include sexuality in their affirmative action statements. However, do these schools have active affirmative action officers who are advocates for the issue of sexuality on the campus? Is sexuality, as part of the affirmative action charge, a status protected as equally as ethnicity and gender? This information is not as readily available to a candidate as other information about the school.

Out gays and lesbians represent the present challenge to the boundaries of the academic club. The academy will have to expand its institutional comfort zones to accommodate the queer. In that process both the academy and the queer professoriat will change.

THE JOB MARKET AND UNDERGRADUATE QUEER INSTRUCTION

Shelton Waldrep

In a job market that has become increasingly competitive, the pressure to amass publications and other professionalizing gestures is enormous. Yet the academy's approach to those who do queer work is often predictably homophobic.[1] We all hear of the occasional student who, first time out on the market, is courted by several high-powered schools and finally chooses one prestigious place over another—all because he (rarely she) is gay, out, and has acquired some sort of early publicity. These instances are rare, however, and eclipse the many more examples of students who struggle with their vitae, their advisers, and their families' attitudes to decide how and when best to present themselves as working in the realm of queer studies. Rumor and personal testimonies can provide any job seeker who asks with numerous stories of candidates who suspect or even know that their chances at a job at various institutions were scuttled because of their identification as queer—in whatever form—in their vitae, abstracts, writing samples, transcripts, or job letters.

Indeed, the desire to control how our work in queer subjects does or does not act as a label is taken away from us as soon as we set it on paper and send it off. A few years ago a friend who was about to go out on the job market for the first time and go for interviews at the MLA convention stopped by my office at Duke University, where I was the managing editor of the *Lesbian and Gay Studies Newsletter*. He wanted to make sure that his vita could include a book review that he had completed and that was to appear in the next issue. He wanted, in other words, his vita to include a reference to a publication in a queer journal—to be stamped with it, as a message to his potential employers. That he wanted to make sure his vita contained the signal either that he was out or worked in queer areas or both stuck with me because in many ways it is the obverse of the problem that most job seekers face: how to define themselves around the site of their queer work—or, rather, how their queer work defines them. The act of self-identifying becomes a rhetoric over which one has little control and for which the only real choice is whether or not to do it. There is no safe way to enter the job market, and the portrait that one constructs of oneself can never truly be one's own.

The challenge of the job market, therefore, is not simply a question for students to ponder; it is also tied to the actions of administrators and committees and to changes in how and why departments hire queer theorists. Those on the other side of the table at the interviews should ask themselves these difficult questions: How is the work of younger scholars—particularly of those who work at the margins—supported by our institution? Is our department or program seriously interested in fostering the research of someone doing queer studies not only now but twenty years from now? What are the pressures felt by scholars—younger or older—who work in this area? Are we hiring these people because we want to fill a quota or because we are seriously committed to the type of work they are doing? Are we hiring them because we are acceding to demands from students and administrators or because the courses they can teach are ones that we will support in our own curricular decisions?

At Duke University I served on two committees that attempted to develop a curriculum for an undergraduate major in gay-lesbian-bisexual studies. Among other things, I found that although there exists a brave tradition of scholars who have attempted to foster queer pedagogy in often marginalized colleges and universities, most institutions that have begun to integrate queer theory into their graduate courses and curricula are still woefully unable to define and put into place queer studies for the largest segment of their student body: the undergraduate women and men, gay and straight, who see queer studies not only as a potential career path but also as very much a part of their emerging identity.[2] My point is that institutions must reconsider how they hire job candidates and reconsider as well what those candidates will do if they are hired. Queer studies is on the brink of a transformation as it becomes institutionalized and incorporated into the academic community. Who will be hired and what kinds of candidates will be desirable for positions related in any way to queer studies may be guided by how *undergraduate* instruction shapes a base in this academic field, creating a financial impetus for more hires in the future.[3] Yet it is far from clear what such programs will look like.

The job market is already a series of land mines for the uninitiated. Incredible pressure is placed on candidates to maximize their job possibilities—a force whose calculus increases each time an attempt on the market is made. For hiring committees, queer vitae need be neither a battle flag nor a white flag; rather, they can be an opportunity to find out what candidates have to offer and how their work might help to rethink disciplinary boundaries. To work in a new area is necessarily to engage in new professional responsibilities. The sooner we realize that this challenge rests as much with those who do the hiring as with those who hope to be hired, the better the chances are that the situation for graduate students working in queer areas will change.

NOTES

The contributors thank David A. H. Hirsch for his invisible hand in this article.

[1] I use the term *queer* as a sign for bringing together feminist, lesbian, and gay studies—historically separate—and for also suggesting its political importance as a reclaimed word of opprobrium.

[2]Questions about queer pedagogy have recently been raised by several books devoted to the subject. See Haggerty and Zimmerman; Malinowitz.

[3]Though I see a growing need for experts in the area of queer studies, my optimism must obviously be read in the context of a shrinking job market that has not been mitigated by any efforts on the part of the MLA as an organization.

WORKS CITED

Abelove, Henry, Michele Aina Barale, and David M. Halperin, eds. *The Lesbian and Gay Studies Reader*. New York: Routledge, 1993.

Haggerty, George E., and Bonnie Zimmerman. Introduction. *Professions of Desire: Lesbian and Gay Studies in Literature*. Ed. Haggerty and Zimmerman. New York: MLA, 1995. 1–7.

Malinowitz, Harriet. *Textual Orientations: Lesbian and Gay Students and the Making of Discourse Communities*. Portsmouth: Boynton, 1995.

Miller, D. A. *The Novel and the Police*. Berkeley: U of California P, 1988.

Sedgwick, Eve Kosofsky. *Epistemology of the Closet*. Berkeley: U of California P, 1990.

Preprofessionalism:
What Graduate Students Want

JOHN GUILLORY

The question of my subtitle—what graduate students want—is simply answered at the present time: they want a job. Since the dire state of the job market is well known, I forgo here a recitation of morbid statistics. I welcome the fact that both graduate students and professors are beginning to comment publicly on the subject of the market, and I would endorse a number of recent proposals for alleviating some of the consequences of the market's decline (e.g., see Bérubé and Nelson 1–32). But these proposals are not my primary concern. I am interested rather in the relation of the market to the desires invested by graduate students in the profession of literary study. These desires are not comprehended by the concept of a job. One consequence of our current crisis has been that the very uncertainty of this object of desire, the job, permits the object to stand in for many other objects as well, some of them reasonable and attainable, others, as I hope to demonstrate, largely phantasmic. When a student cannot find a job, it's not only the desire for a job that is frustrated but also every desire whose gratification is thought to be contingent on the job. I ask first, then, What are these other desires? And second, How does the job market, its uncertainty and arbitrary brutality, affect the formation and expression of those other desires from the moment students enter graduate school? I would argue that these desires have been deeply determined by the threat of unemployment, at least since the late 1970s, when the conditions for the present crisis were firmly established.

The author is Professor of English at Johns Hopkins University. A version of this paper appeared in the Spring 1996 issue of the ADE Bulletin.

Of the desires contingent on employment, it is easiest to identify those that may be simply called professional. These are what we would expect them to be: the desire for security, at the least, then for interesting work, and often also for professional success, for prestige, and the rewards of prestige. The desire for success is in my view entirely legitimate. The question I raise has to do with the relation of the market to its expression in graduate school. It is a question of professionalization, or the means by which graduate students internalize a model of professional discourse and behavior. Among the determining influences on the course of professionalization in recent years has been the job market itself, which for some time now has been driving graduate students to "professionalize" very early, perhaps too early. The result is the penetration of graduate education by professional practices formerly confined to later phases of the career, the obvious examples being publication and the delivery of conference papers. This development has become so marked as to constitute a new professional domain, what I will call preprofessionalism. Graduate students are preprofessional not only because they are not yet professors but also because their engagement in professional activity is premature, undertaken without any certainty that it will culminate in an appointment. The premise of graduate education as a course of study is undermined by the new domain of preprofessionalism, which looks more like a curious sort of on-the-job training. Students do everything that their teachers do—teach, deliver conference papers, publish—without the assurance that any of these activities will secure them a job.

In a recent President's Column of the *MLA Newsletter*, Patricia Meyer Spacks has called attention to the deformation of graduate education resulting from preprofessionalism. I would agree with her judgment that preprofessionalism inhibits students from developing long-term intellectual projects and thus propagates intellectual shallowness. I would also agree with Erik Curren, past president of the Graduate Student Caucus of the MLA, that graduate students are hardly to blame for cultivating "precocious professionalism" (61). What the market demands, incredibly, is a graduate student who is already in some sense a successful professional before that student can be considered for a position as a professor. In such a context, "professional desire" is contorted into the form of prematurity, of desiring something now—professional success— that can only be had later. This prematurity is phantasmic: it telescopes professional careers into the time period of graduate school and conflates graduate education with self-marketing, as though getting a job were somehow the culmination of a successful career.

But there is another, equally important, set of desires invested in literary study. These desires are political—by which I mean something specific and not, I think, especially surprising. Many of those entering the profession in the 1970s, 1980s, and 1990s possessed strong, usually left-of-center political convictions, and they saw literary study as a life in which a kind of political desire might be gratified. Whatever the reasons for this circumstance, it is scarcely to be disputed that literary study was indeed strongly invested with political desire beginning in the 1970s; this investment has only intensified in recent years. Literary study is no longer a refuge for progressive intellectuals, a profession in which one does no social harm, so to speak; in literary study now, many social problems are actively addressed by foregrounding a political thematic in the classroom and in publication—a thematic defined by the familiar categories of race, class, gender, or sexuality. And of course this turn in the profession toward a politically valenced practice of literary study has elicited the familiar charge of "politicization" from the media.

It is the emergence of an intensified investment of political desire in literary study—as a motive of teaching and publication—that I link to the decline in the job market. I don't regard the market as the simple cause of that politicized agenda, but I do believe it is a condition for the politicization of certain intellectual practices (see Guillory). The so-called politicization of criticism is driven by the increasing social marginality of literary study, its increasing irrelevance to the socioeconomic conditions of our society. The short-term rise and fall of the job market for PhDs is only a rough index of this marginality; the decline in the market value of literary study (in relation to other socially valued knowledges, professional or technical) is long-term, and that trend makes literary study peculiarly vulnerable to market forces. The result is what Roger Chartier, in his study of the historical motif of "frustrated intellectuals," calls the gap between "subjective aspirations and objective chances" (128). This gap is in turn a condition for moments and modes of politicization in the history of intellectuals.

At a certain point in the decline in the market value of literary study—and that point is marked by our recent crisis—the relation between professional desire and political desire becomes one of resonance, of mutual intensification, especially in the domain of graduate education. The ideologues of the right would have it that these desires are contradictory, that the desire for social justice is incompatible with the desire for professional success. This moralism unfortunately has its correlative on the left, in the inability to acknowledge that these two desires are coincident because they seek the same means of fulfillment: the career of the teacher of literature. And the same monstrous contingency—the market—stands in the way of both desires.

If the declining market value of literary study demarcates a terrain of social marginality, this marginality is constantly converted by literary critics into the occasion of political expression. The greater the marginality, the greater the motive to politicize. At the same time, politicized expressions are inhibited from easily circulating outside this domain, by virtue of its marginality. The condition of social marginality accounts for the difficulty literary critics experience in gaining access to the public sphere of political discourse.[1] Thus political expression is driven back into the spaces of the professional field itself, into the classrooms, the conference halls, and academic publishing. In those spaces, the agenda of politicization unites with the process of professionalization. If politicized critical discourse is inhibited from circulating outside the profession, it now circulates within it as the sign of professional identification and legitimation, as the most highly valued content of the profession's discursive forms, indeed as the cutting edge of criticism. Paradoxically, the same discourse is perceived in the media as delegitimizing, as a flight from the traditional task of literary study. What I am trying to grasp here is an aspect of our profession that is conspicuously evident and influential in the domain of preprofessionalism. Because graduate students suffer most from the consequences of the social marginality of the literary profession, their practice is subject to the greatest pressure to become both hyperprofessionalized and hyperpoliticized. The form of their practice is only too professional—it is often prematurely professional; the content of their practice is only too political—it is often reductively political. The newest institutional structure of preprofessionalism, the graduate student conference, is at once the means by which graduate students professionalize themselves in preparation for the market and the vehicle for the most politicized current modes of criticism. I hasten to say that I am not dismissing these new institutional forms or their contents. My point is, rather, that they are determined: graduate students are condemned to suffer most the symptoms of a pathology that afflicts the profession universally. For the agendas of professionalization and politicization characterize significant portions of the profession as a whole, and these agendas are formed and deformed by the same social condition of marginality that graduate students face in its most extreme expression, a collapsed job market.

In speaking of the long-term decline in the market value of literary study, I do not mean to minimize the effects of the current crisis of the job market. But I do mean to provide a context for understanding the crisis that does not reduce it simply to a question of the overproduction of PhDs. The concept of overproduction grasps a fact about the present situation, the gap between "subjective aspirations and objective chances," but does so from a perspective that sees this gap produced by the decisions of literature departments. If departments do not control objective chances (the market)—and of course they do not—one might comprehend the gap in another way: as the underemployment of those seeking careers in the teaching of literature. In our society, many more people would like to teach literature than there are jobs teaching literature. When regarded in this way, the crisis looks like a local instance of a much larger crisis of employment. Indeed, the crisis is global and in the media has a name, "downsizing," a euphemism that signifies the harsh but supposedly necessary means by which corporations must make themselves competitive in a new world market. This notion is thoroughly ideological. What is new about the global employment crisis is not some form of capitalism but a further development of capitalism's inexorable logic of accumulation, which operates according to the principle of productivity. The globalization of capital has exacerbated the pressure on corporations to increase productivity, or the ratio of profits to production and labor costs. In the view of most corporations, productivity can always be improved by reducing the workforce. Several developments have determined such reductions in recent years, among them the utilization of new laborsaving technologies, the new mobility of capital and production across national boundaries, and the bureaucratic reorganization of corporations through mergers and acquisitions. While the firing of manual labor (both skilled and unskilled) is a long-standing practice of corporations, what is new is the downsizing of professional-managerial fields, many of which grew in previous decades because their labor was crucial to increased productivity. The resources of technology and organization have now been developed to such a degree that it has become possible to replace technical and managerial workers by these resources. Hence for the first time since its emergence in the late nineteenth century, the professional-managerial class is shrinking.

William DiFazio and Stanley Aronowitz have recently analyzed these developments in a book entitled *The Jobless Future*. They state grimly that "there is absolutely no prospect, except for a fairly small minority of professional and technical people, to obtain good jobs in the future" (9; see also Rifkin). The condition of a contracting labor market for virtually all fields will obtain for some time to come, perhaps a long time. Nevertheless one might wonder why this fact is relevant to the crisis in literary study, given that our profession has such a remote connection to the market of commodities. I propose a way of thinking about the relation between the long-term decline in the value of literary study and the short-term rise and fall of the labor market that we have seen in the 1980s and 1990s. First of all, one must ask: Is the size of the profession an expression of its social importance? Can the fluctuations of the job market be taken as the measure of this importance? The absolute size of the literary professoriat has certainly increased by many magnitudes since the late nineteenth century. But this increase is not necessarily an expression of the increased social importance of literary study; it is, rather, correlated with a growth in the size of the university system. The American university grew over the past century to accommodate social mobility into emergent professional-managerial fields, and many departments in the humanities grew to accommodate this enlarged student population. Perhaps a better measure of the significance of literary study is the ratio of English majors to other majors in the university system. We can at least suppose with some assurance that the size of the literary professoriat will correlate to the size of the English major. Yet

here again it would be difficult to draw any conclusion about the social significance of literary study from short-term fluctuations in the aggregate size of the
English major. We know from statistics collected by the United States Department of Education (see Franklin) that the size of the major increased during
the 1960s, decreased during the 1970s and early 1980s; it increased once again
during the second half of the 1980s. Doubtless these fluctuations exerted corresponding pressures on the job market for PhDs in English; but I would argue
that these pressures are short-term in their effects and that in order to understand such a phenomenon as the job market, we must understand how long-
term social developments interact with short-term events.

The long-term condition of the university's conversion from a predominantly liberal arts institution to one in which the liberal arts occupy a much
smaller share of the professional-technical curriculum underlies the constitu-
tively paradoxical situation of literary study: even as the professoriat has grown
larger (in terms of gross numbers), it has become more socially marginal. This
underlying weakness is concealed during periods in which the major grows or
hiring increases, just as it suddenly takes on the appearance of apocalypse when
the major contracts or the job market declines. Nowhere has this paradox of
literary study been more evident than in the discrepancy between the competitive hiring at the senior level during the mid-1980s, spurred by an influx of
Reagan defense moneys into the universities and by an upturn in the size of the
major, and the ongoing conversion of full-time positions at the junior level into
part-time or adjunct positions (especially in composition). If the professional-
managerial class is itself now vulnerable to downsizing after a century of
growth, this circumstance has had the short-term effect over the last decade of
drawing some students out of these fields into the humanities and into literary
study. The fact that this short-term effect has not arrested a now longer-term
conversion of full-time into part-time positions indexes the underlying weakness of literary study. The condition of the job market appears more than ever
as a crisis today, because the market seems to have resisted the pressure of a fa-
vorable short-term condition, an increase in the size of the English major (to
which we add as well the short-term condition of a wave of retirements). In
fact, we know that the job market, with brief fluctuations up or down, has been
depressed since the late 1970s.

The disparity between subjective aspirations and objective chances seems
more intense because the depressed job market was preceded in the late 1950s
and 1960s by a rapid growth in the size of the profession. This growth was pro-
pelled in part by the expansion of the professional-managerial class, especially
in the 1960s, but also by a brief turn a few years later away from business and
technical fields among many university students, no doubt the "countercul-
tural" types now slated by the Republicans for an old-fashioned purge. While I

grant the significance of this influx of students for investing the profession with political desire, I am equally impressed by the extent to which the profession during this period internalized certain bureaucratic modes of behavior. These techniques of professionalization seemed to follow from the fact of growth itself, partly as a way of dealing with the administrative problems of size. I believe that the current form of what I have been calling professional desire was established at this time. The form is mimetic of those technical and managerial professions more directly integrated into the socioeconomic system. In imitation of the dominant forms of technobureaucratic organization, departments began to judge their collective success by the measure of growth and to judge the success of their individual members by an increasingly quantitative measure of productivity, one confined exclusively to the realm of publication. This is the norm of professionalization that has now penetrated graduate study. I offer a hypothesis about the relation between the underemployment of PhDs—the effect of long-term downsizing—and the overproduction of PhDs, which is the effect of internalized norms of growth and productivity, expressed institutionally in the establishment of new graduate programs and the expansion of old ones. The severity of the current employment crisis is attributable to the fact that these two processes have now converged: the employment crisis of the professional-managerial class has downsized the field of literary study (and the humanities in general) because the field was historically vulnerable. Meanwhile, the resulting decline of the job market, which would have been bad in any case, was worsened by the surplus PhDs whose institutional function during the last decade was to contribute to the illusion of growth in literature departments.

About the global crisis of unemployment there is nothing that members of our profession can do. As for the overproduction of PhDs, there is only one thing we can do, and that is to produce fewer. But we will lose a crucial opportunity if the job crisis does not become also the occasion for inquiry into the modes of professionalization we have internalized in our practice. In particular, the norms of growth and productivity need to be thoroughly reexamined.

With regard first to growth, graduate education appears now to be a kind of pyramid scheme. The prospect of its collapse has revealed something extraordinary, that the growth of literary study consists largely in the growth of graduate programs and in the transformation of graduate students into a public for literary criticism. Professors of literature now write and teach for graduate students; graduate students have become their constituency and collectively now exert a considerable pressure on the profession, moving it in certain directions, along the cutting edge of criticism. Hence the most symptomatic professional desire one can harbor today is expressed in the desire to teach graduate students in preference to undergraduates. It is this desire that in part drove the expansion of graduate programs in the 1970s and 1980s. Newly minted professors look forward to teaching in departments with graduate programs, reproducing the same professional desire that emanated from their teachers. One can see, then, how the pyramid scheme works, if to be fully professionalized means to teach graduate students. The number of graduate students would have to increase geometrically for this desire to be gratified for all of us. But this is to say that the desire itself is phantasmic.

With regard to the norm of productivity, a similar argument might be made. Let us acknowledge that to demand publications from graduate students as a requisite for job candidacy seriously deforms the experience of graduate school. And yet the penetration of this norm of productivity into graduate education only extends the logic of professionalization already internalized in the professoriat. The norm of productivity, according to which every professor is accountable as a research scholar, is clearly a phantasmic mode of professional desire. All of us know that much literary criticism is not worth reading, because it is produced only as product, as proof of productivity. But rather than take inventory here of the ill effects of this professional phantasm, I make a different point: Literary critics do indeed produce knowledge, but this knowledge is not integrated into the market of commodities. The books and articles we write, strictly speaking, are spurious products when considered according to the norm of productivity. This is why state legislatures are increasingly likely to consider as the product of university teaching the numbers of students taught, not books written. In sum, the status of knowledge in the profession needs to be renegotiated, and along with it the rationale for literary study in the university.

If professional desire is subject to such phantasmic deformations, the same must be said of political desire. Politicized discourse can circulate in the microsociety of the profession as a knowledge-product and therefore as a validation of professional identification. That the content of such products is sometimes merely an expression of opinion, of good politics but indifferent or redundant scholarship, scarcely matters to its function as the embodiment of either political or professional desire. However pleased we may be with the political good will of our discourse, this discourse pales in the context of the ongoing employment crisis. Surely it is time to begin reflecting on the sociology of the profession, on the social space it occupies in the socioeconomic order. In this space, the uncertainty of the market gives unlimited play to the expression of fantasies about the profession. What I call preprofessionalism is nothing other than the realm in which the profession's fantasies, both professional and political, are acted out. The kind of sociological analysis I have in mind will demand that we suspend some of our investments in specific agendas of professionalization and politicization in order to clarify what is merely phantasmic in those investments. The decline of the job market is a reality check, then, and perhaps an opportunity.

NOTE

[1]When it does occur now, access to mass media by literary critics has been made possible by the attack on literary study in the media. The attack has enabled some literary critics to enter the mass public sphere as the defenders of literary study.

WORKS CITED

Bérubé, Michael, and Cary Nelson, eds. *Higher Education under Fire: Politics, Economics, and the Crisis of the Humanities.* New York: Routledge, 1995.

Chartier, Roger. *Cultural History: Between Practices and Representations.* Trans. Lydia G. Cochrane. Ithaca: Cornell UP, 1988.

Curren, Erik D. "No Openings at This Time: Job Market Collapse and Graduate Education." *Profession 94.* New York: MLA, 1994. 57–61.

DiFazio, William, and Stanley Aronowitz. *The Jobless Future: Sci-Tech and the Dogma of Work.* Minneapolis: U of Minnesota P, 1994.

Franklin, Phyllis. "From the Editor." *MLA Newsletter* 20.4 (1988): 2–6.

Guillory, John. "Literary Critics as Public Intellectuals: Class Analysis and the Crisis of the Humanities." *Rethinking Class.* Ed. Wai Chee Dimock and Myron T. Gilmore. New York: Columbia UP, 1994. 107–49.

Rifkin, Jeremy. *The End of Work: The Decline of the Global Labor Force and the Dawn of the Postmarket Era.* New York: Putnam, 1995.

Spacks, Patricia Meyer. "The Academic Marketplace: Who Pays Its Costs?" *MLA Newsletter* 26.2 (1994): 3.

The Public Duties of Our Profession

Invited by the American Society for Eighteenth-Century Studies to address the topic The Public Duties of Our Profession, I approached the task with mixed emotions. On the one hand, I was grateful to be invited; on the other, I was exasperated by the topic.

Why was I exasperated? I brooded to myself like some mother hen of introspective banalities. I then realized that my exasperation was less with the topic per se than with the related topic of the public intellectual. My exasperation with the topic of the public intellectual has one major source. Briefly, too many people who clamor for public intellectuals are indulging themselves in bouts of wrongheaded nostalgia. They lament the loss of a tradition that Ralph Waldo Emerson or Walter Lippman or Margaret Mead or the New York intellectuals can variously embody. According to this golden-age narrative, when such intellectuals spoke, they spoke to the public, and, equally important, the public listened. The narrative, continuing, tells us that the rise of jargon-ridden academics who make a fetish of their narrow academic specialties has now vanquished this noble tradition.

Although this nostalgic narrative is not wholly mistaken, it is hugely misleading, because it ignores the fact that many public intellectuals are alive and well in the United States today. They have what public intellectuals must have: a large vision to convey; a community or circle that supports this vision; and, finally, clear and compelling rhetorical strategies in every contemporary medium to reach audiences beyond their circle. Among these public intellectuals are feminists, African Americans, neoconservatives and conservatives, participants in the public humanities movement, some documentary filmmakers, and such

The author is University Professor of English at Rutgers University, New Brunswick, and Director of the MacArthur Fellows Program at the John D. and Catherine T. MacArthur Foundation.

PROFESSION 1996   100 individual figures as Edward Said and Camille Paglia. Obviously, they quarrel ferociously. For example, feminists are a favorite neoconservative, conservative, and Paglian target. Nevertheless, they are together our public intellectuals.

Not everyone can be a public intellectual. It demands a particular set of talents. However, all academic professionals have public duties. By academic professionals I mean people who earn their daily bread by teaching and learning and who subscribe, to one degree or another, to certain conventions and norms. One norm particularly germane to these remarks is that a modern academic professional ought to acknowledge intellectual and scholarly debts. What, then, are our public duties? Or, more precisely, what are our publics and what is our obligation to them?

Our first public is our students. They may be in our classrooms—whether in physical space or cyberspace—or outside our classrooms, for example, in a library. No matter what the location, teaching is hard work. Today, certain factors exacerbate its intrinsic difficulties. Our students, reflecting the demographic diversities of the world, have different traditions, backgrounds, and expectations about education. But despite their differences, they are all citizens of era media. Our average first-year student will have spent more time in front of the TV set than in a school classroom. The media shape student attention spans, databases, idioms, and attitudes toward expertise. I feel that I am less a prof than a talking head.

No matter how hard it might be, we must teach with grace, a concern for cosmopolitanism and complexity, a trust in freedom of inquiry, and respect for the personhood of each student. Our teaching should exemplify an I-thou relationship, a morally charged psychological reality that digitalization can never achieve. We must also, I believe, toil to bring as many able students as we can into our classrooms. If we are in public institutions, as I am at Rutgers University, the taxpayers are our employers and teaching well is proof of our accountability to them. Teaching well is also a public service.

Our second public is our colleagues, our fellow professionals. Whether we share disciplinary and departmental allegiances or not, we share a commitment to teaching and learning and to the institutions that sustain them. Our responsibility to our colleagues is to behave toward one another as we behave toward our students—with grace, a concern for cosmopolitanism and complexity, a trust in freedom of inquiry, and respect for the personhood of each individual. This is often easier said than done, especially in times of great change, of digitalizing and downsizing, and of anxiety about such changes. However, if we are to govern ourselves fairly, the need for creative collegiality is at its greatest during such times.

For people in the humanities, a third public consists of ghosts. Only in some metaphysical schemes or Gothic tales does this public speak back. Who these ghosts might be metamorphoses from field to field. For those of us in literatures and languages the ghosts are the writers and speakers who have gone before us; the brave, brilliant, often nutty, creative users of languages. They, their textual presence, their histories, their inventions and imaginings, their foibles and follies, their terrors and nightsweats and daffodils—these are our responsibility. If we do not care for the language crafters and their tongues, who will? Moreover, if we do not act as general stewards of the word, who will? I might add that this is a fascinating moment to be a general steward of the word, to serve texts as well as hypertexts, the written as well as the spoken word. If we are revisionary stewards, controversy will often result; there will be political consequences; powerful people will get mad, be punitive, look for scapegoats. Ultimately, the best way to conquer controversy is to do good work and defend it energetically, shrewdly, patiently, vividly, persuasively.

For me, as a professional, these three publics are the most important. I must work with them and for them as best I can. Unless I do so, I cannot speak to non-professionals about my profession with much plausibility. However, I am more than a professional. To be a professional is a major but by no means the only component of my identity. This thing, my identity—this compound of flower, flowerpot, and dirt—has many other elements. Among them is my United States citizenship. My professionalism and my citizenship often commit me to the same values—for example, a belief in freedom, a commitment to democratic governance. My professionalism and my citizenship often lead me to the same conclusions—for example, my belief in the value of the now imperiled National Endowment for the Humanities, my belief in intellectual property rights, and my belief in the value of well-supported public education. However, as a professional, I work and have obligations in one loose, porous sphere, that of teaching and learning. My credibility flows from my competence in that sphere. As a citizen, I work and have obligations in another loose, porous sphere, that of political and civil society. My credibility flows from my competence in this sphere.

Ah, I can hear the murmurs now, she's abdicating from politics. She's retreating from politics. Moreover, she's forgetting that professionalism has its politics. Nonsense to both charges. First, I am not retreating from politics. I am only advocating that we remember that we are people with multiple, multiplex identities, that we have one set of obligations as professionals and another set of obligations as citizens. It would be a mistake to submit to another nostalgic dream, that is, the dream of an organic, unified self that permits us to behave in the same way at every time and in every place. In brief, a resolution appropriate for the membership of the American Society for Eighteenth-Century Studies or the MLA to consider might not be appropriate as a referendum for the citizens of Washington State to consider. And vice versa. Second, I am not forgetting that professionalism has its politics. That politics has provided me with many of the comedies, farces, and tragedies of my mature years. However, the proper goal of professional politics is the well-being of teaching and learning. Oh, that we were better goalies. I can say this without mixed emotions.

A New Tour of Babel:
Recent Trends Linking Comparative Literature Departments, Foreign Language Departments, and Area Studies Programs

MICHAEL HOLQUIST

The Department of Comparative Literature, in which I hold an appointment, is housed in Connecticut Hall, built in 1750 and the oldest building on our campus. The Center for International and Area Studies, where I also have an office, is housed in the newest building on campus, Luce Hall, which opened in February 1994. The two buildings are located at opposite ends of the campus, and as I walk from one to the other it has struck me from time to time that the temporal and spatial distance between the two makes an irresistible metaphor for the split between activities characteristic of the occupants of both structures. As a comparatist I am surrounded by scholars occupied with questions of literary theory, analysis, and history; they are ineluctably humanists. In my appointment (or, as I sometimes conceive it, my guise) as chair of the Council on Russian and East European Studies, I spend time with economists, sociologists, political scientists, diplomatic historians, and specialists on international security issues who deal with questions of global environment, arms control, and the medical infrastructures of emerging nations; they are no less ineluctably social scientists.

On those trips across campus I have often reflected on the difficulties both worlds have experienced in trying to relate to each other. This contemplation

The author is Professor of Comparative Literature at Yale University. A version of this article appeared in the Fall 1995 issue of the ADFL *Bulletin.*

has occasionally been lugubrious, but recently hope has arisen for a new rap-
prochement between humanists and social scientists because of changes in both
areas. Taking the instances of comparative literature and Russian and East European studies, in what follows I will sketch some of the events that have led to
greater interaction between the two discourses.

This is not the place to rehearse a complete history of comparative literature
as a discipline, but it is useful to remember that the field is a relative latecomer
within the spectrum of disciplines organized around methodical comparison.
Comparison was a basic gesture in Aristotle's biology, of course, but it was only
with the Enlightenment that systematic contrast and comparison became the
central feature of so many different methodologies. The work of Linnaeus,
Cuvier, and others led to such new disciplines as comparative anatomy (Grew,
1672), embryology (admitted by the French Academy in 1762), taxonomy (de
Candolle, 1813), morphology (Goethe, 1817), and paleontology (Lyell, 1838).
As the sheer act of comparison gave skeletons a history, a whole new sense of
time's immensity dawned. Comparative anatomy and geology laid open the
great age of the earth. In what turned out to be one of the more problematic
innovations in the comparative method, in 1829 Abel Villemain, seeking to
make literary study scientific, coined the term *littérature comparée*.

The effect of the comparative method in literary scholarship was no less
revolutionary than it had already proved to be in physiology and anatomy. The
transfer to the cultural realm of a master trope from the natural sciences is no
innocent thing: often, as with *littérature comparée*, it portends a shift in the balance of power among the fundamental categories by which a society separates
"culture" from "nature." It could be argued, in fact, that the Enlightenment
turn to comparative method across several disciplines played a role in the "discovery" of culture as we now know it: as two distinguished anthropologists
have pointed out, "The concept of culture, in the sense of a set of attributes
and products of human societies, and therewith of mankind, which are extraso-
matic and transmissible by mechanisms other than biological heredity . . . did
not exist anywhere in 1750" (Kroeber and Kluckhohn 145).

It was only slowly, however, that scholars became aware of the consequences
of introducing relative values into culture as well as into nature. Early work in
comparative literature was as much characterized by positivism and hierarchy
as were natural sciences such as comparative anatomy. Thus, binaries
abounded, as in the East-West dichotomy at the heart of an extended Orientalism. One effect of this adherence to clear-cut dichotomies was an enviable lu-
cidity. To begin with, such an arrangement restricted the number of texts
available for comparison to a manageable list of classics in the West. And non-
Western areas could be seen not to count for very much, since they either had
no literature (as was the Hegelian prejudice about Africa) or, if it could not be
denied that they indeed had a literature, even if only in the remotest past, their

texts could be assigned to historical linguistics (as with India) or ignored (as was generally the case with China). Before the gaggle of new nations came roiling onto the scene after the Treaty of Versailles, the field confined itself, horizontally, to the comparison of western European works and, vertically, to only the "highest" expressions of western European culture. It was a golden age of *Stoffgeschichte*, in which titles such as "The Theme/Motif/Image of the Quest/ Shield of Achilles/Joseph and His Brothers/and So On in German/French/ English Literature from [period x] to [period y]" were typical.

After 1919, these extended bibliographic exercises masquerading as motif studies were challenged by a number of different groups in Europe whose work was more speculative. These scholars paid more attention to such extrahistorical considerations as forms of genres, the structure of repetition in verse, and above all the nature of the sign in language. One might, as did Boris Eikhenbaum, write about American and Russian literature, but the emphasis was less on thematic similarities or differences—the way water imagery was treated in one country's literature as opposed to another's, say—than on the formal features of defining differences between, for example, the genres of the short story and the novel. Much of this more formally oriented work was first accomplished in central and eastern Europe.

It is not by chance that the changes in the paradigm of comparison were first manifest in countries whose ambiguous position between Asia and Europe had made them unpopular as areas of concentration in comparative literature. Shocks to the old binarized models of comparison were arguably first felt in these lands because the East-West standard model could not account for them. But perhaps no less important, the Slavic lands were being reshuffled politically, as the old paradigm of south, west, and east Slavs gave way to newly independent countries after 1919, engendering new senses of identity that created strains on prior models of comparison. Thus it is not surprising that it was a citizen of one of those new nations who gave the shift in the comparative method its most influential (if belated) formulation: René Wellek of Prague, an ancient city but the new capital of the freshly minted state of Czechoslovakia.

It was the year after the Second World War and its further reshaping of the geopolitical map that Wellek could celebrate "The Revolt against Positivism in Recent European Literary Scholarship" and propose seven years later to a new American audience "The Concept of Comparative Literature" as a successor to such a by-then widely abandoned positivism. But only six years later, Wellek would himself have to acknowledge the discipline was in turmoil in his much cited "The Crisis of Comparative Literature"; in 1972 Wellek ultimately characterized this crisis in even more urgent terms as "The Attack on Literature." The military rhetoric had intensified because earlier, in 1959, the since-discredited word *crisis* could be invoked to describe what then was merely the clash of different methodologies—in Wellek's vocabulary, the clash between "intrinsic" and "extrinsic" approaches.

Since then, of course, the situation has grown more fraught. One way to gauge how far we have come is to recognize that the source of our anxiety has shifted from a concern originating in contradictions between different methodologies to the more basic question of what in our present state of incivility might constitute a methodology at all. In other words, while various forms of comparative study have come and gone, rarely before has it been felt necessary to interrogate the possibility of comparison itself. The crisis in comparative literature was only one aspect of a larger dilemma that now began to emerge: a shift in the space of interpretation.

The most obvious way this dilemma manifests itself within the academy in the West is through the recent debates about the place of identity studies, gender criticism, cultural criticism, and multiculturalism. Whatever else these topics might nominate, the urgency with which they are debated reminds us again that the concept of canon always boils down to a set of questions about how to make a comparison, a structure previously taken for granted. Baldly stated, the reason scholars in the past could be confident of their method was that they could be certain about what they were comparing.

In the disciplines of natural science that first adopted comparison as a systemic methodology for gaining new knowledge, one could be certain of one's subject if only because of its indubitable materiality: the jawbone of an Indian elephant might be different from the jawbone of a hairy mammoth, but the essential boniness of each was never in question. In retrospect, comparative literature appears to have been in crisis from the moment of its inception, because of its extension of the comparative method from the realm of nature to the realm of culture. Such immaterial subjects of analysis as tropes, genres, themes, and narrative forms—all heavily freighted in cultural values—introduced a new complexity in the constitution of the objects being compared.

Not only was the ratio of comparison made less secure, so too were the very poles to be compared: what might be called the basic arithmetic of comparison began to shift. The previous hegemony of two began to melt into a new necessity for three. In traditional comparative studies, the basic unit comprised two things that were then put into a meaningful relation to each other through an act of comparison. In line with the most advanced assumptions of the Enlightenment in which the comparative method's origins are complicit, the active role of the subject making the connection between them was obscured by the invisibility of the subject, whose presence was always assumed but not stated. The dualism enabled by this hidden subject in turn made possible the fiction of objective science. Insofar as the subject's activities resulted in the value-free judgments of natural science, the specificity of the subject could theoretically be considered unimportant—indeed, had to be systematically discounted; the subject merely instantiated a particular act of a universal mind in the unfolding of a larger truth.

The sheer unmediatedness of this model of comparison began breaking up in the new uncertainties that followed the First World War: the crisis in comparative literature went a long time unrecognized until finally a subject of one of the nations that came into being after 1919 perceived it. The crisis in comparative literature is deeply intertwined with the history of postcolonialism and particularly with the ideology of nationalism that grew apace after the breakup of the empires and monarchies that had defined space before the Treaty of Versailles.

It turned out that 1919 was the first act in the three-act tragicomedy of modern postcolonialism, the second act being the further redrawing of boundaries after the Second World War, and the third the breakup of the Soviet empire in our own time. At Versailles a completely different order of geopolitical space opened, as the old empires and their colonies splintered into a myriad of new nations. The small number of great-nation hegemonies that defined the simple ratio of center-periphery relations before 1919 shattered into a clamorous horde of newly invented polities. Each proclaimed a self-determination that rendered the old categories of comparison unequal to their new variety and scale. Different ratios were called for as, to give only one instance, central Europe broke up into a dizzying tarantella of new and rapidly shifting alliances, such as the Little Entente, which pitted the three victorious Danubian powers (Czechoslovakia, Romania, and Yugoslavia) against the three defeated remnants of empire (Bulgaria and the truncated versions of the formerly imperial states of Austria and Hungary).

These newly drawn nations constituted a map (and a clock) that could not be read in the time and space of Old World imperialisms. A new chronotope was created after the First World War. The *salon des miroirs* in which the Treaty of Versailles was signed was, for all its pomp, still a smoky back room and thus an apt setting for the creation of the new world that emerged there, a world of appearances whose borders were created precisely by smoke and mirrors. In the second act of postcolonialism, the farcical redrawing of the maps of Africa and Asia after the Second World War, the complexities of comparison were further compounded as old peripheries became new centers, creating a confusing matrix of neo- and postcolonialism. And since the opening of the third act, the breakup of the Soviet empire after 1989, the indexes of difference have increased exponentially. In such a welter of shattered categories, the old certainties that had enabled earlier enthymematic, either-or acts of comparison have lost their power to underwrite bipolarity.

Or so it would seem. But the chronology of events and the chronology of paradigms successively invoked to explain those events have failed to coincide. As Einstein is reputed to have said about the effect of relativity theory, "Overnight everything changed, except the way people think." For decades after the Big Bang of 1919 that initiated a new world of geopolitical complexity, the ratio between the new cultural realities of that world and the theoretically impoverished models of comparison for representing it remained incommensurable. If I may invoke a specular metaphor one last time, the *salon des miroirs* created a situation in which scholarly methods were cast into a carnivalized house of distorting mirrors. Traditional models no longer sufficed to calibrate the ramifying variety and complexity of the emerging worlds: the number two was, and of course still is, a cipher whose capaciousness was never adequate, as became apparent in the need to invent new versions of complexity, such as the brutalizing attempt to move to the threeness of dividing the globe into First, Second, and Third Worlds.

This greater variety and complexity in geopolitics is reflected as well in the difficulties that have attended comparative studies since the end of the First World War: the borders between disciplinary languages and the practices they shape are becoming less marked than they were once assumed to be. This blurring of boundaries may be—and within a given discipline often is—perceived as a crisis.

A recent response to the situation in comparative literature has been to expand the number and kind of subjects to be compared; the confusion of borders on maps and borders in discourses has recently been seen in a more positive light, an optimism resulting in what is sometimes called cultural studies. But even when conceived as a source of answers to the current dilemma, cultural studies has proved difficult to define. As the mountain of books attempting to explain it rises, the phenomenon itself becomes ever more elusive.

It might be useful, at least for the present, to think of cultural studies as a way of grouping the increasing number of works that bring together insights formerly apportioned among the social and human sciences. More to the point, cultural studies might be thought of as nominating new filiations of the kind that the Social Sciences Research Council and the American Council of Learned Societies joint committees have sponsored in the last decade, providing models for just how productive such discursive border crossings can be. Following are three examples of how the borders of the social and human sciences are currently being breached to the advantage of both sides:

1. In *Imagined Communities*, a book increasingly cited across the whole spectrum of the social sciences as an authoritative text on nationalism, Benedict Anderson organizes his argument around the ideas of two literary scholars, Walter Benjamin and Erich Auerbach.
2. A growing number of trauma centers at research hospitals across the country are convening research groups including not only physicians and psychiatrists but also sociologists, literary scholars, and historians.
3. A leading American psychologist seeking to understand the effects of rapid social change in the former communist countries of eastern Europe has organized his research around concepts from the literary scholar Mikhail Bakhtin and from Lev Vygotsky (author not only of the psychological classic *Thought and Language* but also of a study of *Hamlet*).

The phenomena figured in these three instances might be visualized as composing something like a Russian stacking doll (*matryoshka*). The metaphor has a certain historical logic, insofar as it is precisely the collapse of the Soviet Union that more than anything else has given new urgency to the cross-disciplinary tendencies these examples manifest. We might say, then, that this *matryoshka* has at least three layers. One is the new linkage among social science and humanities disciplines (in the cases cited, among political science, sociology, and psychology on the one hand and between history and literary studies on the other). Another is made up of the connections between American and foreign scholars. A third layer consists of a new perception of how politics relates to culture.

What these three layers represent is a new geology of scholarship: they map a territory different from the one that was previously divided between the social and human sciences. This shift in the tectonics of disciplines makes itself apparent dramatically in the new alignments developing between international studies and humanistic studies. Samuel Huntington, director of the Olin Institute for Strategic Studies at Harvard, has recently made the point in the canonical pages of *Foreign Affairs*: "World politics is entering a new phase. . . . It is my hypothesis that the fundamental source of conflict in this new world will not be principally ideological or primarily economic. The great divisions among humankind and the dominating source of conflict will be cultural" (22). This emphasis on culture is one way in which changes that have already occurred in relations among the disciplines making up area studies have been recognized.

As one who trained as a philologist but who now directs a center for Russian and East European studies I can describe more specifically how the developments impelling Huntington to make his hypothesis have shaped changes in the congeries of disciplines once stigmatized as kremlinology.

The collapse of the Soviet Union is cause for wonder and dismay. But for the small band of specialists who were devoted to the academic study of the Soviet Union, the shock of its disappearance has a particular pathos. The depth of the effect on such scholars may be felt in the words of one of the most prominent among them: James H. Billington, a leading historian of Russia, a longtime director of the Kennan Institute, and the current librarian of Congress, recently told a meeting of the American Academy of Arts and Sciences, "We are living in the midst of a great historical drama that we did not expect, do not understand, and cannot even name" (31).

The geopolitical shape of what was once the Soviet Union has changed irrevocably. But so has the shape of the academic disciplines devoted to the study of what was once the Soviet Union. The most intimate form that the collapse has assumed for experts in the area is the breakup of their own discursive paradigms. Billington is not exaggerating when he says we do not even know what to call the historical drama now unfolding. It has not been a revolution (certainly not—even in what is already the *former* Czechoslovakia—a velvet revolution). Nor has it been a consistently applied reform from above, dictated by a single person or group with a coherent telos. Various metaphors for change have been proposed, such as the collapse of the Ottoman Empire and the medical trope of Oliver Sacks's *Awakenings*. But it is still too early to fix these events in a useful new metaphor. One other model for recent events has already proved its inutility: whatever else is happening, we are not experiencing "the end of history."

In this age of what Thomas Kuhn might recognize as a period of unnatural science, an increasingly popular approach has been to conceive the current discursive crisis as a shift from something called area studies to something called cultural studies. Area studies was—and, although in transition, still is—a way to name a conglomeration of professional specialties (particularly in the social sciences) organized outside the academic departmental structure and centered on specific areas of the world. Russian and East European studies is, then, one of several professional formations (along with Latin American studies, Near East studies, etc.) pursued primarily by economists, political scientists, sociologists, and historians. Slavic departments have played an ambiguous or a merely service role in area studies, acting mainly as places where social scientists can pick up the languages they need to practice their specialty. The humanities in general and the study of literature in particular were always uneasily accommodated in this clustering. During the cold war, which saw the emergence of area studies in American universities, social scientists frequently felt that literary scholars had little to contribute to the kind of understanding of the Soviets required during a period of confrontation. The emphasis was on more or less recent events that could be related to policy issues.

It was always a canard to understand kremlinology as a discipline devoted merely to monitoring the appearance of Politburo members as they jockeyed for position at Lenin's tomb during May Day celebrations (or, even worse, to equate it with "counting tanks"). Nevertheless, there was always a certain tension between area specialists—or, as they were sometimes more barbarously called, areal specialists—and specialists in hard-core academic disciplines. As hapless chairs of Russian and Soviet and east European centers would tell you, the more an economist, say, knew about the specific details of a particular region, the less highly regarded he or she was by theoretically minded colleagues in the indubitably academic confines of micro- or macroeconomics.

Professionals organized in departments of economics, political science, and so forth, then, were slightly suspicious of area specialists, who were usually clustered in extradepartmental Title VI centers. But in one discipline the suspicion went the other way: area experts were always somewhat dubious about the contribution that literature specialists might make to area studies. Government funding agencies, like the Department of Education, and local centers of area specialists at particular campuses had the sense that there was something soft, or, as was sometimes said, nonstrategic, about literary scholarship; it had, in short, little to contribute to policy studies.

One way you can tell things are changing is in the reevaluation of this judgment that is taking place both in Washington and on campuses across the land: the culture of eastern Europe, an area of study that social scientists preoccupied with real-world issues of finance and politics always left to literary scholars, is increasingly being perceived as a subject that has been neglected to the disadvantage even of hard-line social scientists. In his most recent book, *Out of Control*, and in an even more recent interview, one of the paladins of the cold war, Zbigniew Brzezinski, is at pains to explain recent political events in terms of ethics and culturally held values, drawing a distinction between Western civilization and the civilizations of the rest of the world (Interview 58).

But how do these developments relate to the work of the MLA? The new respect scholars in the social and human sciences are showing for one another is having an effect beyond area studies. When political scientists such as the two distinguished representatives I have invoked here call for new attention to culture, they are pointing to an aspect of literary scholarship that is more highly specified in the three examples above. Huntington and Brzezinski suggest that the fundamental differences among societies can be grasped only by looking at the stories people tell themselves about themselves—and about others—that define them *as* selves. Certainly Anderson, the social scientist cited in my first anecdote, holds this view: his whole theory of nationalism is based on the premise that the power holding individuals in the embrace of the community of the nation is at bottom narrative. Like Renan, Anderson argues that a first condition for any nation is that it get its history wrong, meaning that the community must, if it is to cohere, see itself as the product of a past that has conduced ineluctably to its present constitution. It must willfully exercise a certain collective amnesia, forgetting the vagaries and contingencies of the actual past in favor of a more compelling and teleological tale. In this way the randomness of experience can be given the comforting mantle of necessity.

This account of Anderson's theory gives no hint of its subtlety but may suggest why two German philologists should play so important a role in *Imagined Communities*. Both Auerbach and Benjamin provide elegant hypotheses about the way in which particular literary narratives can model larger assumptions about time and space in the communities from which the narratives spring. Auerbach wandered across borders all his life, writing about European literature in Turkey, where he became a member of the MLA, and ending up in the United States after the Second World War. Benjamin committed suicide in an all too lugubrious realization of the metaphor of border crossing when he felt he would be turned back by Spanish customs officials to face the fate that befell Jews in Nazi-occupied France. Both philologists argue that literary texts are the most intense and most comprehensive expressions of the cosmologies of the cultures in which they are enshrined, so that if one wishes to know a given society, its literary texts (even in societies where the category literature does not exist and privileged narratives are myths or orally transmitted wisdom tales) are indispensable. Thus, when Anderson defines nationalism as a phenomenon that derives from and creates a new cosmology for its adherents, it is not surprising he should turn to Auerbach and Benjamin and identify novels and newspapers as sites where the new sensibility is both mirrored and, more to the point, actively shaped.

Since the official acknowledgment of post–traumatic stress disorder (PTSD) by the American Psychiatric Association in 1980, there have been a growing number of collaborative efforts involving medical doctors, psychiatrists, sociologists, historians, and literary scholars to understand this long-recognized and widely recognized phenomenon. PTSD is "a response, sometimes delayed, to an overwhelming event or events, which takes the form of repeated, intrusive hallucinations, dreams, thoughts or behaviors stemming from the event, along with numbing that may have begun during or after the experience, and possibly also increased arousal to (and avoidance of) stimulants recalling the event" (Caruth 2–3). The disorder was first noted during the First World War, as the number of cases of shell shock reached almost epidemic proportions on some fronts, but only recently has it become clear that "the pathology consists . . . solely in the *structure of its experience* or reception: the event is not assimilated or experienced fully at the time, but only belatedly, in its repeated *possession* of the one who experiences it. To be traumatized is precisely to be possessed by an image or event" (Caruth 3).

Another way of understanding trauma might be, then, to conceive it as an especially intense form of a problem that in its less pathological manifestations is familiar to all of us as the difficulty of assimilating our past to our present so as to form a coherent identity. Trauma is, in other words, a particularly urgent form of narrative: how to construct a beginning, middle, and end from the chaos and horror of experience. Trauma is a rich area of investigation because in it "the traumatic event is not experienced as it occurs, but becomes fully evident only in connection with another place, and in another time" (Caruth 7).

Trauma studies involve interdisciplinary work by medical researchers, social scientists, historians, and literary scholars, all of whom have different reasons for cooperating. Clinicians have discovered that getting a better grasp on narrative theory aids them in understanding—and treating—disorders that are rooted in a person's ability to put the story of his or her identity into a livable order. Historians have become involved (there is now a journal devoted to psychohistory) because much of what Freud and others in the clinical community have reported on trauma provides a new perspective on such massively traumatizing events as war or, paradigmatically, the Holocaust. And literary scholars have found a new way to ground the fictions they study in the deepest layers of lived experience, for the skills they have learned in studying complex emplotment in literary works (think of *Tristram Shandy* or the French *nouveau roman*) have much to offer their colleagues in other fields who seek to unravel the mysteries of how trauma occludes the ability of patients to tell their own stories to themselves.

The effects of such developments on the internationalization of scholarship are no doubt obvious, but let me cite some of the more pertinent ones. Not only is much of the theory driving trauma studies derived from different countries (Austria, Israel, France, the United States), but the whole impulse of the movement is directed toward better understanding of events whose scope is ineluctably international: the effects of wars and political repression, as well as different artistic movements in various countries that have evolved new formal means for representing such events in literary texts. The scholar I quote so frequently in this section, Cathy Caruth, has a PhD in comparative literature and now teaches English. That she was chosen to edit two issues of *American Imago*, the official journal of the Association for Applied Psychoanalysis, is exemplary, as is these issues' inclusion of scholars from a wide variety of disciplines and countries, devoting attention to questions of international concern.

A specific example of how new forces are shaping the boundaries of both nations and disciplines is provided by the work of James Wertsch, an American psycholinguist who has written several studies probing the construction of national identity. Because national identity can only be studied comparatively, Wertsch has joined colleagues in a number of other countries: Japan, Sweden, Brazil, and, since his major focus is on eastern Europe, Russia and Estonia. In his most recent work, he has addressed the problem Billington addresses in his lecture to the American Academy: the recent history of eastern Europe, especially Russia, where changes are so great and so manifold that they beggar all traditional schemes for investing contingency with an aura of necessity. With Estonian and Russian colleagues (Peter Tuulviste, of Tartu University, and Mark Rozen, of the Institute for Psychology in Moscow), Wertsch interviewed large numbers of people to gather data on how they contextualize recent events in their lives. The project also involves close attention to how national history was taught in the past in Estonian and Russian schools (and how that teaching compares with the teaching of national history in the United States) and how it is now presented in Estonian and Russian textbooks.

Wertsch's work has certain affinities with trauma studies, insofar as it concerns the reception of experience that can only be described as traumatic. And he too finds himself necessarily working with not only other scholars in his discipline but also historians and literary scholars, since much of the analysis of his data once again involves questions of organizing narrative—at the personal level of biographies in individual subjects and at the level of history in textbooks that examine connections between the national past and the present. His work represents another constellation in the expanding universe where social and human scientists find themselves necessarily thrown together on an international scale.

I have not made the obvious point that, in all the cases I have cited and in many other instances of collaboration between humanist scholars and colleagues from different disciplines and countries, the humanists involved are members of foreign language or comparative literature departments. The new cooperation between disciplines represents a kind of interdisciplinary scholarship that has grassroots origins in that it does not develop out of some grand scheme that is then applied to selected problems: rather, the new problems we are facing in the post–cold war era have themselves called into being the need for cooperation across professions.

WORKS CITED

Anderson, Benedict. *Imagined Communities*. 2nd ed. London: Verso, 1991.

Billington, James H. "The Search for a Modern Russian Identity." *Bulletin of the American Academy of Arts and Sciences* 45.4 (1992): 31–44.

Brzezinski, Zbigniew. Interview. *Brown Journal of Foreign Affairs* 1.1 (1993–94): 51–60.

———. *Out of Control: Global Turmoil on the Eve of the Twenty-First Century*. New York: Scribner's, 1993.

Caruth, Cathy. Introduction. *American Imago* 48.1 (1991): 1–9.

Huntington, Samuel P. "The Clash of Civilizations?" *Foreign Affairs* 72.3 (1993): 22–49.

Kroeber, A., and C. Kluckhohn. "Culture: A Critical Review of Concepts and Definitions." *Papers of the Peabody Museum of Archeology and Ethnology* 47 (1952): 145–54.

Wellek, René. "The Attack on Literature." *American Scholar* 42 (1972): 27–42.

———. "The Concept of Comparative Literature." *Yearbook of Comparative Literature*. Ed. W. P. Friedrich. Vol. 2. Chapel Hill: U of North Carolina P, 1953. 1–5.

———. "The Crisis of Comparative Literature." *Proceedings of the Second International Congress of Comparative Literature*. Ed. W. P. Friedrich. Vol. 1. Chapel Hill: U of North Carolina P, 1959. 148–56.

———. "The Revolt against Positivism in Recent European Literary Scholarship." *Twentieth Century English*. Ed. W. S. Knickerbocker. New York: Philosophical Library, 1943. 67–89.

Reading Literature: From Graduate School to Elementary School

CHARLES MUSCATINE

Ever since its appearance on the academic scene about thirty years ago, the intellectual movement known as deconstruction has been recognized as a direct challenge to the traditional conception of literature as Literature and therefore to the previously established ideas of reading and of literary criticism taught in the graduate schools. At least a dozen other movements have appeared since, variously reinforcing or adapting or overrunning deconstruction and one another but mostly moving in the same direction, in their various ways making good the early challenge and transforming advanced literary studies, it would seem, forever.

I am myself one of the victims of this transformation, having grown up in the New Criticism and in a sort of liberal humanism and, after some years devoted to the administration of an undergraduate curricular experiment, having awakened like Rip van Winkle one morning in the early eighties to find the scholarly village completely changed.

But I do not intend to deplore Theory, as this new body of thought has come collectively to be called. I remember too well the pathos that surrounded the old historicists, in our view, and the righteous enthusiasm, if not amusement, with which we young New Critics dismantled their practice. I intend to be, like Rip, both good-natured and generous. It is clear to me that Theory has not only transformed, it has revivified and renourished literary scholarship in our time, providing new and exciting terrain for the activities of thousands of young scholars for whom the landscape of the early sixties already seemed to

The author is Professor Emeritus of English at the University of California, Berkeley.

offer little room and little intellectual nutrition. It is also clear that Theory has provided us sharpened insights into the connections among language, literature, culture, and politics that we will not soon want to dispense with. If there is a lot of it with which I disagree, and a lot that I simply do not understand, I still have confidence that the healthily anarchic freedom of our graduate schools, where critical analysis as an activity is stronger than ever before, will continue to permit Theory to grow, to change, and gradually to sift out what isn't true or doesn't work.

I have had a certain concern, however, about the effect of Theory in the schools, about how the new graduate curricula could be expected to coexist with those of the elementary and secondary schools. *Coexist* is a more modest and more pessimistic term than I would actually like to use. I would like to be able to imagine the reading of literature in kindergarten to graduate school as—potentially, ideally—a continuum, a coherent if complex educational sequence for students, and a source of professional identity and effectiveness for teachers. It would be more than satisfying were there to be an intellectual correlative to the institutional symbiosis that already binds elementary teachers to graduate faculty members through complex channels of graduate and teacher education.

My initial pessimism has come from two sources. The first is the deep and perennial distinction in America between the preconditions of teaching in the schools and those in the colleges and universities. The obvious differences in maturity and legal status between schoolchildren and college students and the differences of governance and control between schools and colleges mean that professors by and large have a lot more freedom than teachers do and a lot easier job of teaching. Summarizing the problem (with a somewhat idealized view of the American university), one might well ask, How can institutions presumably licensed to maintain a continual and honest critique of our culture be intimately conjoined with institutions obliged to affirm, support, and even inculcate the dominant traits of that culture?

The problem is an old one, but one that we have long confronted or sidestepped in repeated and occasionally successful attempts to create open intellectual connections between schools and universities. These include "articulation," agreements about college entrance requirements, various activities of the NCTE, and arrangements such as the NEH Summer Seminars for teachers, the National Humanities Faculty, and the ACLS Teacher Curriculum Development Project. The results have not been spectacular, but the first problem—of unequal freedom—has not prevented us from trying and hoping.

But the second problem would seem to have made matters much worse, and that is that—whether by historical accident or historical necessity—the intellectual content of Theory would seem to be much more inimical, much less assimilable, to the work of the schools than the ideas it is replacing or has replaced.

The New Criticism had important traits that made it comfortable and congenial for us to think of in its possible transposition to the schools. Its central discipline of close reading of "good literature" could be imagined as a seamless educational sequence from elementary to graduate school. It was based on the assumption that literature had a special character that distinguished it from other forms of writing and on a fairly wide agreement on a canon, on what works were most worth reading. It had, then, a strong sense of the "values" of literature and had gone some distance in working out a technique and vocabulary—including such terms as *unity*, *complexity*, and *maturity*—in which the evaluation of literature could be related to the results of literary analysis. Applying literary analysis to describable traits of relatively stable texts presumed the possibility of agreement about the meanings—even complex meanings—of texts. The meaning of the work—the work standing with its own ontological integrity about midway between the author's indeterminable intentions and the idiosyncratic responses of readers—was available to analysis and rational argument, based on textual, linguistic, and historical evidence, by readers willing to equip themselves to read and to recognize and discount as much as possible their own personal idiosyncrasies.

A project that lent itself to determining what readers of literature could agree on was adaptable prima facie to pedagogy on all levels, and of course there are a lot of other points of compatibility. A canon of Literature with a capital L makes for a secure definition of the field of English, of the professional discipline, and of the curriculum. The search for definable meaning and the possibility of reasoned analysis based on evidence open out to widely valued training in critical thinking. An emphasis on values is conducive to the cultivation of literary taste and judgment—clearly desirable for young students. The whole approach comfortably asserts the value of studying literature for its own sake, and, as I say, we have had some modest successes in using it to integrate kindergarten through graduate school.

I feel a certain nostalgia for the New Criticism; but I don't want to reinstate it, and I don't expect it to make a comeback: it appears today remarkably naive. But this brief sketch of what was in place forty years ago will serve as a foil to what has happened. How, by contrast, are the leading ideas of deconstruction, feminist criticism, neo-Marxist and neo-Freudian criticism, cultural criticism and the new historicism, ethnic studies and postcolonial criticism, gender studies, reader-response criticism, and their cognates relatable to teaching in the schools?

It is clear that a few of these ideas have already taken root in the schools and are flourishing. Multiculturalism, which makes unanswerable arguments for racial and gender equality, is deeply congenial to widely held ideas about education's role in a democracy. With it, the older idea of a special literary canon that happens to exclude the writings of women and minorities is patently undergoing serious modification. This gives teachers a wider choice of materials and, from works that speak directly to the actual condition of a wide range of students, a chance to make a powerful initial case for the appeal of literature.

The abolition or at least the amplification of the old canon will be mourned by only a handful of political conservatives. But many of the other educational implications of Theory—despite their illuminative and regenerative effects on the graduate school—would seem harder to assimilate to schoolteaching. What are English teachers to make, if anything, of the wholesale reconception of language, of discourse, and even of reality on which much of Theory is based? What can be done pedagogically with the new instability of language, the new indeterminacy of meaning, the new dissolving of literature into a great congeries of other "texts"—all of equal cultural importance? Schoolteachers are struggling with perhaps diminishing success to teach students to *construe* written works; what are they to do with deconstruction, destabilization, dislocation, decentering, and other emphases on the inherent instability of reading and understanding?

At the very least, the blurring of the old distinction between literature and other written works and of that between written works and other texts—pictorial, auditory, architectural, cinematic, and so on—will be disorienting and disorganizing. A new emphasis on interdisciplinarity, on crossing or redrawing boundaries between fields, promises to be healthy and invigorating in a university environment where professors have some curricular freedom, research time, and flexibility of relations with other departments. In the more restrictive environment of schools, it may well blur the sense of the teacher's professional field and of his or her proper job of work.

The widespread denial by Theory of aesthetic values has sources and ramifications far too complex to be detailed here. But it is easy to see how this general position, coupled with the idea of the reader's displacing the banished author as the principal creator of the text, could play out in the schoolroom as a debilitating subjectivism and relativism. Reinforced by Theory's erasure of the distinction between high art and pop art, high culture and pop culture, it could do damage to any conception of education in the judgment of value.

Much of recent Theory, as we all know, plays itself out not so much in terms of literature as in terms of ideology, culture, and politics. A defense of education in value judgment would be expected to be interpreted by Theory as a not-so-covert argument for political elitism. Indeed, most of the ideas that we have been contemplating have important correlatives for Theory on the planes of ideology and culture, if they do not in fact already constitute ideology and culture. So what do we make, educationally, of the idea that our whole enterprise is inherently political?

When we think of the ideal of education for citizenship in a democracy, education as inherently political seems like a familiar and easily useful concept.

But much of recent Theory does not look at our profession or our culture in peacefully unitive, consensual terms. It holds that the creation and criticism of literature are never disinterested, but always exercises of power, and that the struggle for power is as inherent in our work as it is in our combative, contestive, conflictual culture. The key terms of philosophical and literary theory—*difference, deconstruction, instability, decentering,* and the like—are virtually interchangeable with the key terms of political and cultural criticism: *domination* and *resistance, struggle, opposition, subversion, contestation.*

Even if one were to accept the fact of "inescapable cultural difference, division, and dissonance" and thus to accept "the eruption of radical cultural contention and disagreement as a normal rather than a perverse condition" in the academy, one might be disposed to wonder—and to worry—how it would play out in the schools (Graff and Robbins 433, 428).

Whatever we think of it, postmodernist theory *is* playing out and *will* play out in our schools, with a slow, geological certainty—not only through direct academic interest and influence but also because both Theory and our schools in part breathe in the same culture. But I think that there is some room in which to influence this process for the good. The schools are most likely to adopt the best of Theory, and avoid the worst, if they, their staffs, and clientele—meaning all of us—begin by rejecting Theory's own contentiousness and settling down with good will to further the process of refining Theory itself.

It may be that we can have it both ways—not in the spirit of political compromise but because the educationally practical truth of Theory is very likely to be partial. A lot of philosophical, critical, and social theory is not progressive but historically pendular, and we can expect the pendulums in time to swing back. Some theory can be appreciated and accepted as theory and then in practice be safely ignored, just as you can safely sit on a wooden bench that physics identifies as electrical particles. Much theory is so radical and exclusive that it must turn out to be only partially useful. Thus we can throw out the old canon, and even "canonicity," and still find ourselves needing to teach a lot of formerly Great Books. It may turn out that while all texts are indeed the creatures and creators of cultures, some have special traits that permit them simultaneously to transcend their cultures and speak more than one language. It is probably true that the reader, in reading, in important ways creates the work, makes its meaning, but it would be very hard on society if similar meanings, or sectors of meaning, were not available to be shared and agreed on with other readers. Similarly, it may be that all literature is ideological and serves mostly the interests of the dominant class; but the interests of the dominant class may turn out to be not entirely contemptible. We can acknowledge with Theory that personal and political life is permeated by the operation of Power and still recognize that some people at some times reject or transcend the imperatives of Power—and even of Desire.

Rejecting contentiousness, we should also beware of its opposite, that unreflective fascination with the new and the stylish, the bandwagon effect, that is already a plague in upper academia itself.

If some of the ideas congenial with Theory that are already settling into the schools are widely accepted and clearly salutary, others seem to me to have been welcomed on insufficient reflection. There are good examples in the most recent version of "Standards for the English Language Arts," by the International Reading Association and the National Council of Teachers of English.

The authors of "Standards" have obviously adopted Theory's submerging of the conception of literature within a series of other expressive forms of all kinds. The first standard comfortingly recommends that "students read and study a wide range of texts, including fiction and nonfiction, classic and contemporary works, and texts that build their understanding of the culture and history of the United States." But the word *literature*, used with conspicuous infrequency in the fifty-seven pages of the document, is replaced by a range of undifferentiated "texts." The careful, disciplined reading of literature fades into a multiplicity of "approaches" and "strategies"—within different "literacy communities"—that in their variety and recommended flexibility promise a disorienting and blurring effect on the teacher. Visual texts and "viewing" (while no doubt essential to cultural criticism) are given questionable place alongside literature and reading. The relativism and subjectivism promoted by Theory are also overly conspicuous: there is much about student response, little about training in discrimination and judgment.

In general, the standards fail to present the study of literature as a unique discipline with its own subject matter and supporting body of knowledge and its own techniques of analysis. We should carefully reconsider whether this is what we really want.

WORKS CITED

Graff, Gerald, and Bruce Robbins. "Cultural Criticism." *Redrawing the Boundaries: The Transformation of English and American Literary Studies.* Ed. Stephen Greenblatt and Giles Gunn. New York: MLA, 1992. 419–36.

International Reading Association and National Council of Teachers of English. "Standards for the English Language Arts." Draft.

Always in Flux—Literary Forms, Cultural Norms, and Language Patterns: The Example of "Yekl"

MARTHA BANTA

As one who regularly teaches American literature at UCLA at the upper-division level, I offer certain observations that I believe are applicable to the classroom situations many of us encounter in our daily rounds. Since I stress teaching practices, I need to mention some of the particulars of the UCLA case; then I can move toward what I hope are useful generalizations.

To be sure, UCLA has its share of students who specialize in "time-of-day" courses, as in "I'm majoring in 1:00–3:00 PM." Nevertheless, most students care greatly about the choices they make for a major, and there are a great many who have elected to concentrate on the reading of literature. The UCLA English department houses the nation's largest concentration of literature majors—some 1,200. In addition, the department has recently established a brand new field of emphasis whereby students can focus on the various literary forms out of which we construct that critical mass called American literature. Many nonmajors sign up for our courses, further swelling the enrollment figures. You can imagine the staffing problems this creates, but I won't discuss that issue here. Rather, I bear down on some of the implications of this dramatic demonstration of the laws of supply and demand in action.

The UCLA catalog lists thirty-three American literature courses, broken down into historical periods, themes, and genres. As expected, courses that cover contemporary works are hot items. So what about my own territory of teaching: one that spans the fifty years that come on the heels of the Civil War—that is, "the old stuff"? Is what got written between the 1870s and the

The author is Professor of English at the University of California, Los Angeles.

First World War considered a dead spot on the enrollment charts? Hardly! Think waiting list; think ambushes in the hallway from students who plead that their lives will be ruined if they can't get into the class. Up to a point, these reactions come from typical first-week craziness, the thrill and tension on which many students thrive. Beyond panic, however, is their very real desire to read literatures emerging from that specific period whose historical circumstances and literary creations anticipate aspects of their own experience. Consider but one fact with major literary consequences: the massive inflow of European immigrants into the United States at the turn of the century, who brought with them new customs, new ideas, and new vocabularies for living in a new land.

Take a look at the names on the enrollment printout I get on the first day of class. Of the sixty-five names, about one-third are instantly recognizable to an Anglo eye and readily pronounceable by Anglo lips; but to read off these three score names in rapid succession is an exercise both instructive and exhilarating. It is direct proof—if proof were needed—of the multicultural makeup of today's classrooms. Granted that the UCLA student body offers a somewhat extravagant example of this fact, since UCLA has become the most racially and ethnically diversified of all the University of California campuses. But we're all aware (or should be) that comparable diversity is on display throughout the country's secondary schools and colleges.

One consequence is the challenge put to teachers like me when making out a course syllabus. As a firm believer in the need for students to acquire a solid grasp of real knowledge about how literature works, I do my best to pick titles representative of the changes taking place between 1870 and 1910 in what was being written (and how it was written). I try to select readings that inscribe the arc formed by the authors' choices of stylistic modes, genre types, and narrative structures, as well as to make certain that the readings reflect the cultural adjustments taking place across the American scene.

The making of a workable reading list is easier said than done when one envisions a classroom filled with students whose attributes sprawl across the demographic charts: students with an array of cultural, social, and economic backgrounds and foregrounds; students with a range of linguistic aptitudes— fluently bi- or trilingual, adept in American English only, or gallantly working with English as their second language. Try to make up a representative reading list for this rainbow coalition.

The pragmatics of course planning that I have discussed here constantly condition what we try to do to fulfill our duties as teachers. I turn now to the issues I take into the classroom whenever I attempt to demonstrate the ways in which literary forms are of a piece with prevailing cultural norms and language patterns.

I teach a survey in American literature from the Civil War to the First World War (one of the winsome ways college catalogs mark off historical periods in terms of wars we have fought). I find I cannot teach literature without treating literary history as well. I believe students need to know that Hart Crane's poetry comes after Walt Whitman's—how else to understand the ways by which Crane draws on the Whitmanian tradition, even as he adds his own modernist licks; they need to realize that Emily Dickinson's miniaturistic enigmas came before the experiments in style of Gertrude Stein; they need to see that the road leading to the novels of Richard Wright and Toni Morrison began with the tracks laid down by Frederick Douglass and W. E. B. Du Bois. What is more, I cannot touch literary history without getting into cultural history, intellectual history, and history history. Further, I feel that my job is unfinished unless I take into account the dramatic shifts in the American vernacular taking place during this volatile period as the nineteenth century careened into the twentieth.

Four examples: (1) Walt Whitman's *Leaves of Grass* gets roasted at times because of the poet's penchant for tossing in words from different languages, but by 1855 Whitman well knew the importance of incorporating Spanish and French into the local mores of speech. Linguistic absorptions had brought new energy to the language of Shakespeare's England. They continued to act as the source of the exuberant American English celebrated in Whitman's epic poem. (2) During the post–Civil War years, when European travel became economically feasible for a growing number of Americans, the genre of the international novel developed by William Dean Howells, Henry James, and Edith Wharton tested the survival skills of innocents abroad. These newly cosmopolitan narratives used language for dramatic purposes to either encourage or block communication between the fictional representatives of different national cultures. (3) When Mark Twain headed out West—travels that inspired the tall tales of the rambling narrative *Roughing It*—he learned that the clothes, customs, and vocabularies that were correct east of St. Joe, Missouri, did not work once he ventured into areas where he encountered words like *coyote* and *blind lead*, words not found in the *Webster's Dictionary* he had lugged along on his overland stagecoach ride. (4) The Creole tales of George Washington Cable and Kate Chopin and the dialects embedded in Charles Chesnutt's stories and Paul Dunbar's poems drawn from the black experience introduced important linguistic layers and cultural complications. They mark yet another significant chapter in the long history of American writers' attempts to substitute their own powerful language tradition for the "colonialized" British speech that held the United States in thrall even after the Revolution.

Turn-of-the-century American vocabularies increased exponentially. They reflected discoveries taking place in science and technology, but along with *X ray, dynamo, telephone, Kodak, movies, skyscraper*, and *the el*, other words leave less innocent records of social upheavals and maladies: *Jim Crow, skid row, nabobs, the Pinkertons, sweatshop*. Then consider the enormous importance of the two-way street of language that resulted when Yiddish, Polish, Gaelic, and Italian were added to the pool of Yankee speech. And recognize the marked effect on the era's literature as authors began a self-conscious exploration of shifts taking place in the value given to words once thought to be sacred. Stephen Crane's Henry Fleming is forced to test *heroism*, *glory*, and *patriotism*. The characters in stories by Charles Chesnutt and Anzia Yezierska confront the problem of applying to themselves words such as *equality* and *freedom*. Theodore Dreiser's businessmen relearn the meaning of *individualism* in the midst of corporate structures. Mary Wilkins Freeman, Edith Wharton, Kate Chopin, and Charlotte Perkins Gilman tell stories that place the word *home* (ringed by *mother*, *wife*, *breadwinner*) under assault by newer terms such as *apartment*, *the working woman*, and *divorce*.

I conclude with two episodes extracted from the kinds of stories to which my students are particularly responsive, precisely because such narratives tell how the peoples witnessing a turbulent cultural mix are able or fail to speak with one another.

Episode 1: Although *Ramona*—Helen Hunt Jackson's novel of 1884, her exposé of race prejudice in Old California—is written in English, her characters are identified as speaking in English, Spanish, and several Indian dialects, as well as "Tennessean," languages that reflect cultures often at odds with one another. Perhaps the most terrible moment in this tragedy of noncommunication is when a brutish Yankee accuses Alesandro, the noble Indian married to Ramona, of stealing his horse. Alesandro cries out "Señor, I will explain," but before he can utter the words of his innocence, he is shot through the throat (344). He dies, choking on his own blood, his own unspoken words.

Episode 2: The short story "Yekl," published in 1896, was Abraham Cahan's first attempt to write for an English-speaking audience. A master of Yiddish, Hebrew, Russian, and English, Cahan had already achieved fame as the founder of the all-important *Jewish Daily Forward* when William Dean Howells urged him to bring scenes of New York City ghetto life to the attention of the mainstream audience. "Yekl" brilliantly captures what it means for a Yiddisher to absorb Yankee speech patterns, what results when the resident American vernacular begins to incorporate Old World terms within its own vocabulary, and how Cahan conveys to English-language readers the processes of speech formation taking place within their own complex cultural situation.

Three years before the opening of the narrative, Yekl Podkovnik immigrated to Boston from Russia. Quickly changing his name to Jake, shaving his beard and earlocks, and adopting Yankee clothes, mannerisms, and values, Jake has moved on to New York, where we find him talking away while working in a cloak shop. Cahan first tells us what Jake's speech sounds like:

> He spoke in Boston Yiddish, that is to say, in Yiddish more copiously spiced with mutilated English than is the language of the metropolitan Ghetto

in which our story lies . . . and his r's could do credit to the thickest
Irish brogue.   (2)

Thereafter, when Cahan records Jake's conversation, readers can see what that
conversation looks like; we witness the process out of which new speech patterns
are being formed. Cahan also places asterisks next to Hebrew terms that refer
English-only speakers to the bottom of the page for explanations. A footnote an-
nounces that "English words incorporated in the Yiddish of the characters . . . are
given in italics" (2). The words we read may be set down in English, but we are
to understand that they are being spoken in Yiddish riddled by phonetically rendered additions from the Yankee speech that Jake enthusiastically embraces. You
can see this for yourself from the following wonderful conversation:

> "When I was in Boston," [Jake] went on, with a contemptuous mien in-
> tended for the American metropolis, "I knew a *feller*, so he was a *precticly*
> friend of John Shullivan's. He is a Christian, that feller is, and yet the two of
> us lived like brothers. May I be unable to move from this spot if we did not.
> How, then, would you have it? Like here, in New York, where the Jews are a
> *lot* of *greenhornsh* and can not speak a word of English? Over there every Jew
> speaks English like a stream."
>
> "*Say*, Dzake," the presser broke in, "John Sullivan is *tzampion* no longer,
> is he?"
>
> "Oh, no! Not always is it holiday!" Jake responded, with what he consid-
> ered a Yankee jerk of his head. "Why, don't you know? Jimmie Corbett *leaked*
> him, and Jimmie *leaked* Chollie Meetchel, too. *You can betch you' bootsh!* John-
> nie could not leak Chollie, *becaush* he is a big *bluffer*, Chollie is."   (2)

In a later scene, Jake pleads with Mamie (the woman he wants to marry) not
to speak English in the presence of Gitl, the wife who has just arrived most in-
conveniently from Russia, for fear Gitl will guess at their intimacy. Stubbornly,
the thoroughly Americanized Mamie continues to speak English, forcing Jake
to reply in kind in an argument that finds him appropriating invectives such as
"For Chrish' shake!" (51), whose use the goyim would consider profane but he
does not. Cahan presents these dialogues brilliantly on the page, capturing the
cadences of Yiddish and English (both proper and slang) at the historical moment when they first flowed into that multilayered American speech we now
take for granted.

What have we here in these examples? Very "American" tales that show how
literature provides us with complex narratives about American lives in transition between the old and the new. We have here a robust body of writing en-
riched by its keen sense of cultural mutations and linguistic explorations:
forever in flux—merging, converging, evolving. Many of my students are actually experiencing this process; the rest realize they cannot know literature without a sense of the cultures out of which it sprang. They come to appreciate that

they are unable to understand those cultures unless they get a feel for the part language plays on the social scene; they also appreciate that one of the best ways to understand this interplay is to engage enthusiastically in the precise, informed study of literature.

At whatever level we teach, high school or college, literatures and languages work together in the classroom; they work together, else they wither and die separately.

WORKS CITED

Cahan, Abraham. *"Yekl and the Imported Bridegroom" and Other Stories of Yiddish New York.* New York: Dover, 1970.

Jackson, Helen Hunt. *Ramona.* New York: Penguin-Signet, 1988.

Literary Literacy; or, The Cook, the Cop, the Nurse, the Computer Scientist, and Me

SANDRA M. GILBERT

Eliot, T. S. An English author of the twentieth century, born and raised in the United States. Eliot wrote poems, plays, and ESSAYS, and urged the use of ordinary language in POETRY. He was much concerned with the general emptiness of modern life and with the revitalization of religion. Among Eliot's best-known works are the poems "The Love Song of J. Alfred Prufrock" and "The WASTE LAND," and the play Murder in the Cathedral.

Woolf, Virginia. An English author of the twentieth century who experimented with STREAM-OF-CONSCIOUSNESS narrative technique. Her works include the NOVEL To the Lighthouse *and the ESSAY "A Room of One's Own," which is about the problems of female artists.*

[B]road, shallow knowledge is the best route to deep knowledge.
                              —E. D. Hirsch et al., *The Dictionary of Cultural Literacy*

Almost a decade ago, the literary critic and composition theorist E. D. Hirsch, a professor at the University of Virginia, struck it rich with a best-seller entitled *Cultural Literacy: What Every American Needs to Know.* Apparently riding the crest of the same backlash against theoretical innovation, identity politics, and multicultural pedagogy that motivated such other polemics as Allan Bloom's well-known *The Closing of the American Mind* and William Bennett's *To Reclaim*

The author is Professor of English at the University of California, Davis.

---

a Legacy, as well as, more recently, Charles J. Sykes's *Profscam*, Roger Kimball's *Tenured Radicals*, and Dinesh D'Souza's *Illiberal Education*, Hirsch urged teachers to remember that reading and writing have always (and perhaps only) been facilitated by shared knowledge of a common intellectual inheritance; he claimed, in other words, that what he calls "cultural literacy" is a precondition for serious educational experiences. Noting in the subsequently published *Dictionary of Cultural Literacy* that we "only make social and economic progress by teaching everyone to read and communicate, which means teaching myths and facts that are predominantly traditional," Hirsch insisted that "disadvantaged students" in particular "are the very ones who suffer when we fail to introduce traditional literate culture into the earliest grades" (xv).

In his castigation of those "who evade [the] inherent conservatism of literacy in the name of multicultural antielitism" as "in effect elitists of an extreme sort," Hirsch deployed a rhetoric that was in some ways as combative as the more ideologically charged locutions of Bennett and Bloom. Yet unlike those thinkers, he frankly aligned his own goals with those of the liberals whose methods he attacked, explaining almost apologetically that "the social goals of liberalism *require* educational conservatism" (xv). At the same time, however, he rather damagingly admitted that "cultural literacy is a necessary but not sufficient attainment of an educated person," for "cultural literacy is shallow; true education is deep" (xv).

Although I have myself for the past twenty years been doing intellectual work in feminist and gender theory that entails just the sort of canon revision Hirsch appears to deplore, I'm sympathetic not only with his goals and his definition of a common intellectual background as "cultural literacy" but also with his conviction that such "cultural literacy" is an essential precondition of "true education." As a feminist critic and teacher, in fact, I consider it crucial that students in my field understand the nature of the canon with which women readers and writers have for centuries been confronted. And as—in another part of my life—a poet and essayist, I count on my own readers' sharing enough of my knowledge to get my references, comprehend the contexts of my themes and structures.

Yet although I'm keenly aware of my own multifaceted professional reliance on "cultural literacy," I must of course note that everything I do is directed toward (or depends on) the creation of an audience possessing that enigmatic quality Hirsch names "true education." Indeed, my interest in the mystery of "true education" is what motivates this essay and, along with so-called cultural literacy, I'm sure it's what I share with most readers of *Profession*.

It's not insignificant, however, that even while Hirsch exploits the resonance of the words "true" and "education," he leaves vague the concept for which they stand. His trademark notion of cultural literacy can be (and has been!) patented, despite (or perhaps because of) the fact that it's both substantively and strategically "shallow." But from Plato to Machiavelli and on, philosophers have had trouble agreeing on the cryptic lineaments of "true education." Thus I realize that any pronouncement of mine will risk sounding hubristic or professionally self-serving. Nevertheless, I want to suggest that "true education" is inextricably entwined not just with the dynamics of a shallow cultural literacy but also with a more hard-won mastery that—partly to acknowledge indebtedness to Hirsch and partly as a tool with which to debate him—I'll call "literary literacy."

What constitutes literary literacy, and how can we formulate its advantages? In exploring this question, I'd like to begin by telling the story of a recent venture of mine that became a powerful learning experience for me, an experience that helped me understand a little more than I had before about what I am calling literary literacy and hence about the nature of true education.

In June 1995 I spent four days as a visiting scholar at a faculty development seminar for teachers at Southern Maine Technical College, a small community college in South Portland. One of a number of such projects funded by the increasingly beleaguered National Endowment for the Humanities, this particular four-week interdisciplinary seminar was focused on early-twentieth-century modernism, a phenomenon the group approached through readings in physics (Einstein), psychoanalysis (Freud), the history of industrialization (Henry Ford), and literature (Woolf, Eliot, Hurston), among other topics. I had been invited as a literary consultant to help lead discussions of *Mrs. Dalloway*, *A Room of One's Own*, "The Love Song of J. Alfred Prufrock," and *The Waste Land*, but I also joined in conversations about *Their Eyes Were Watching God* as well as, more generally, the Great War of 1914 to 1918, the first "wave" of feminism, the Harlem Renaissance of the late twenties, the relation between gender and genre, and the rise of an aesthetic avant-garde during the first third of our century.

The twenty or so participants in the group (which was about two-thirds male) came from an extraordinarily broad spectrum of fields, pretty accurately representing the emphases of the institution where they teach. As I recall, there were at least three people from law enforcement, including a retired police chief from the city of Portland, two from culinary arts (including the star of a local TV cooking show), two from nursing, two from computer science, one from psychology, one from mathematics, two from physics, one from physical education, and two from counseling, as well as several from English and history. In short, humanists, especially literary critics, were strikingly in the minority—as were feminists.

Southern Maine Technical College occupies an exceptionally beautiful and historically interesting site on the shore of Casco Bay. The guest house where I stayed is a Yankee merchant's mansion, elegantly refurbished and efficiently staffed by the school's department of hotel management; virtually next door, the ruins of several eighteenth-century forts face the water, the splendid views of Portland Head Light, and the islands made famous by Harriet Beecher Stowe and Sarah Orne Jewett. But no doubt because humanists were such a minority in the group and because I was the last "expert" visitor (the seminar had already met for three weeks when I arrived), I was at first too anxious about my own share in the project to savor the pleasures of this setting. I remember scrambling over the ramparts before my first meeting with the participants, nervous and puzzled about how in so little time I could impart anything significant that would help elucidate such difficult texts as *Mrs. Dalloway* and "The Love Song of J. Alfred Prufrock."

It must be obvious that I wouldn't be telling this story if my worst fears had been realized. In fact, almost as soon as I encountered this dauntingly diverse set of scholars at the casual, coffee-and-muffin breakfast that preceded every morning's three-hour formal session, I was struck by the enthusiasm with which they approached the material that had brought us together. Of course, they were professional educators, so they themselves had done their homework diligently. But besides time-consuming reading, most had clearly devoted considerable energy both inside and outside the seminar room to tracing the often very complicated concerns that linked the figures whose careers they were surveying. Coming to the literary segment of their course from three weeks of increasingly sophisticated research into the often baffling concepts of modernism and the modern, they were now looking forward with some trepidation but also considerable anticipation to discussing the formidable works they had been assigned.

What made their eagerness particularly impressive was that indeed only the handful of humanists I mentioned earlier had ever spent any extended time with the texts we were about to examine. To be sure, E. D. Hirsch might have been satisfied with almost every participant's cultural literacy, for most had at least heard of T. S. Eliot as a rarefied experimental poet, and some knew enough about Virginia Woolf to wonder whether, as in Edward Albee's title, they should be "afraid" of her. Few of them, in other words, would have needed to be instructed that Eliot "was much concerned with the general emptiness of modern life" or that Woolf "experimented with stream-of-consciousness narrative technique," in the words of two of my epigraphs, for, in the words of the third, most possessed a comparatively "broad, shallow knowledge" of modern literature before entering the seminar room.

Yet while such a grasp of facts might have helped many hold their own in a game of Trivial Pursuit, it hadn't constituted any sort of route to a "deep knowledge" of literature. In fact, it's probably fair to say that the superficial cultural literacy of the nonhumanists in our group was precisely what caused them to quail before the monuments of modernism we were about to study. Most knew just enough about the difficulties of Eliot and Woolf to fear both.

No doubt for this reason, these participants were not only relieved but also as pleased as the humanists were by the serious discussions of "Prufrock" and

Mrs. Dalloway that marked the beginning of a real route to deep knowledge. Intelligent as they were, the idea of "literature" had disquieted them. Yet when we read "Prufrock" aloud, noting its complex aesthetic strategies along with the range of historical issues it could be said to embody, or when we went around the table discussing different views of Woolf's novel, most confessed not just enlightenment but also delight in what we were doing. One after another, they said they hadn't quite understood how, why, and what "literature"— a subject most hadn't studied since high school, if at all—might mean to them and their students.

We had little time, of course, in which to cover a great deal of rich material, and I have little space here in which to summarize our conversations. I'll therefore have to omit any real report of how we dealt with the quick protocinematic cuts the group noticed in *Mrs. Dalloway*, with the novel's resonant representations of madness, and with its subtly nuanced treatment of the differing implications the Great War had for the men and women who lived (or didn't live) through that social and political trauma. Let me just say a few words, however, about the ways in which we saw "The Love Song of J. Alfred Prufrock" as an aesthetic structure embodying the same cultural history, along with the crucially "modern" mindset(s), that the participants in the seminar had been exploring through their other readings that month.

We talked, to begin with, about the status of "Prufrock" as a work produced by a poet keenly conscious of his position as an individual talent inheriting not just a single massive literary tradition created by a succession of monuments of unaging intellect but also a set of traditions and countertraditions into which he placed himself warily and sometimes wearily. More specifically, we scrutinized the referential and prosodic strategies through which Eliot both aligned himself with and distanced himself from the history of which he was so deeply aware. Starting with his dramatic monologue's odd title ("The Love Song" of the prosaic and starched-sounding "J. Alfred Prufrock" rather than, say, the romantic "Love Song of Har Dyal"), we examined its shockingly bathetic comparison of the evening to "a patient etherized upon a table" (3), its mystifyingly jingly refrain ("In the room the women come and go / Talking of Michelangelo" [13–14]), and the beautiful, almost Arnoldian blank verse of its final epiphany ("We have lingered in the chambers of the sea / By sea-girls wreathed with seaweed red and brown / Till human voices wake us, and we drown" [129–31]).

But given the modernist matters on which the participants in the seminar had been concentrating, we also spent some time meditating on the distinctive cityscape Prufrock traverses, his path determined by a coercive labyrinth of streets that lead like an "argument / Of insidious intent" to the unspeakable "overwhelming question" that is at the heart of his dilemma (8–9, 10). Given the readings in Freud that the seminarians had done, we turned our attention also to the undersea world in which Prufrock half wishes, half fears to experience himself as a desirously scuttling shell, "a pair of ragged claws" (73). And given the discussions of transformed gender roles, of "sex-change," in which we had engaged, we mused on the meanings of the role reversal in which he anxiously imagines himself "pinned and wriggling on the wall" (58), the passive object of aggressive female gazes, even while he himself dissects female subjects into arms, bracelets, perfumes, and dresses, representations of self as arbitrary as the necktie that encircles him, the morning coat that enfolds him, and the streets in which he is entrapped. In exploring the textual history of the poem, moreover, we discussed the implications of its original title—"Prufrock among the Women"—along with the function of the ellipses right after "lonely men in shirt-sleeves, leaning out of windows" (72), which are not (as some readers think) merely a stylistic mannerism or an indication of a "thought-break" but instead signal the deletion of a key passage where the protagonist visits an unnervingly erotic red-light district whose women are bursting out of corsets and beckoning from sinister doorways.

Our discussion of the poem was increasingly intense, but perhaps the mounting interest the group was feeling in gaining what Hirsch calls a true education in literature and what I am defining as literary literacy was best dramatized by the TV chef–culinary arts instructor who sat next to me that day. After a break, he came in brandishing a piece of paper he said he'd found on the stairs outside the seminar room. On it was written (although I don't remember exact words) something like the following verse:

> Girls, girls, girls,
> Girls in skirts and girls with curls,
> I love to kiss
> Those seaside girls.

The four lines were followed by the signature "T. S. Eliot."

"So here's a poem that has T. S. Eliot's name on it," the chef said challengingly. "Do you think we should be studying it in our seminar?"

Of course, I replied that that was in fact an excellent question. "Authorship, evaluation, canon formation" were the particular words and phrases I began to murmur too.

The chef (in my title here he's the "cook") persisted. "If *I've* written these lines, they're no good, right?" he speculated. "But are they worthwhile reading if T. S. Eliot wrote them?"

At this point the retired police chief (the "cop" in my title) also chimed in, as did the nurse and the computer scientist. How can we know whether lines of poetry are really "poetry"? they wondered. How do we decide whether such lines merit serious attention? they asked. What criteria do we apply in making such decisions? Would we study lines by the cook or the cop if we thought they'd been written by a certified poet? Or would the cook, the cop, the nurse, and the computer scientist *be* poets if they wrote certain kinds of lines?

Clearly the participants in the seminar had become not just scholars and readers of literature but students of literary theory.

And suffice it to say that although their questions were in some sense unanswerable (or infinitely answerable), we spent a good deal of time discussing the issues of authorship, evaluation, and canon formation that such queries imply. For me, as for them, these were central matters that drew us together in a quest for true education in the meaning as well as the substance of literary literacy.

I have related the history of this seminar and its doings as though it took up several weeks or even months (as it well might have), but in fact we only worked as a group for three or four days. Yet I believe those few days were significant to all of us, for during that time we engaged profoundly and productively in what the pioneering critic-teacher Louise Rosenblatt has called "transactions" with literature—that is, in appraisals and analyses of the body of knowledge called "literature," whose very energetic but enigmatic existence also entails the activity I've been calling literary literacy.

I think I can say, without being smug, that the participants in the seminar learned something from talking to me and the other humanists in the group. I know I learned something from them, first and foremost that "literature"— whatever we may mean by this often vexed and vexatious term—ought to be approached and analyzed by students at every educational level. (Yes, I certainly believed that before I went to Portland in June 1995, but I didn't until then have quite such confidence in the multilevel sophistication I'm defining here.)

What I might as well term the "economy" of our group was exhilarating and intensified my confidence. On the last day we met, the computer scientist took me out on his boat for a trip around Casco Bay, where he showed me Jewett's Green Island and Cow Island. The cop promised me that the next time he led a group of law enforcement students to London (a tour he regularly guides) he'd be sure to bring them to the Imperial War Museum *and* discuss the literature of the Great War with them there.

And the cook gave me a box of quechua, an ancient grain grown in the Andes since the time of the Incas. Quechua, he explained, is a perfect protein that can be prepared in any number of ways, in all of which (not unlike literature) it is usually delicious and always remarkably nourishing.

WORKS CITED

Eliot, T. S. *Selected Poems*. San Diego: Harvest-Harcourt, 1988.
Hirsch, E. D. *Cultural Literacy: What Every American Needs to Know*. Boston: Houghton, 1987.
Hirsch, E. D., et al. *The Dictionary of Cultural Literacy*. Boston: Houghton, 1988.

An Obscure Destiny, This Business of Teaching English

JOSEPH R. URGO

What is education for? Why do people go to college? Why do college graduates go to graduate school?

The story "Old Mrs. Harris," in Willa Cather's collection *Obscure Destinies* (1932), centers on the fate of Mrs. Harris's granddaughter, Vickie Templeton, the eldest child of a Colorado family in decline. Vickie receives a scholarship to attend the University of Michigan at Ann Arbor and discusses the matter with her worldly neighbor, Mr. Rosen. Mr. Rosen asks her why she wants to go to college. Vickie answers, "To learn." Rosen presses further: "But why do you want to learn? What do you want to do with it?" Vickie responds, at a loss: "I don't know. Nothing, I guess." Rosen won't let go. "Then what do you want it for?" Vickie holds her ground: "I don't know. I just want it." To Vickie's surprise, this reply pleases Mr. Rosen, and his pleasure relieves the tense exchange between them. "Then if you want it without any purpose at all," he says, "you will not be disappointed" (158).

The dialogue between Mr. Rosen and Vickie Templeton will strike a familiar chord among readers of *Profession*. In literary studies we take for granted the idea of open-ended education, and we refer to it in various ways: knowledge for its own sake, the pursuit of learning, the habit of inquiry. The concept is an article of faith among educators in the liberal arts. Most will even recognize Mr. Rosen's quotation from Michelet, which Cather used on more than one occasion in her writing: "Le but n'est rien; le chemin, c'est tout" ("The end is nothing; the road is all"). Mr. Rosen writes down the quotation on a piece of paper

---

The author is Associate Professor of English and Humanities at Bryant College.

---

and tells Vickie to take it with her to college "as an antidote, a corrective for whatever colleges might do to her" (159). What is it that colleges will do to her? Are colleges still doing it to students?

I chair the Department of English and Humanities at Bryant College in Rhode Island. Bryant is a business college with the motto "Education for Business Leadership." We have business majors in accounting, applied actuarial mathematics, computer information systems, finance, management, and marketing. Although we offer majors in liberal arts fields (communications, economics, English, history, international studies), the vast majority of our students take degrees in business. In 1994 the college received national accreditation for its business programs from the American Assembly of Collegiate Schools of Business (AACSB). Ironically, the most recent AACSB accreditation standards (which the college must meet by 2004) demand fewer credit hours in business and more credit hours in liberal arts; at least half of any student's program of study must be in what the AACSB calls "general education." It appears, then, that only half of the curriculum can be specifically "for" something ("for business leadership"); the other half must be something else.

The achievement of the national accreditation led to a thoroughgoing curriculum reform in which over thirty percent of the faculty participated. The reorganization of the business curriculum demanded that materials be presented in fewer credit hours; the reorganization of the liberal arts curriculum allowed for the creation of distribution requirements and a wide variety of program minors. Needless to say, this restructuring has greatly altered the curricular landscape here, revitalizing the role of the Department of English and Humanities, moving us from service to partnership. After all, the AACSB has implicitly insisted that the motto "Education for _____" be left at least half blank, leaving open the possibility that education may not be for anything in particular or, ultimately, that education may be for education.

Graduate programs in English and related areas might learn something from the AACSB. One of the most serious degradations of education in our present system is the stress on the destination (sometimes collapsed into an emphasis on "outcomes"). Of course, the issue is not new; Cather saw the problem earlier in the century, as have many others. In setting its accreditation standards, the AACSB has attempted to counter a tendency in business education to overemphasize the first job at the expense of the career path, or the road with the more obscure outcome, or destiny. Liberal education at its best prepares students for uncertainty by rewarding the very qualities that technical training means to reduce: provisionality, indeterminacy, and the suspension of decision. The emphasis on securing the first job subverts the educational process by implying that education is equivalent to qualification or, in the language of the school corridors, a hurdle to jump over. For example, when graduate programs in literary studies equate the decline of the job market with failure of programs, they trivialize their missions as educational institutions. Anyone who goes to college or graduate school to get a job will inevitably be (to quote Mr. Rosen) disappointed—in the job, in the education, or in both.

Incoming freshmen at Bryant are asked to choose (or predict) their major. Dutifully, most check off one of the majors listed on the form. In recent years, however, many began to leave that question blank. Undaunted, the office of undergraduate programs added the category "undeclared" to the choices. Roughly a third of all incoming freshmen check off this category, now enshrined as an acceptable answer. Mr. Rosen would be pleased. Equally pleased is the English and humanities department. "These are our students," one colleague said at a department meeting. Very few check off English as a major. Most of our majors come from the ranks of the undeclared, and we try our best to maintain the value of contingency or provisionality in their educational program.

People who graduate from college with a degree in accounting will either be accountants or be disappointed. The certainty of the correlation between the field and the career (accounting-accountant; finance–financial analyst) makes the road and its end virtually the same. But what about the English and humanities offerings? The career placement office is always trying to pin down what it is that English majors might do in their careers (journalism? publishing?), and the English department is always trying to leave that section of the form (or of the viewbook or brochure) ambiguous. The fact is that people who major in one of the liberal arts get an education in, of, and for itself. Once that education is under way, we think they can do or learn how to do almost anything.

English professors at business and other technical colleges do something that I doubt English professors at liberal arts colleges do: explain continually, to students, parents, trustees, and their colleagues "on the other side" (i.e., in business departments) why students should take courses with such titles as Studies in Comparative Literature or Women and the Creative Imagination. At one curriculum meeting, for example, a marketing professor asked, "Why shouldn't all the books studied in a course on the novel have business themes?" Another asked, "Why, once a student has taken an English course, does that student still write poorly?" If students can learn a computer program once and for all, why can't they learn to write once and for all?

"Once and for all," like "happily ever after," is of course antithetical to everything we try to do in literary studies. Nonetheless, the argument that education is a road whose destination doesn't matter is getting tougher to defend, because the arguments for job training and professional preparation are in actuality arguments against education, against intellectual inquiry, and against the spirit of unfettered imagination. And so to defend the obscure destinies of education appears to be an assault on the values of efficiency and productivity—articles of faith in the business world, in the academy, and in the national culture. The frequency of observations in *Profession* and elsewhere about the paucity of opportunities in the academic job market and the declining number of jobs for literature and language PhDs enforces the notion that education ought to be for something, whether that something is business leadership or a tenure-track job. I am afraid that such thinking is potentially disastrous for teaching anything to anybody.

AACSB requirements that increase the liberal arts component at business schools are responding to developments in the business world, to what might be called a postjob environment. As William Bridges argues in *Jobshift: How to Prosper in a Workplace without Jobs*, the era of lifetime employment is passing rapidly. In a postjob world, workers prepare themselves for a succession of task-oriented term assignments within multiple career paths. The assumption behind the latest AACSB educational requirements is that, while a business education will ensure competency in the present environment, an engagement with the liberal arts will prepare students for the obscure destinies of a jobless world.

The concept of the job can be traced to the nineteenth century in the United States, to the industrial revolution and the development of factories and managerial bureaucracies. Much resistance arose to such work organization at the time; then for a while in this century it felt normal to work a forty-hour week at the same institution for thirty years. As the industrial era now yields to the information age (or whatever it ends up being labeled), places of employment will yield to employment situations, and workers will become small businesses themselves, moving from task to task, migrating with opportunities. The literary crisis of the self may finally reach closure as subjectivity is equated with having options. In any case, it is important to see the disappearance of tenure-track jobs and the rise of the itinerant professor (with and without tenure) not as some academic aberration but as part of a wider, more encompassing job shift in contemporary capitalism.

The question for graduate programs in literary studies is how to educate for such a world. At present, many graduate programs in English are preparing students not for academic job shifts but for a shrinking number of "permanent" jobs. As a result, graduate education makes cynics of its students and nurtures hostility in the coming generation of scholars who should, and do, resent sacrificing their educations to premature job training. For example, emphasizing the academic job market has meant that the publish-or-perish ethic has trickled down to the first-year graduate seminar. By stressing publication, graduate programs have encouraged ahistoricism (who has time for the past?) and greatly truncated research methods. Whereas graduate education was once the place to learn the scholarship one needed to begin a career, it is now the place to launch that career. What suffers? Scholarship suffers. I am sure all the readers of this journal have read published essays in their fields in which the writers have not done their homework and old arguments are rehearsed in new words. I don't know that graduate schools have the motto "Education for Assistant

Professors"; maybe they do. If the only purpose of graduate education in literary studies is to produce assistant professors of English, then we should close down half of those programs. A graduate program that declares such a mission has abandoned the field of education and entered the realm of technical and professional training.

Much of what constitutes teaching literature at a business college amounts to holding the line against this confusion of training with education. The size of the faculty at Bryant College has nearly doubled since 1986, the percentage of teachers with PhDs has increased dramatically, and the college has experienced a sea change in its identity and direction. As English department chair, I often advocate the obscure destinies of the educational process. Freshmen who read the want ads, choosing their majors on the basis of the current needs of corporate America, are foolhardy (as are graduate students who design their dissertations according to the MLA *Job Information List*). The only advice I know to impart to students is "Do what you're good at; study what gives you pleasure." If students immerse themselves in what they love now, they will probably grow accustomed to liking what they are doing and perhaps even end up doing something they enjoy, whatever it is. If they do what they think they must do to get a job (read: to survive), they will learn to abhor education. They will see it either as a hoax (because the elusive job market will shift by the time they graduate) or as a waste of time, since they are forced to study things that do not bring pleasure. As a result, education becomes a hurdle, a hoop, or a gate.

Ultimately, the interpretation of education as job training is rooted in and embodies the American tradition of anti-intellectualism, the antagonism toward any activity that is not practical, productive, or profitable. When you factor in the growing cost of higher education and the decline in federal funding for tuition assistance, that antagonism is fueled by real hardship. Thus we can expect those outside the academy to insist that education be *for* something. Those on the inside, however, cannot afford to capitulate, at least not entirely. A good portion of education, in order to maintain its integrity as education, must be for itself. As Vickie Templeton said, "I just want it." The obscure destinies of our students are perhaps their most important possession, the one thing that makes education possible.

WORKS CITED

Bridges, William. *Jobshift: How to Prosper in a Workplace without Jobs.* Reading: Addison, 1994.

Cather, Willa. *Obscure Destinies.* New York: Vintage, 1974.

Beyond the Wars of Religion: How Teaching the Conflicts Can Desecularize American Education

M. D. WALHOUT

In a recent article entitled "What (If Anything) Hath God Wrought? Academic Freedom and the Religious Professor," the Berkeley law professor Phillip E. Johnson complains that Christianity, while retaining "great vitality in the culture at large," is "effectively marginalized and shut out of academic discourse" (19). In support of his contention, Johnson cites the 1991 case of *Bishop v. Aronov*, in which a federal appeals court held that the University of Alabama was justified in preventing a professor from telling his students that he was a Christian, even in voluntary, after-hours sessions. "Just as women students would find no comfort in an openly sexist instructor," the court reasoned, "an Islamic or Jewish student will not likely savor the Christian bias that Dr. Bishop professes" (Johnson 16–17). That a federal court can equate Christianity with bigotry, Johnson notes, is a sign of a major shift in American culture, even though "many persons in academic life do not seem to realize that this cultural shift has occurred and still seem to imagine that a major threat to academic freedom is coming from a religious establishment that no longer exists" (19).

The demise of the religious establishment that once dominated American higher education is chronicled in George M. Marsden's *The Soul of the American University*. "On the one hand," says Marsden, "it is a story of the disestablishment of religion. On the other hand, it is a story of secularization" (6). Disestablishment led to the hiring of Jews, Catholics, agnostics, and even atheists at Protestant universities; secularization led to the banishment of religion from those same universities. The failure to distinguish between these

The author is Associate Professor of English at Seattle Pacific University.

two cultural tendencies, Marsden suggests, was the fundamental mistake made by the liberal Protestant educators who severed the religious ties of their universities around the turn of the century. As a result, "the largely voluntary and commendable disestablishment of religion has led to the virtual establishment of nonbelief, or the near exclusion of religious perspectives from dominant academic life" (6).

But the exclusion of religious perspectives would appear to violate the secularized university's own ideals. "The principal threat to academic freedom these days," Johnson believes, "comes not from ministers, or trustees, or university administrators, but from the dominant ideologies among students and faculty" (19). Marsden makes a similar point:

> One of the strongest current motives for discriminating in academia against even traditional religious viewpoints that play within the procedural rules of universities is that many advocates of such viewpoints are prone to be conservative politically and to hold views regarding lifestyle, the family, or sexuality that may be offensive to powerful groups on campuses. Hence in the name of tolerance, pluralism, and diversity, academic expressions of such religious perspectives may be discriminated against. (432)

Neither Johnson nor Marsden, please note, has any desire to turn the clock back to the days when the Protestant establishment dominated American higher education. They simply request the freedom to express religious viewpoints while observing the procedural rules of academic discourse—a request I consider entirely reasonable. The question is whether today's secularized universities are open to such a possibility.

This is where Gerald Graff's program for "teaching the conflicts" comes in. In *Beyond the Culture Wars*, Graff argues that "the best solution to today's conflicts over culture is to teach the conflicts themselves, making them part of our object of study and using them as a new kind of organizing principle to give the curriculum the clarity and focus that almost all sides now agree it lacks" (12). No one will deny that religion plays a major role in today's conflicts over culture. Few, moreover, will deny that such conflicts should become objects of study, perhaps even organizing principles in curricula. The question is whether professors should be free to advocate religious viewpoints in the classroom, as Johnson and Marsden propose. Does Graff's program for teaching the conflicts imply that religious advocacy should be encouraged? While he doesn't address the question directly, I think the answer has to be yes.

The question that Graff does address directly is that of political advocacy in the classroom. He takes on those conservative critics of the university who, declaring that politics has no place in the classroom, condemn the political correctness of radical professors. Rather than perpetuate the myth of the politics-free classroom, Graff proposes, these conservative critics should simply acknowledge their own political agenda. "Instead of pretending we can eliminate political conflict from teaching," he recommends, "we should start making use of it" (170). But it is not just the conservatives who meet with Graff's disapproval. In an essay coauthored by Gregory Jay, he challenges the radical proponents of "critical pedagogy," the goal of which is to raise the political consciousness of students in order to generate social change. The problem with critical pedagogy, Jay and Graff argue, is not that it brings politics into the classroom but that it reduces politics to indoctrination, forestalling open debate. "Teaching the conflicts," they insist, "starts with a different vision of how to organize teaching. Instead of attempting to transform the consciousness of students directly, the strategy of conflict pedagogy is to present students with political conflicts while giving them space to choose their own positions" (209).

Graff's defense of open political debate in the classroom, I would suggest, should apply to metaphysical debate as well. On the one hand, there are those secularists who proclaim that religious convictions have no place in the classroom, fearing, perhaps, that opening the door to the religious right would mean the end of academic freedom. On the other hand, there are members of the religious right who would indeed limit academic freedom, replacing today's "secular humanist" curriculum with one based on "traditional" values. From the standpoint of teaching the conflicts, neither of these alternatives is acceptable. If the myth of the politics-free classroom is an illusion, the same goes for the myth of the metaphysics-free classroom. For to exclude from the outset all religious assumptions—a principle Marsden refers to as "methodological secularization" (156)—is to proceed as if metaphysical naturalism were true. By the same token, the freedom to advocate metaphysical naturalism in American universities must be protected against threats from the religious right.

But what about those who still object that much if not all of what gets taught in the classroom—or should get taught there, at least—is politically and metaphysically neutral? Graff's response to this objection, as one might expect, is to teach the demand as part of the conflict over the nature of knowledge. I would agree that much of what is and should be taught is not dependent on particular political ideologies or metaphysical theories. Given the pluralism of the contemporary university, however, the decision about whether a particular body of knowledge carries political or metaphysical baggage must not be made *in advance*, that is, before the participants in the debate have had their say. Those participants will often disagree, at the beginning of the discussion, about whether ideological baggage is attached to a particular body of knowledge. Under these circumstances, to presuppose that a particular body of knowledge does or does not carry ideological baggage is to prevent open discussion. Even when open discussion is encouraged, of course, there is no guarantee that the participants will ever reach agreement. But one thing seems clear: they will be less likely to understand one another if the baggage remains unexamined.

Another common objection to Graff's program for teaching the conflicts is that there is no neutral standpoint from which to determine what the conflicts are, which of them should be taught, and who should teach them. In the absence of a neutral standpoint, the argument goes, such determinations will inevitably be made by those in power, who tend to be hostile to conservatives and Christians (or to radicals and atheists—take your pick). Ward Parks has even suggested that Graff's program is little more than a coverup for the institutionalization of political correctness. "It is obvious which conflicts Graff regards as significant," he complains: "those involving race and sex" (97). Graff's response to this objection is that teaching the conflicts doesn't require neutrality. All it requires is that those in power be genuinely committed to teaching the conflicts, including the conflict over what conflicts should be taught. The proof of this commitment is in the curricular pudding. Racial and sexual conflicts must not be taught to the exclusion of other conflicts that divide our culture, including the conflict between religion and secular humanism.

The teaching of that conflict at secularized universities would benefit religious believers and nonbelievers alike. On the one hand, it would enable believers not merely to express their core beliefs without fear of discrimination but also to have those beliefs taken seriously in the world of the academy. Some, no doubt, would continue to prefer the consensual religious education offered by the nation's many sectarian universities. It may be that the primary reason such institutions have survived is that religious viewpoints are not adequately represented at mainstream universities. On the other hand, teaching the conflicts would also enable secularized universities to extend the ideals of tolerance, pluralism, and diversity to religious believers and to reengage the core beliefs of students and professors in the educational process. If it is true, as Marsden suggests, that the secularized university has sold its soul to the modern economy, a little metaphysics might help to redeem that soul.

Here is an illustration of how teaching the conflicts can lead to rewarding discussion of religious viewpoints. One of Graff's now famous examples of academic conflict is an admittedly reductive staging of a debate between an older male professor (OMP) and a young female professor (YFP) over Matthew Arnold's "Dover Beach," which ends with the famous lines:

> Ah, love, let us be true
> To one another! for the world, which seems
> To lie before us like a land of dreams,

So various, so beautiful, so new,
Hath really neither joy, nor love, nor light,
Nor certitude, nor peace, nor help for pain;
And we are here as on a darkling plain
Swept with confused alarms of struggle and flight,
Where ignorant armies clash by night.   (90)

OMP ventures the opinion that Arnold's poem is "one of the great master-pieces of the Western tradition." YFP, however, insists that "Dover Beach," with its male speaker seeking refuge from the troubles of the world in the love of a woman, is "a good example of how women have been defined by our culture as naturally private and domestic and therefore justly disqualified from sharing male power." OMP retorts that "Dover Beach," like all great poetry, transmutes such "transitory issues" as Victorian gender roles into "universal human experience." To which YFP replies, "What you take to be the universal human experience in Arnold . . . , Professor OMP, is male experience presented as if it were universal" (38–39).

Notwithstanding Graff's disclaimer, his "Dover Beach" scenario has been much maligned. Parks, for example, complains that

> YFP gets most of the lines in the dialogue, and Graff gives her the last word on every point; she is progressive in her views, professional in her manner of address, and trenchant in her logic. OMP, by contrast, is an academic buffoon, fustian, isolated, angry, unable to formulate a coherent argument and presenting his objections in a simplistic fashion that leaves him wide open to attack. . . . One can imagine the outrage a white male scholar would have occasioned if he had used comparable stereotypes of women or blacks in the course of rebutting the arguments of feminists, Afrocentrists, or other "victim group" advocates.   (93–94)

Parks weakens his argument by indulging in some stereotyping of his own—feminists and Afrocentrists are reduced to whining "victim group" advocates—but he is right about Graff's scenario: the deck is stacked against OMP. If I may be permitted to add my own complaint to the pile, I would say that the deck is stacked against Christianity as well. Later in the same chapter, Graff suggests that the literary canon of the 1950s reflected "the Christian conservatism of Eliot and his followers," including, presumably, the New Critics (48). "Dover Beach" belonged to that canon; OMP is evidently one of its last defenders. In demolishing OMP's defense of "Dover Beach," then, YFP is implicitly demolishing the Christian conservatism reflected in the traditional canon.

Now imagine, if it's not too difficult, a Christian feminist professor (CFP). CFP might be willing to grant that OMP's defense of "Dover Beach" is descended from the Christian conservatism of Eliot and the New Critics. What

CFP would deny, however, is that OMP offers anything like an adequate Christian interpretation of Arnold's poem. For one thing, the experience of Arnold's speaker is anything but a "universal human experience." On the contrary, it is the highly particular experience of an agnostic Victorian humanist, as the previous stanza suggests:

> The Sea of Faith
> was once, too, at the full, and round earth's shore
> Lay like the folds of a bright girdle furl'd.
> But now I only hear
> Its melancholy, long, withdrawing roar,
> Retreating, to the breath
> Of the night-wind, down the vast edges drear
> And naked shingles of the world.   (90)

If what OMP means by universal human experience is just that "Dover Beach" is, thanks to Arnold's craftsmanship, capable of moving readers of different eras, cultures, and genders, then CFP might well agree. But the only way such universal appreciation can occur, she will insist, is through knowledge of the historical particularities Arnold presupposed, including the erosion of Christian belief in the wake of evolutionary theory and the higher criticism of the Bible—not to mention, as YFP observed, Victorian gender roles. From CFP's point of view, the problem with YFP's reading of "Dover Beach" is not that she is preoccupied with gender roles and other "transitory issues," as OMP charges, but that she is not preoccupied enough. For it is precisely the ebbing of the sea of faith that prompts Arnold's speaker to seek consolation in his lover's arms, as though she must ease the burden of his despair.

The point of this alternative reading of "Dover Beach" is simply to remind readers how often interpretive disagreements lead to, or follow from, metaphysical differences. Graff himself implies that what divides OMP's ahistorical reading of "Dover Beach" from YFP's historical reading is, at least in part, the influence of Eliot's Christian conservatism. In response, I have tried to sketch a more adequate Christian interpretation of the poem. But this is precisely what Graff's example is supposed to do: generate richer, more nuanced interpretations through the juxtaposition of conflicting readings. I see no reason to halt the process just because religious viewpoints are in danger of being expressed by professors like CFP. On the contrary, open discussion of religious viewpoints would make it clear that there are religious as well as secular alternatives to the once dominant Christian conservatism of Eliot and the New Critics, itself a more nuanced position than Graff implies. In this way, teaching the conflicts can serve to complicate our sense of the conflicts themselves—surely a good thing in a polarized society.

WORKS CITED

Arnold, Matthew. "Dover Beach." *Selected Poetry and Prose*. Ed. Frederick L. Mulhauser. New York: Holt, 1953. 89–90.

Graff, Gerald. *Beyond the Culture Wars: How Teaching the Conflicts Can Revitalize American Education*. New York: Norton, 1992.

Jay, Gregory, and Gerald Graff. "A Critique of Critical Pedagogy." *Higher Education under Fire: Politics, Economics, and the Crisis in the Humanities*. Ed. Michael Bérubé and Cary Nelson. New York: Routledge, 1995. 201–13.

Johnson, Phillip E. "What (If Anything) Hath God Wrought? Academic Freedom and the Religious Professor." *Academe* Sept.-Oct. 1995: 16–19.

Marsden, George M. *The Soul of the American University: From Protestant Establishment to Established Nonbelief*. New York: Oxford UP, 1994.

Parks, Ward. "Teaching the Coverup." *Academic Questions* 7.1 (1993–94): 91–99.

RESPONSE TO MARK WALHOUT

Having recently made visits to several church-based colleges and universities, I'd had a chance to ponder some of the issues Mark Walhout raises in his essay. Invariably in these places I have sensed a strong desire to reassert the original religious mission of the institution but also deep uncertainty about how this can be done without retreating into sectarian dogmatism. If the college reasserts its "Jesuit mission," its "Benedictine mission," its "Lutheran mission," or whatever, it risks losing its hard-won intellectual reputation, which was achieved through secularization. But if the college fails to reassert its religious mission, it loses touch with what distinguishes it from any other college. Caught in a classic double bind, the college is damned if it recommits itself to its religious roots but is equally damned if it does not.

As I've suggested in talks at these colleges, a way out of the impasse is to organize courses and units around the question itself of the religious mission of the institution. Such a strategy would reactivate the college's distinctive religious mission, but it would do so without dogmatism, since the mission would be reconceived as an issue for classroom debate rather than as orthodoxy. For colleges faced with a crisis of institutional identity, organizing introductory courses or concentrations around the crisis would be a way to make the crisis itself and its history an object of study, using it, in Walhout's words, "to reengage the core beliefs of students and professors in the educational process."

In other words, a great deal depends on what "reinstating the religious mission" of the institution is taken to mean. If it means that only an institution-wide consensus on core beliefs will do, the outcome figures to be unattractive. Either the core beliefs will be narrowly enforced or defined so vaguely as to be meaningless. However, if reinstating religious mission means encouraging collegial debate about that mission and making such debate central in the curriculum, a church-based institution has a chance to turn its identity crisis into a source of educational strength. This is the strategy proposed by Walhout.

What I had not considered until reading Walhout's essay is the rather different situation that presents itself in secular colleges and universities. American higher education as we now know it grew originally out of a fierce struggle between faith and secularism. Until the last decades of the nineteenth century, most American colleges were denominational institutions that had been established to train ministers, promote piety, and advance the fortunes of the founding sect. The turn of the century saw the decline of the religious college and the emergence of the secular university dedicated to scientific research, vocational training, and a campus culture of sororities and fraternities, sports, and other social activities that ultimately facilitated business contacts. Religion—like the Greek and Latin studies that had gone hand in hand with it—retreated from its central position in the college curriculum and became one "field" among many. The parties to the old debate between secularism and faith were still present in the new university, but the great struggle had ended as religion retreated into departments that coexisted with secular departments.

Walhout points out that with the cessation of debate over the educational role of religion, secularism won by default. Citing recent work by Phillip E. Johnson and George M. Marsden, he observes that to express religious convictions in class is now to risk being accused of bigotry. Walhout's observation rings true: at the 1995 Conference on the Role of Advocacy in the Classroom, a divinity scholar remarked that hers is the only academic discipline that forbids its professors to believe in what they profess.

Of course, as Walhout acknowledges, the situation is reversed in colleges dominated by the Christian right, where students and faculty members who entertain "secular humanist" beliefs can face exclusion or ostracism.[1] The avoidance of debate between religious studies and other departments in secularized institutions is mirrored in the avoidance of debate between secular and fundamentalist institutions. Instead of taking an active role that might help raise the quality of public discourse, higher education has vacated the field, leaving the debate over religion to politicians and the media, where it readily sinks into shouting and sloganeering.

But exceptions to this evasion can be found—usually in the deep South, where conflicts over religion are so persistent that they can't be shoved under the rug. On a visit to a Mississippi college a few years ago, I was startled when asked how the college should respond to local citizens who equated the liberal arts with liberalism and saw the humanities as a euphemism for secular humanist atheism. Though debating such issues is not what those citizens had in mind, at least here was a community where "liberal arts" and "humanities" meant something and something was at stake in teachers' and students' attitudes to them. (Other than Christian fundamentalists, the only people I had known to get worked up about "humanism" were poststructuralists and Marxists.) Might not an educational institution do something creative with such a situation?

One southern campus I visited that did was the University of North Carolina, Greensboro, which had developed a freshman seminar unit around the theme of Darwin versus Genesis. In the early 1990s I spent two fascinated hours observing a symposium at which students presented papers on various issues raised by the readings, responded to one another's papers in panel discussions and to comments from the student audience of approximately a hundred, performing these tasks at a high intellectual level. Their instructors reported that these symposium meetings provided excellent points of reference when the classes reconvened afterward in small sections. Contrary to what one might expect, the student debates I witnessed did not remain locked into the binary oppositions in which they began. When discussions are well organized and moderated, "none of the above" positions can emerge—like that of Walhout's Christian feminist professor who displaces the opposing terms of my hypothetical debate on "Dover Beach."

The questions raised by religious pedagogy are clearly similar to those that have lately erupted over classroom political advocacy. Organizing courses and units around controversies is a creative way of negotiating the double bind of all advocacy pedagogies, where teaching with passionate commitment can too easily become indoctrination. What Walhout is suggesting, I take it, is that once classroom religious issues are organized around debates, beliefs can be strongly asserted without anyone's feeling coerced by theological correctness. Strong counterarguments will now be not only present—rather than sequestered in other classrooms and campus buildings—but empowered by the debate structure. This is the argument that Gregory Jay, Donald Lazere, and I have made about the issue of politics in the classroom (Jay and Graff; Lazere). That is, teaching the conflicts, far from encouraging a wishy-washy neutrality, enables instructors to become more open about their political commitments with less danger of students' feeling bullied.

To be sure, proponents of various current forms of radical or critical pedagogy—feminist, Marxist, Freirean—vigorously deny the charge that they indoctrinate students, and they point out, often justifiably, that their classes are based on dialogue, not coercion. The charges of indoctrination against these teachers are indeed frequently unfair, often based on conjecture or myth rather than on evidence. Yet even the most politically open and "dialogical" classroom can be subtly coercive, for the political orientation of the teacher implicitly seems the "right" one, and the whole responsibility for countering the class's dominant politics is left to the students.

It is all well and good for us to urge our students to disagree with us, but students have no way of being sure that we are serious as long as the classroom walls protect us from those colleagues down the hall or across the quad who are in the strongest position to disagree with us. However much I may exhort my students to disagree with me, a curriculum that systematically shields me from the criticisms of my colleagues sends them the very opposite message. Students would be more likely to believe that it's all right to disagree with their teachers if they had more experience of their teachers' disagreeing with one another.

I grant that organizing such disagreements in the curriculum is not easy. Like recent conflicts over politics, conflicts over religion are rooted in the deep divisions that polarize our society. At a Catholic university near New York City, I was told by an administrator, "There are two things here that you can't argue openly about—abortion and homosexuality." Yet I couldn't help noticing that these were precisely the two topics everyone on campus seemed to be talking about in private and reading about in the campus newspaper. Why couldn't what the university was already arguing about in dormitories and in the campus media become the subject of a course, or a theme linking several courses?

Clearly, the worry is that engaging such conflicts would deepen fear, tension, and anger. But once these feelings are already present in a college's atmosphere, they will probably only get worse if the conflicts are *not* engaged. Making the religious-secular conflict an object of cross-curricular discussion may be difficult and painful at first, but in the long run it should be a relief.

Gerald Graff
Professor of English, University of Chicago

NOTE

[1]In *The Myth of Political Correctness*, John Wilson surveys many recent cases of such "conservative correctness" at religious colleges, cases that go underreported, as Wilson points out.

WORKS CITED

Jay, Gregory, and Gerald Graff. "A Critique of Critical Pedagogy." *Higher Education under Fire: Politics, Economics, and the Crisis of the Humanities.* Ed. Michael Bérubé and Cary Nelson. New York: Routledge, 1995. 201–13.

Lazere, Donald. "Teaching the Conflicts about Wealth and Poverty." *Left Margins: Cultural Studies and Composition Pedagogy.* Ed. Karen Fitts and Alan W. France. Albany: State U of New York P, 1995. 189–208.

Wilson, John. *The Myth of Political Correctness: The Conservative Attack on Higher Education.* Durham: Duke UP, 1995.

Kiddie Lit in Academe

BEVERLY LYON CLARK

1996. I want to attempt the kind of essay where it is as fruitful to read between the lines as to read the lines themselves, the kind of essay that formally embodies the contradictions among and within the discourses by which we are spoken. In this process I want to explore my approach-avoidance relation to children's literature, an approach-avoidance that is emblematic—especially the avoidance part—of the desires of the profession at large. To do so I sketch both the cultural construction of an American children's literature critic in the last three decades and the cultural construction of American children's literature criticism in the last century.

The nineteenth century was a time "when majors wrote for minors," to cite the title of a Henry Steele Commager essay published in 1952, a time when "almost every major writer . . . wrote for children as well as adults, and . . . for over a century the line between juvenile and adult literature was all but invisible" (10). As Jerry Griswold points out, the best-sellers between 1865 and 1914 were as likely to be *Heidi* as *Madame Bovary*, *Alice's Adventures in Wonderland* as *Our Mutual Friend* (vii). They were in fact more likely to be *Little Women* than *Portrait of a Lady*, more likely to be *Treasure Island* than *Moby-Dick*.[1]

1964. As an adolescent, I write a puppet play for a Girl Scout Roundup in Idaho: I call the play "Alice in Western Massachusetts Land." Fortunately the script has not survived. Its high point, I think, was making a connection between cheeses produced in the town of Cheshire and the Cheshire Cat. I can't remember now what the connection was. Somehow, during the performance, I get confused about the time and miss my share of the puppeteering.

The author is Professor of English at Wheaton College.

To gauge the nineteenth-century status of children's literature, consider the most popular American magazine for children. The *Youth's Companion*, published from 1827 to 1929, achieved a circulation that in 1885 outstripped that of all other United States magazines, for children or adults (Greene 511). Skimming Lovell Thompson's anthology of highlights from the magazine, I find contributions by almost all the authors considered major in the nineteenth century: Washington Irving, Ralph Waldo Emerson, Henry Wadsworth Longfellow, William Cullen Bryant, John Greenleaf Whittier, Oliver Wendell Holmes, Harriet Beecher Stowe, not to mention Richard Henry Dana, Catharine Maria Sedgwick, Louisa May Alcott, Emily Dickinson, Hamlin Garland, Mark Twain, Bret Harte, Sarah Orne Jewett, Edith Wharton, Jack London, Willa Cather, Susan Glaspell, Robinson Jeffers, Robert Frost, Stephen Crane . . .

Likewise, the leading "adult" journals of the day—among them, the *Atlantic Monthly*, *Harper's New Monthly Magazine*, *Nation*, *Scribner's Monthly*, *Literary World*—devoted considerable space to reviewing children's literature. As Richard L. Darling concludes in a study that addresses the decade and a half following the Civil War, "At no other time have such fine critics, such gifted authors, such discerning minds, devoted so much intelligent energy to a critical examination of children's books. What critic with the stature of William Dean Howells has reviewed children's books in the twentieth century?" (250).

1970. I graduate from college, an English major, having taken the maximum number of courses allowable in English. None is in children's literature. It wasn't offered. With the exception of a course in what is called Negro literature, which I go off campus to take, none is in American literature either. I'd read enough Hemingway and Crane (The Red Badge three times) in high school. At the same time, I now see, I was trying to live up to my cloistered image of the serious scholar. I tried a course in medieval philosophy. It didn't take. The course in Milton sat better; I went on to write an undergraduate thesis on "L'Allegro" and "Il Penseroso."

By the 1920s, as Paul Lauter has suggested, the arbiters of American literature were no longer literary clubs and magazines but the emerging professoriat, almost all white males. Richard Brodhead might demur that the key arbiters at this time were not yet the professoriat but rather nonacademic critics—yet the latter were also college-educated white males. Meanwhile the canonical authors of American literature had shifted from the likes of Longfellow, Whittier, and Stowe to Melville, Twain, Thoreau, and James. Elizabeth Renker argues that American literature created itself as a profession by shedding femininity and appropriating the language of science, a change fueled by two world wars. It "achieved institutional maturity" (358) by shedding juvenility as well, as Renker acknowledges only implicitly, metaphorically. If nineteenth-century America was pervaded by the metaphor of America as child, then America's emergence as a world power in the twentieth century was marked by a desire to put away childish things.[2]

Or at least that desire was urgent for the white male professoriat. Among African Americans there was, instead, a concern to uplift the race. As such scholars as Dianne Johnson (now Johnson-Feelings) have documented, many of the figures active in the Harlem Renaissance—including Langston Hughes, Arna Bontemps, Jessie Fauset—wrote for children.

All the authors whose currency rose during the canon ferment of the early twentieth century, all those who made it into the canonical mainstream, were white men. Most of them—in particular, Melville, Thoreau, and James—did not write for children.

1975. I attend a party of graduate students. I've been reading James, Crane, Nabokov. Jan Alberghene, who will go on to preside over the Children's Literature Association, talks about her rereading of Cherry Ames. Cherry Ames? I wonder in disbelief.

Important milestones in the professionalization of English include the proliferation of graduate study in the last quarter of the nineteenth century, spearheaded by Johns Hopkins University (founded in 1876), the establishment of the Modern Language Association in 1883, and the publication of *PMLA* beginning in 1884.[3] Skimming the contents of *PMLA* since its inception, I find little on children's literature before 1966. In the earliest decades, when philology and folklore vied with source study for preeminence—and when the journal published minutes of conference presentations—there may be discussion of a talk on the European (of course) sources of Uncle Remus or on the balladic nature of cowboy songs of the Mexican border. The respondents to A. Gerber's talk on Uncle Remus refer to versions of tales they heard in childhood, but they use their childhoods only to authenticate their own authority—their childhoods functioning as "a pure point of origin in relation to language" (Rose 8)— and they go on to discuss whether the tales came from France by way of Haiti and how much Joel Chandler Harris might have fabricated his versions. Certainly there is no indication that either Gerber or John A. Lomax, the proponent of cowboy ballads, conceived of his subject as children's literature. Similarly, in 1915 Ronald S. Crane concluded a seventy-page disquisition on the history of *Guy of Warwick* with a paragraph that finally admitted children to the pages of *PMLA*. He laments that by the eighteenth century, when scholarly interest in the tale was quickening, the lay audience consisted only of children: "To such uses had come a story once read and admired by all Englishmen!" (194).

1976. I decide to include a chapter on Lewis Carroll in my dissertation. One of my committee members has in fact published on Carroll, in a mainstream journal. Maybe it's permissable to allow one crossover author from what has been called the golden age of children's literature some attention in adult discourse—especially if that author can be conceived as a "pure point of origin" for more recent literature. Maybe it's permissible if the author is not American and hence not entangled in our twentieth-century anxiety of immaturity, our attempts to free ourselves from associations of America with childhood. Attention to Carroll allows us to project childishness onto a representative of the parent country. Maybe, finally, it's permissible for the professoriat to engage fleetingly with Carroll if he can be construed as simply a don on holiday.

The first article to focus on children's literature in *PMLA*—aside from pieces on the more ambiguously situated Twain—is Donald Rackin's, in 1966. It deals with Carroll. The second, James R. Kincaid's (1973), and the third, William A. Madden's (1986), likewise deal with Carroll. Only in 1991 does an essay appear that unabashedly includes the word *children's* in its title. Sarah Gilead too addresses Carroll, among other figures.

1979. There is a chance that I can continue to teach at Wheaton—can go from soft money to a regular full-time appointment. I volunteer to teach the course in children's literature. One source of support for the course is the college librarian: she is committed to building a strong collection in children's literature, finding extra funding even as departmental library budgets are reduced.

If during much of the nineteenth century few social or circulating or even public libraries allowed children to borrow books, by the end of the century most United States public libraries were catering to children, sometimes with separate children's rooms and specially trained librarians. As early as 1877 Minerva L. Saunders—perhaps the first librarian to allow children under twelve to use public library books—set aside a corner of the Pawtucket, Rhode Island, library for children, even providing special small chairs for them. By 1878 the librarian Caroline M. Hewins, of Hartford, Connecticut, was publishing a list of titles recommended for children; her 1882 *Books for the Young* was the first publication of the Publishing Section of the American Library Association (ALA). In 1890 Mary Bean opened a separate children's room in the Brookline, Massachusetts, library. In 1898 the Pratt Library School added a course for training children's librarians. In 1901 Anne Carroll Moore chaired the first meeting of the Section for Children's Librarians of the ALA, and in 1906 she became the first head of the children's department of the New York Public Library. Standard histories of the public library may feature the names of men—Justin Winsor, Melvil Dewey, William Frederick Poole—but all the leaders among children's librarians seem to have been women.[4]

1980–84. I read criticism of children's literature. The first books I stumble across are collections geared to the interests of librarians. I just don't connect to the enthusiasm for bibliotherapy or to the annotated bibliography in paragraph form that seems to constitute most surveys of children's literature.

Librarians not only have provided a haven for children's literature but also have played a vital role in shaping it. In 1922 the ALA started awarding the Newbery Medal for the outstanding contribution to American children's literature during the previous year; in 1938, the Caldecott Medal for outstanding illustrations in children's books. Both awards continue to be enormously influential, especially given that until recent cuts in library funding 80%–90%

of children's book sales were to libraries, and even now 50%–60% continue to be (Dunleavey 31). I've heard, from a prominent reviewer and a prominent editor, that winning the Newbery or the Caldecott can lead to sales of 60,000 to 100,000 copies.

One of the ways the award givers have shaped the field is by being responsive to women writers: 67% of the Newbery winners have been women, a percentage at least twice that for any comparable award for adultstream—mainstream—literature (see Clark 171). The award givers have been less responsive to issues of race. As Donnarae MacCann notes, pointing to the awarding of the Newbery Medal to *The Voyages of Doctor Dolittle* even as W. E. B. Du Bois's pioneering children's journal the *Brownies' Book* ceased publishing because of insufficient circulation, "The increasing institutionalization of children's literature . . . helped extend the lifespan of the white supremacy myth" (64–65).[5]

1982. I attend the Institute for Reconstructing American Literature, an institute attentive to gender, racial, ethnic, and class challenges to the canon. Its activities will culminate in, among other things, the Heath Anthology of American Literature. *I take on the role of advocate for children's literature. Part of me looks on in disbelief. No one hears me anyway.*

One reason literary critics look down on children's literature—even critics attuned to other kinds of marginalization—is the urge to dissociate America and American literature from youthfulness, an insistence on our cultural independence of the parent country. A related reason is the wish to achieve "institutional maturity," as Renker puts it; professionalization seems to require a sense of maturity. Also suspect are the very popularity and (perish the thought) profitability of much children's literature.

Yet another reason for critical condescension is that children's literature is associated with librarians, a group that the professoriat generally treats more as handmaidens than as fellow scholars and teachers. I use the term *handmaidens* advisedly: most librarians and library staff members are women. Although it wasn't until 1852 that the Boston Public Library hired a woman clerk, in 1891 female librarians started outnumbering their male colleagues at the annual ALA convention. By 1910 78.5% of United States library workers were female; by 1920 almost 90% were (Garrison 173, 26).

What librarians publish as part of their professional work, their research, is apt to be collections of interviews with or essays by authors (underscoring that authors are people too) or else bibliographies, including bibliographies of books that can help a child deal with divorce, with the death of a grandparent, with being disabled. I suspect it would be hard to find a field more heavily bibliographied and indexed than children's literature. But neither such collections nor bibliographies carry great prestige with literary critics.

1986. I am awarded an NEH fellowship for college teachers to do research in children's literature, presumably on the themes of reading and writing. I sometimes think that I got the fellowship because the readers were too unfamiliar with the field to realize how little I knew.

Not only does the work of librarians carry little prestige but, except on the occasional acknowledgments page of a critical tome (in tandem with the now notorious expressions of gratitude to the scholar's wife), it is ignored by literary critics. The MLA screens over 4,000 journals to locate articles on language and literature for its CD-ROM and print bibliographies—journals that include, just to look at the letter *a*, *Asian Music, American Anthropologist,* and the *Annual of Armenian Linguistics.* The MLA also screens *Children's Literature,* the *Children's Literature Association Quarterly, The Lion and the Unicorn,* the *English Journal,* and (as of 1991) *Children's Literature in Education.* Currently it does not screen most of the children's literature journals that have strong associations with librarianship or education, such as *Journal of Youth Services in Libraries, Horn Book Magazine, School Library Journal, Language Arts, New Advocate, Canadian Children's Literature, Interracial Books for Children Bulletin, Voice of Youth Advocates, Junior Bookshelf,* or even the prestigious British journal *Signal.*

The "major" research university where I went to graduate school has subscribed to more than thirty thousand journals. Of the above-mentioned journals important to scholars of children's literature it has subscribed only to the *English Journal* and *Children's Literature.* It canceled its subscription to *Children's Literature* in 1985.

1992. My paper on Little Men *is named Best Paper of the Conference at the June meetings of the Children's Literature Association. The article from which it derives, however, is rejected by the three mainstream journals to which I send it the following year. The rejection comments either suggest that the piece will not be of interest to the journal's readers or displace onto the essay characteristics of its purported topic, as if the essay too is a child, a little thing, undeveloped. One anonymous referee writes—and I quote exactly—that the essay "troubles me through its imbeddedness in kidlit data as mixed with gender issues, an amalgum which doesn't always make for general interest."*

So where does that leave the relation between children's literature and the academy now? I find myself switching back and forth between two answers, one upbeat, the other less so. Right now I'm thinking that it's saner and probably more accurate to stress the upbeat answer (I've placed that *Little Men* essay in a prestigious journal), so I'll give it last.

The first answer is provided by juxtaposing two essays published not long ago in general-interest journals, essays whose titles are suitably suggestive. In "The Trashing of Children's Literature," Francelia Butler, the founding mother of the discipline, discusses the resistance that proponents of children's literature, mostly women, have experienced in academia. She notes that the MLA did not offer a session on children's literature at its annual convention until 1969. She recounts the trials of starting *Children's Literature* at the University of Connecticut, how in working on the journal she was "threatened for moonlighting"—working on such a journal clearly wasn't advancing the cause of scholarship. She might almost be responding to John R. Dunlap, the author of the second article, "Kiddie Litter." He opens with a potted—and dated— history of children's literature. He closes with a peroration on the serpent lurking in the garden. In between, he dismisses the "wooden characters" in Robin McKinley's *The Hero and the Crown* as "little more than backdrop for a feminist yawp" and claims that in Virginia Hamilton's *M. C. Higgins the Great*—one of the most important children's books of the past three decades—"an episodic plot is dominated by a heavy-handed symbolism." The problem with award-winning books of the past several decades, he makes quite clear, is that "the 'field' of children's books is disproportionately populated by maiden aunts and bluestockings" (20).

The second answer, my closing answer, goes as follows: Despite the profession's disengagement from children's literature earlier in the century, there are now promising signs of change. The MLA may have been slow to grant divisional status to children's literature, doing so only in 1980, seventy-nine years after the ALA created its Section for Children's Librarians, but at least it has now done so. I'm heartened, further, that the MLA has now published Glenn Edward Sadler's volume on children's literature. I'm heartened that prestigious presses are bringing out books by American children's literature critics—witness Oxford's publication of books by Jerry Griswold and Dianne Johnson-Feelings and Yale's publication of books by Lois Kuznets and Lynne Vallone. Emblematic of the move into academic respectability is that Jacqueline Rose's pathbreaking *The Case of Peter Pan*, first published by Macmillan more than a decade ago, has now been reissued by the University of Pennsylvania Press. I'm heartened as well that adultstream journals like *Nineteenth-Century Literature*, *College English*, *American Literature*, *Signs*, *Differences*, and *New Literary History* are now publishing the occasional article on children's literature. When they don't address Carroll, these articles tend to focus on *Little Women*, and most are by women. Maybe we won't reenact the usual process of professionalization, whereby the profession gains its spurs by divesting itself of femininity. Not to mention juvenility.

Certainly children's literature can offer literary criticism and cultural studies radical new perspectives on reader response and on the interface between the verbal and the visual. Rose underscores, for instance, the rupture between writer and addressee, "the impossible relation between adult and child," and claims that children's literature is "one of the central means through which we regulate our relationship to language and images as such" (1, 138–39). It can also offer radical insights into what it means to be spoken by a discourse of maturity and what it means to be culturally constructed as a critic.

NOTES

[1]Henry James's work appears on none of the lists of best-sellers (works whose total sales equaled one percent of the population) or better-sellers (works that almost did) compiled by Frank Luther Mott for books sold in the United States before 1945. *Moby-Dick* did eventually achieve best-seller status, but only because of its twentieth-century sales; it was "a very poor seller indeed when it first appeared" (Mott 131).

[2]See Griswold 13–15. For parallel arguments focused on British literary traditions, arguments that address the emergence of the "serious" novel as it dissociated itself from children and women around the turn of the century, see Hughes; Reimer.

[3]For an account of this professionalization, see Graff.

[4]For historical background on United States library service to children, see Long; Nesbitt. Bowker's essays provide profiles of some of the important founding mothers. More general histories of libraries and librarians include those by Ditzion and Garrison.

[5]MacCann and others have been particularly critical of librarians, yet literary critics have been even slower to respond to issues of race. I look at the creation of the Coretta Scott King Award in 1970; at the New York Public Library's periodic bibliographies of *The Black Experience in Children's Literature*, beginning in 1974; and at volumes edited by MacCann and Woodard; Bacon; Hirschfelder. I'm tempted to think that the librarians—and other educators whose focus is young children (witness the NCTE volume by Sims)—have felt more need to be responsive to all child readers.

WORKS CITED

Bacon, Betty, ed. *How Much Truth Do We Tell the Children? The Politics of Children's Literature.* Minneapolis: MEP, 1988.

Bowker, R. R. "Some Children's Librarians." *Library Journal* 1 Oct. 1921: 787–90.

———. "Some More Children's Librarians." *Library Journal* 1 May 1922: 393–96.

Brodhead, Richard H. *The School of Hawthorne.* New York: Oxford UP, 1986.

Butler, Francelia. "The Trashing of Children's Literature." *Ms.* Sept.-Oct. 1992: 61.

Clark, Beverly Lyon. "Fairy Godmothers or Wicked Stepmothers? The Uneasy Relationship of Feminist Theory and Children's Criticism." *Children's Literature Association Quarterly* 18 (1993): 171–76.

Commager, Henry Steele. "When Majors Wrote for Minors." *Saturday Review* 10 May 1952: 10+.

Crane, Ronald S. "The Vogue of *Guy of Warwick* from the Close of the Middle Ages to the Romantic Revival." *PMLA* 30 (1915): 125–94.

Darling, Richard L. *The Rise of Children's Book Reviewing in America, 1865–1881.* New York: Bowker, 1968.

Ditzion, Sidney. *Arsenals of a Democratic Culture: A Social History of the American Public Library Movement in New England and the Middle States from 1850 to 1900.* Chicago: American Library Assn., 1947.

Dunlap, John R. "Kiddie Litter." *American Spectator* Dec. 1989: 19–21.

Dunleavey, M. P. "The Crest of the Wave?" *Publisher's Weekly* 19 July 1993: 30–33.

Garrison, Dee. *Apostles of Culture: The Public Librarian and American Society, 1876–1920.* New York: Free, 1979.

Gerber, A., et al. "The Tales of *Uncle Remus*, Traced to the Old World." *PMLA* 8 (1893): xxxix–xliii.

Gilead, Sarah. "Magic Abjured: Closure in Children's Fantasy Fiction." *PMLA* 106 (1991): 277–93.

Graff, Gerald. *Professing Literature: An Institutional History*. Chicago: U of Chicago P, 1987.

Greene, David L. "The *Youth's Companion*." *Children's Periodicals of the United States*. Ed. R. Gordon Kelly. Westport: Greenwood, 1984. 507–14.

Griswold, Jerry. *Audacious Kids: Coming of Age in America's Classic Children's Books*. New York: Oxford UP, 1992.

Hirschfelder, Arlene B., ed. *American Indian Stereotypes in the World of Children: A Reader and Bibliography*. Metuchen: Scarecrow, 1982.

Hughes, Felicity A. "Children's Literature: Theory and Practice." *ELH* 45 (1978): 542–61.

Johnson, Dianne. *Telling Tales: The Pedagogy and Promise of African American Literature for Youth*. New York: Greenwood, 1990.

Johnson-Feelings, Dianne, ed. *The Best of the* Brownies' Book. Oxford: Oxford UP, 1996.

Kincaid, James R. "Alice's Invasion of Wonderland." *PMLA* 88 (1973): 92–99.

Kuznets, Lois Rostow. *When Toys Come Alive: Narratives of Animation, Metamorphosis, and Development*. New Haven: Yale UP, 1994.

Lauter, Paul. "Race and Gender in the Shaping of the American Literary Canon: A Case Study from the Twenties." *Feminist Studies* 9 (1983): 435–63. Rpt. in *Canons and Contexts*. New York: Oxford UP, 1991. 22–47.

Lomax, John A. "Cowboy Songs of the Mexican Border." *PMLA* 25 (1910): xvi–xxvii.

Long, Harriet G. *Public Library Service to Children: Foundation and Development*. Metuchen: Scarecrow, 1969.

MacCann, Donnarae. "Effie Lee Newsome: African American Poet of the 1920s." *Children's Literature Association Quarterly* 13 (1988): 60–65.

MacCann, Donnarae, and Gloria Woodard, eds. *The Black American in Books for Children: Readings in Racism*. 2nd ed. Metuchen: Scarecrow, 1985.

———, eds. *Cultural Conformity in Books for Children: Further Readings in Racism*. Metuchen: Scarecrow, 1977.

Madden, William A. "Framing the *Alices*." *PMLA* 101 (1986): 362–73.

Mott, Frank Luther. *Golden Multitudes: The Story of Best Sellers in the United States*. New York: Macmillan, 1947.

Nesbitt, Elizabeth. "Major Steps Forward." *A Critical History of Children's Literature: A Survey of Children's Books in English*. Ed. Cornelia Meigs. Rev. ed. London: Macmillan, 1969. 384–90.

Rackin, Donald. "Alice's Journey to the End of Night." *PMLA* 81 (1966): 313–26.

Reimer, Mavis. "'These Two Irreconcilable Things—Art and Young Girls': The Case of the School Story." *Nobody's Baby: Feminist Theory and Children's Culture*. Ed. Beverly Lyon Clark and Margaret R. Higonnet. Baltimore: Johns Hopkins UP, in press.

Renker, Elizabeth. "Resistance and Change: The Rise of American Literature Studies." *American Literature* 64 (1992): 347–65.

Rose, Jacqueline. *The Case of Peter Pan; or, The Impossibility of Children's Fiction*. 1984. Philadelphia: U of Pennsylvania P, 1993.

Sadler, Glenn Edward, ed. *Teaching Children's Literature: Issues, Pedagogy, Resources*. New York: MLA, 1992.

Sims, Rudine. *Shadow and Substance: Afro-American Experience in Contemporary Children's Fiction*. Urbana: NCTE, 1982.

Thompson, Lovell, ed. *Youth's Companion*. Boston: Houghton, 1954.

Vallone, Lynne. *Disciplines of Virtue: Girls' Culture in the Eighteenth and Nineteenth Centuries*. New Haven: Yale UP, 1995.

LETTERS

The pursuit of formal beauty above and against all human values was such a well-recognized artistic credo of fin de siècle France that one is astonished that one of its better known manifestations should today evoke such cries of outraged morality. Yet Professor Myra Jehlen does not hesitate to stigmatize Flaubert and his *Salammbô* in *Profession 95*. There Flaubert was pronounced guilty of "enhancement of beauty through evil" and paired with Genêt as "two of the evil men of letters"; Flaubert displayed "hatred" toward one of his characters and took "pleasure in pain . . . sadism." The closing sentence associated him with nothing less than "terrorism." Oh déjà vu! Oh 1857 all over again!

Furthermore, "*Salammbô* belongs to a subcategory of orientalism, in which not the rich beauty of the East is celebrated but its festering disease." Sorry, but the two actually went together for Gustave. In the course of his famous coupling with Kuchuk Hanem, Flaubert was not just erotically aroused by this exemplar of Third World womanhood but enchanted with her stench and sweat. She had bedbugs whose "nauseating odor mixed with the scent of her skin dripping with sandalwood." And in the cemetery of Jaffa, he simultaneously "thrilled to the odor of the lemon trees and the corpses" (same letter of 27 March 1853 to Louise Colet, who was probably not as offended as Professor Jehlen would have been to receive it).

Can Professor Jehlen have missed the scene in *Salammbô* where the barbarians stare in horror at the spectacle of infanticide carried out by the "civilized" Carthaginians? This scene, at the end of chapter 13, has always been understood as an inscribed audience response.

Unless one grants that *Salammbô* is a novel of excess, one hasn't a hope of making any sense of it; one can only join the line of tutting Cratylists whom Julian Barnes's narrator addressed with such a fine admixture of pity and scorn in *Flaubert's Parrot*: "But you say he had a 'Sadeian imagination'? I am puzzled. You specify: *Salammbô* contains scenes of shocking violence. I reply: do you think they didn't happen? Do you think the Ancient World was all rose petals, lute music, and plump vats of honey sealed with bear fat?" (149).

What next? Shall Gide be denounced for his concept of the *acte gratuit*? It led to murder, you know. And speaking of murder and *terrorism*, what shall be done about the surrealists, whose most authentic gesture (Breton *dixit*) was to go down into the street and start shooting? Much remains to be policed by the academic morality squad. To paraphrase Sainte-Beuve, "Neo-Victorians and moralists, I find you everywhere!"

Stirling Haig
University of North Carolina, Chapel Hill

To the Editor:

This is to place on record my shocked reaction to Roy Sellars's and Ruth Vanita's naive and misinformed responses (*Profession 95*) to Robert Holub's views on hiring nonnationals. As an American national with a PhD in English literature from a respected British university, who has worked or studied in eight countries, I can assure you that what Holub proposes is not a protectionary measure for the sake of stupid American graduate students, nor is it American xenophobia. It is reality.

When Sellars refers to the philanthropic attitude of European universities who welcome American academics with open arms, I wonder to which European universities he is referring. Every American graduate student in Britain knows that when an American national with a British PhD applies for a British job, his or her application goes straight to the bottom of the pile. Should a non–European Community applicant somehow manage to get a job offer, he or she then faces the grim task of obtaining a work visa. A friend of mine, a brilliant criminologist with an Afghan passport and a British PhD, received a job offer from a British university but could not obtain a work visa. Should he be forced to return to Afghanistan, there is a distinct danger that he will get a bullet in his extremely brilliant brain.

It is European Community policy that a non-EC national can be hired only in such cases where no EC national can fill the position. At least in theory, the chances of an American's getting a position in a university within the EC are zero. Of course there are exceptions, but these remain exceptions. To be fair, Sellars writes from outside the EC, so perhaps when he refers to European universities, he means those that are outside the EC. In this case I would have to agree with him that universities in Romania, Croatia, and other non-EC nations would be open to hiring Americans and other nonnationals.

Regarding Vanita's charges of xenophobia, Holub's proposals are no more xenophobic than those of any country on earth. As a nonnational living in a foreign country, you do not have the right to work, live, or breathe in that country except by the grace of its government, laws, citizens, and institutions. Every human right that you want or expect is given to you at the discretion of those in power. In response to her comments on underprivileged scholars in the developing world, I know of many graduate students in the West living below (sometimes way below) the poverty line while their hard currency debts mount up, and some of those graduate students may never obtain teaching positions. I'm sure that Professor Vanita would be surprised to find out just how much an American scholar is capable of imagining.

While I am fully supportive of the expanding boundaries of which Vanita writes, I simply cannot accept the arguments of these two scholars, which are based more on rhetoric than on fact. Sellars and Vanita seem to view America as some type of Golden Land, run on dreams rather than on political and economic realities.

Ashlynn K. Pai
Toin High School, Wakayama, Japan

Making Faculty Work Visible: Reinterpreting Professional Service, Teaching, and Research in the Fields of Language and Literature

MLA COMMISSION ON PROFESSIONAL SERVICE

EXECUTIVE SUMMARY

BACKGROUND

In May 1992, the MLA Executive Council established the Commission on Professional Service to examine the ways in which faculty work has been defined, evaluated, and rewarded in fields encompassed by the MLA. The formation of this commission was one of several efforts by higher education groups to redefine professional service in higher education and to formulate new guidelines for rewarding it. Over the last few decades, the traditional triad *research, teaching,* and *service* has increasingly become a hierarchy, ranked in order of esteem.

The need for a new conception of professional service is a consequence of the expansion and diversification of faculty roles since World War II. The growing emphasis on research and the dramatic expansion of the student population in the 1960s and 1970s increased role conflicts. New economic, social, and demographic conditions, along with technological changes in the production and dissemination of knowledge, exacerbated those conflicts and created severe strains. As a result, the consensus on values in the academic workplace is eroding.

Members of the MLA Commission on Professional Service: Robert Denham, Roanoke College; Claire Kramsch, University of California, Berkeley (Chair); Louise Wetherbee Phelps, Syracuse University; John Rassias, Dartmouth College; James F. Slevin, Georgetown University; Janet Swaffar, University of Texas, Austin

RESULTS OF THE COMMISSION STUDY: REWORDING THE CONVERSATION

- The commission brought to light many unacknowledged or unrewarded faculty roles and activities within the traditional triad. It concluded that the current model hinders appreciation of the range and diversity of faculty work because much is excluded or trivialized by the categories in use.
- These devaluations and omissions are most striking for the service leg of the triad, which encompasses any faculty work that falls outside teaching and research. The present connotations of service rule out a priori the possibility that it has substantive idea content or significance. There is no way to distinguish substantial contributions in this area from perfunctory ones.
- The commission decided that to incorporate, evaluate, and appropriately reward the invisible or undervalued aspects of service, it is necessary to change both the basic organization and the underlying premises of the faculty reward system.
- Therefore, the commission has devised an alternative model that changes the terms of the conversation about faculty rewards. The basic principle of this new model is that the quality, significance, and impact of faculty work are more important than the category to which the work belongs.

TERMS OF THE NEW CONVERSATION

The new model proposes *intellectual work* and *academic and professional citizenship* as primary components of faculty work. The commission chose these categories because they are fundamental to the academy's mission and well-being. At the same time, the commission recognizes that particular disciplines or special institutional missions may require the inclusion of other dimensions of value relevant to faculty work.

Intellectual Work

Intellectual work comprises faculty members' individual and joint advancement of knowledge and learning in accordance with the academic mission. Such work is not restricted to research and scholarship but is also a component of teaching and service. It should contribute to the knowledge-related enterprises in which a faculty member is engaged as a faculty member and should explicitly invoke ideas and explore their consequences in the world of ideas, the world of action, or both. Significant intellectual work should be an outgrowth of professional expertise rather than of general knowledge or of skills that most educated, intelligent people possess. It must have a public dimension that is amenable to assessment, evaluation, and modification by a critically informed group of peers. Excellence in intellectual work is characterized by such qualities as rigor, skill, care, intellectual honesty, heuristic passion for knowledge, originality, relevance, aptness, coherence, and consistency.

In evaluating intellectual achievement, institutions and professional organizations should include not only discipline-based work and work addressed to specialized audiences but also the broader work of the so-called public intellectual. Evaluations of teaching and scholarship should be differentiated to take into account the more indirect and gradual impact of teaching. The commission urges the establishment of processes that consider such long-term investments and accomplishments.

Academic and Professional Citizenship

Academic and professional citizenship encompasses the activities required to create, maintain, and improve the infrastructure that sustains the academy as a societal institution. Just as research is no longer the exclusive site of intellectual work, service is not the exclusive site for citizenship. Citizenship activities within research and scholarship include participating in promotion and tenure review, evaluating manuscripts, and serving on committees in professional organizations. The definition of teaching is expanded to include such citizenship functions as faculty recruitment, student retention, major advisement, and service on curriculum committees. Joining committees for one's institution or for professional organizations and representing one's institution or field on an external task force or commission are among the activities that constitute citizenship within service.

SITES OF FACULTY WORK

The commission decided to retain the terms *research*, *teaching*, and *service* for continuity, but the new model boldly reinterprets these labels, rejecting any hierarchy that was implicit in the triad. These terms no longer define discrete categories of faculty work or distinct roles of faculty members but describe sites of faculty work, the places where faculty work occurs or is disseminated. Such places include classrooms, committee meetings, the Internet, scholarly conventions, journals, community boards, and so on. The new model is represented as a grid with a values axis and a sites axis, which are described in the last section.

Research

Research, or scholarship, is a site for intellectual and professional endeavors that are produced and legitimated in accordance with the standards of at least one disciplinary or professional community. A dynamic enterprise, scholarship must be made public and open to peer criticism, though it need not be disseminated in traditional formats. By its nature, it is cosmopolitan and transinstitutional rather than local.

Teaching

The commission endorses a concept of teaching that goes beyond individual classroom performance and direct student contact. Recognition and reward for teaching, not to mention efforts to improve teachers' performance and prepare future professors, have been severely hampered in the academy by a restricted conception of teaching that focuses on classroom events and other direct student contact, along with only the most immediate tasks of preparing for or supplementing these events. An augmented conception of teaching includes activities that enrich student learning and promote better teaching. Evaluation should take nontraditional teaching modes into account. Examples of expanded teaching include running a writing center or language lab, attending teaching workshops and conferences, participating in distance learning, and collaborative teaching. Evaluation should also recognize that teaching can be practiced at high and low levels of intellectual investment. Serious intellectual work can be accomplished in teaching by, for instance, monitoring students' learning, translating scholarly knowledge into meaningful and accessible models for learners at different stages, designing modes of assessment, adapting pedagogical approaches to various or nontraditional learners, and creating and sustaining a teaching network.

Professional Service

Service can usefully be divided into two types. *Institutional and organizational service* embraces activities that sustain colleges and universities and enable them to carry out academic goals, including governance. *Applied work* intersects with practical affairs and problem solving, making academic knowledge available in these areas. Beneficiaries of applied work might be government, industry, the law, the arts, and not-for-profit organizations. Examples of applied work include serving on a state or local humanities council, helping a school system revamp its curriculum, working on a community literacy project, writing a script for public television, and consulting on expert testimony for Congress.

A VISUAL REPRESENTATION OF THE NEW MODEL

This new model is represented by a grid or matrix with two axes. The vertical axis corresponds to values and the horizontal axis to sites of faculty work. The vertical axis includes the values of intellectual work and academic and professional citizenship. The horizontal axis maps the three sites: research, teaching, and professional service.

The visual expression of faculty work as a grid has several advantages. It is a graphic demonstration that the character of any particular example of faculty work can be mixed. It clarifies the interrelations among different activities—the overlapping, ambiguities, and connections among work efforts and among sites—and reveals the need for greater flexibility. Finally, it invites the evaluation of different attributes of faculty work in the same way that athleticism and artistry are evaluated in ice-skating: what is the balance between the two attributes? how are they integrated? and what is the level of excellence in each? As a result, evaluation becomes an inquiry that is approached with an open mind.

The new model is provisional, not prescriptive. It is valid across institutions, but its weighting can be varied to allow for diversity among types of institutions. It is a hypothesis to be debated and adapted to fit the mission of different institutions and the nomenclature of different fields.

COMMISSION REPORT

PREFACE

In May 1992, discussions first arose in the MLA Executive Council concerning the role of service in the faculty reward system in the fields encompassed by the MLA. Claire Kramsch, James Slevin, and Phyllis Franklin had attended the conference "Reshaping Institutional Cultures and Reward Structures to Enhance Faculty Professional Service," held at the Wingspread Conference Center in Racine, Wisconsin. Their report to the council gave a sense of the enormous complexity of the existing reward structure, the intellectually challenging issues raised, and the advisability of the MLA's taking a stand vis-à-vis the profession. Council members agreed that it would be beneficial to reexamine current practices and so decided to appoint the Commission on Professional Service, which kept busy for the following four laborious years.

The council gave the commission the following charges:

1. The commission should identify what differentiates service, teaching, and scholarship in the fields the MLA encompasses. The commission should try to determine the definition or definitions of scholarship on which definitions of service are or might be based. It should also consider the status of disciplinary, institutional, and societal service.
2. The commission should describe the traditional service activities that faculty members and institutions count as professional service in the fields the MLA encompasses, and it should consider whether these activities represent the full range of professional service faculty members in our fields actually perform.
3. The commission should consider how professional service should be assessed. What are appropriate criteria for documenting and evaluating faculty achievement in service activities? Should institutions establish assessment mechanisms for service parallel to those for scholarship and

teaching? What are the qualifications of appropriate referees for assessing professional service?

4. The commission should consider how institutions should recognize and reward professional service. What types of rewards or compensation are appropriate at which stages of an individual's career? How should institutions regard service in evaluating untenured faculty members? What role should institutional mission play in determining rewards for service? What are the responsibilities of humanists with regard to professional service?

The MLA commission did not undertake its work in isolation. Questions about the effects of faculty rewards on teaching and questions about what constitutes scholarship have been widely considered within higher education since the late 1980s. After the Wingspread conference, the commission received materials from other disciplinary associations participating in the National Project on Institutional Priorities and Faculty Rewards, directed by Robert M. Diamond from Syracuse University. During the four years of its tenure, the commission organized open hearings on questions concerning professional service at the MLA convention (Dec. 1993), the CCCC convention (Mar. 1994), the Northeast conference (Apr. 1994), the ADFL seminars East and West (June 1994), and the AAHE conference (Jan. 1995). We thank the participants at these hearings who enthusiastically supported the efforts of the commission and provided many of the examples found in this report.

Our own work profited from many lengthy conversations held at the MLA office in New York during these four years. We were conscious of the urgency of our task yet fearful of being misinterpreted, given the political polarities of our times. Moreover, the task itself cut to the heart of the academic enterprise, with all its inherent challenges and paradoxes. We wanted to make quite sure that our final document represented the diversity of higher education institutions. But we were also concerned with providing a general framework for comparing institutional practices and for ensuring the transferability of faculty rewards across institutions. Thus we hoped to reach a definition of faculty rewards that would be valid globally, but with the understanding that these rewards would need to be weighted differently at the local level. We have ultimately left judgment up to the individual institutions, but, in our attempt to rethink the present reward structure, our discussions have been unavoidably colored by our own personal judgment and our own faculty perspectives.

The present document reflects these fundamental tensions. It is the product of our joint reflection on some of the most complex and sensitive issues in higher education. We wish to express our gratitude to Phyllis Franklin, David Laurence, Elizabeth Welles, and the MLA staff for their unwavering support and encouragement when, at times, we despaired. They helped us keep up the strong belief that our work will be of use to our colleagues in the profession and that it may help bring about urgently needed changes in the faculty reward system. The members of the commission present this document in the hope that it can stimulate reflection in its readers and encourage them to take action.

INTRODUCTION

In recent years, changes in higher education have expanded and diversified what we call "faculty work." These changes are due to a variety of historical and societal factors. First, after the end of World War II, the student population in the United States expanded when large numbers of war veterans took advantage of the GI Bill of Rights and went to college; other new groups of students followed in the 1960s. Second, the mission of higher education focused more sharply on research than it had in the past, and concern about achievement in research intensified during the 1950s, especially after the Soviet Union launched Sputnik. With the advantage of hindsight, one can see that conflicts between the ideals of increased student access to higher education and superior achievement in research were probably inevitable. Research places one set of demands on faculty members, academic programs, and institutional resources; accessibility creates other kinds of demands:

In addition to these tensions between the research and the teaching missions of the university, recent years have seen a growing emphasis on its societal mission. Just as scientists are asking themselves, What is the social responsibility of the scientist? so are humanists starting to discuss, What are the social obligations of the humanist or of the scholar in the humanities? What is professional service in the fields of language and literature? Such questions are asked at a time when American colleges and universities are under increased economic pressure to produce and transmit knowledge that is of immediate and practical relevance to the job market. The demographic changes also exert pressure on institutions to diversify their criteria of excellence according to their stated missions and the diversity of their student bodies. The growth of academic technology produces new forms of knowledge and provides new forms of dissemination that require new forms of evaluation. It also generates a greater variety of applied work that does not fit within traditional disciplinary boundaries. Given the growing uncertainties of the job market, junior faculty members want to maintain as great an autonomy as possible; they are keen on developing portable expertise that allows them to retain flexible career patterns with utmost geographic mobility. At the same time, however, institutions are defining their missions more sharply than before, and they increasingly expect their faculty members to serve their specific needs.

These changes in the knowledge mission of the academy have put new demands on scholars and have raised questions about the varied ways in which members of the academic community can and should serve their institutions and the community. They have opened up new options for acknowledging and rewarding the diverse roles that faculty members are now challenged to fulfill at their colleges or universities. The traditional triple mission of the American university—scholarship, teaching, service—has always been in tension in American education because it is an amalgam of different educational visions and intellectual traditions and because it responds to the needs of very different institutions. These tensions have been more or less kept in balance up to now by an invisible consensus among professional peers regarding values and priorities in higher education. Now that this consensus is eroding under new economic, social, demographic, and technological conditions in the production and dissemination of knowledge, the traditional triad of faculty rewards is attracting criticism from both inside and outside academia.

Some critics have focused on the long-standing strain within higher education between teaching and scholarship. They argue that the balance between a faculty member's dual responsibilities as teacher and scholar has tilted, with excessive value being placed on research, to the detriment of teaching. Others contend that in times of budgetary constraints the university's main purpose is to serve society in a concrete, immediate way and that the notion of "professional service," traditionally used to recognize and reward university scholars and teachers, is in need of a redefinition.

Higher education has received public attention on these issues, and it is currently challenged to reexamine its faculty reward structures. Various professional organizations have already issued reports and recommendations. In line with a tradition of self-criticism that is the hallmark of scholarly activity, the Modern Language Association itself has decided to reassess the very definition of knowledge it has been operating on in higher education and to reexamine critically its past practices in the definition and evaluation of faculty work.

In preparing this report, the MLA Commission on Professional Service reviewed the many documents already written on the topic, in particular Robert Diamond and Bronwyn Adam's *Recognizing Faculty Work: Reward Systems for the Year 2000* and others listed in the bibliography. We soon realized that we could not attempt to redefine service without examining teaching and scholarship, for the new demands put on service are intimately linked to the two other traditional dimensions of faculty work. In fact, the attempt to clarify the notion of service brought to light faculty roles and activities that had remained invisible within the usual triad and had therefore been neither acknowledged nor rewarded. Furthermore, it showed that institutions apply a wide variety of criteria on the basis of where each places its priorities and what each decides to reward.

Thus the work of the commission consisted in (1) *broadening* the range of what counts as faculty work in the fields encompassed by the MLA at various programs, colleges, and universities across the country; (2) *making visible* the actual and potential contributions of faculty members to the audiences served by the academy; and (3) *setting the stage* for a conversation among the wide range of participants from the academic communities served by the MLA. The report reflects these three objectives. It offers an alternative model for thinking about the faculty reward system and elaborates and tests this model on several representative fictional cases. In the light of these concrete cases, it discusses the various options available in the evaluation and reward of professional service and concludes by turning or returning to a number of questions and concerns that we believe should be part of the continuing profession-wide conversation to which our report hopes to contribute.

SECTION 1. CHANGING THE TERMS OF THE CONVERSATION

I. Reconsidering the Current Model of Faculty Work

Commission members recognized at the outset of our deliberations that the traditional representation of academic work as research, teaching, or service does not simply differentiate faculty activities in a neutral or objective way but also implicitly ranks them in order of esteem. This hierarchy both reflects and powerfully reinforces the ideal of research as the highest function of the academy. Institutional and professional practices in higher education are systemic, pervasive expressions of the research ideal. Rewards from the institution or profession like status, rank, job security, collegial influence, choice of assignments, sabbaticals, material support, salary, and job mobility, which enable and enhance intrinsic rewards like intellectual satisfaction, are the prime mechanism by which that ideal is communicated and perpetuated.

This is not to say that other values and ideals are absent from American education, which accommodates a great range of educational purposes through the diversity of its institutions. The remarkable success of the research university did not displace earlier visions of higher education entirely but grafted the new ideal onto older ones, preserving but subsuming other goals to the search for knowledge by treating them as derivative or secondary (the "transmission" or "application" of knowledge discovered by research). This model governs, or correlates with, such defining features of professional life as the preparation of graduate students, promotion and tenure policies, the mobility of faculty members, and the organization of disciplines—features that transcend local values and reward systems.

Critiques of this hierarchy of faculty work (and the practices that support it) have provided a symbolic and practical focus for recent discussions of the priorities of higher education. Early reform efforts addressed the problem of values largely through the metaphor of balance, specifically calling for "rebalancing" the relations between research and teaching. This move was intended to rededicate the faculty to teaching and the academy to student learning without seriously weakening the commitment to research. Many academics whose working lives were already devoted to teaching hoped to revise or "correct" the normative model to conform more closely to their actual responsibilities. The strategy of rebalancing therefore entailed efforts to improve teaching, assess it seriously, and give it more weight in promotion and tenure decisions, with implications for redistributing faculty loads and reallocating institutional resources as well. In universities with professional schools, external or public service (called applied work or outreach) was soon added to the rebalancing equations because clinical work or professional practice is central to the intellectual definition of those fields.

As educators discovered, though, rebalancing is a fundamentally flawed gesture toward reform because it does not challenge the basic organization and underlying premises of the model. Without a dramatic shift in perspective, it seems impossible to get away from the power and apparent inevitability of the model's assumptions and connotations, which have become so naturalized as to be invisible. In trying to discern the givens and challenge the underlying assumptions of the current model, commission members used a metaphor that became a major theme in our discussions: the need to make visible and therefore reconsider the value of what has been tacit or disregarded. From one perspective invisibility refers to the degree to which meanings and attitudes have become historically embedded and implicit in our descriptions or models of faculty work. We also spoke of the difficulty in appreciating the diversity and range of actual faculty work, much of which is either erased by categories that exclude it or trivialized as unworthy of close attention. This observation applies most strikingly to activities perceived as service.

Currently "service" is an unwieldy, confused category, encompassing almost any faculty work that falls outside research and scholarship or teaching. Such work divides roughly, in faculty perceptions, into external (societal) and internal (institutional) service. In the fields of language and literature, external service occurs largely outside the bounds of the system and is treated as an add-on, with some slight capacity to enhance the standing of a faculty member engaging in such work at prestigious sites. In contrast, some minimal level of institutional service (generally, committee work) is universally expected as a collegial (not an intellectual) contribution. Yet such service is perceived as sheer labor, at worst despised as thankless scut work. Young professors are told to minimize commitments to service as a waste of time, even a negative mark in their records. At a greater level of faculty investment, service becomes even more problematic in the reward system. For example, there is no place in the conventional system for recognizing and rewarding faculty members who serve with distinction as program directors or department chairs or who make major contributions to a community literacy or humanities project. The academy does not discriminate significantly among those who perform service tasks perfunctorily or poorly, those who carry them out conscientiously, and those who invest intellectual energy in some forms of service as conceptual projects connected to their scholarship and teaching.

In attempting to shed light on these characterizations and assessments of service, the commission members examined the issue of academic values. Putting this point in terms of what is visible and what is hidden, we observed that the present model of faculty work conceals and thereby protects from criticism a set of tacit equations between the type of work done (named teaching, research, or service) and the specific character and values attributed to that work (which are unnamed but assumed). Classification predetermines the benefits and values the work is allowed to claim, so that to name an activity "service" rules out a priori the possibility that it has substantive idea content and significance. Indeed, deciding that something a faculty member has done counts as research, teaching, or service (and therefore is worth more or less) is itself problematic, seeming to be less intrinsic to the qualities of the work than determined by the institutional site where it happens: the campus classroom, popular lecture hall, scholarly convention, departmental committee, Internet discussion list, refereed journal, community board, and so on. The same work carried out or presented in different settings (which are associated with typically different audiences, media, purpose, criteria for access, and so on) is rated differently, on the basis of, primarily, its identification with a faculty role (research, teaching, or service) and, secondarily, the prestige of the site. The mere designation of work as one or another of these roles carries with it a heavy weight of tacit assumptions and value judgments. Probably the most consequential of these is the equation that makes publication (in certain venues) synonymous with scholarship and makes research a metonym for intellectual work.

Given our key metaphor of making visible, it is not surprising that members of the commission found models and diagrams useful for gaining insight and conceiving alternatives (see fig. 1). We used a matrix to reexamine with a fresh and critical eye the adequacy of the categories themselves as descriptions and differentiations of what faculty members do. The matrix, or grid, is a visual equivalent for the position we arrived at in our discussions: it expresses no prejudgments about how academic values correlate with the conventional divisions of faculty work. It takes instead an inquiring stance.

The following discussion explores the proposed matrix and its terms as tools for rethinking received wisdom about faculty work in the fields of language and literature, with emphasis on providing a richer and more judicious account of the varied forms of work typically classified as service.[1]

II. Mapping Academic Values onto Sites of Faculty Work: A New Model

As a visual aid in reconceptualizing faculty work, a matrix has the advantage that it operates as a heuristic by generating questions to be posed about particular examples. The matrix turns the representation of faculty work into an inquiry, requiring that we approach examples with an open mind about their nature and value and the interrelations among different activities. It provides not only a way of "reading" instances of faculty work in terms of a common descriptive system but also the possibility of arguing alternative ways of interpreting and valuing them. The model is open in another sense, as well. Though commission members propose and define terms for the grid, we do so provisionally and with the expectation that these terms and their definitions will be debated, translated, and adapted to fit the missions and nomenclatures of different fields of study and of different institutions. It is a model, not a prescription. Our report presents hypotheses for discussion, not definitive conceptions or language. Here are a few principles that guided our choices and compromises.

The most fundamental decision was to map values (rows) against sites (columns). We use the term *values* to indicate that a particular dimension (or attribute) of faculty work, when named as significant, expresses a quality that can be evaluated. Compare, in ice-skating, athleticism and artistry as dimensions on which a performance or individual skater can be rated. One can ask, To what extent does this performance feature or display artistry? athleticism? How are these valued dimensions of skating balanced and integrated? And what is the quality of excellence in each?

At first glance, *sites* is a more surprising and counterintuitive term for "faculty roles." Although this coordinate of the model is open to alternative specifications, the commission decided to retain in this document the conventional division of faculty work into teaching, research and scholarship, and professional service. We chose to work with these terms for the sake of continuity and maximum usefulness, in part because classification in these categories still exerts such an enormous influence on the way faculty work is perceived and valued. But, while conserving the traditional terms, the commission members wanted to redefine them boldly.

As we conceive them, these traditional divisions are not true logical typologies of faculty work or distinct roles people play. Because physical or metaphoric location of the work or its dissemination (classroom, committee meeting, Internet, journal publication) seems a particularly powerful key to the prototype (influencing our expectations), *site* is a convenient and usefully provocative shorthand or metonym for the cluster of associated features that define the prototype. This metonymy uses location, physical and metaphoric, to stand for the clustering of expectations that defines a faculty role because it often provides a key to how an instance or product of faculty activity will be assigned to a category: for example, whether it is off or on campus, published in a popular magazine or in conference proceedings. The assignment and the metonymy work reasonably well because they signal the typified combination of place, situation, language, participants, instrumentalities, and purpose that governs our expectations and classification practices.

Moreover, the way we understand and use any such categories is more important than their specific labels or content. In practical applications—for example, evaluating faculty performance—these categories are too often treated as natural or inherent in tasks and products themselves. Our model, in contrast, shows that the categories of faculty role (teaching, research, service) are constructed in relation to the objects, activities, products, and faculty lives they interpret. The model presents these distinctions as social conventions that need to be applied with great flexibility and with careful attention to the overlaps, ambiguities, and connections of work in and among different sites.

A. Characterizing the Value of Faculty Work

In figure 1 the vertical axis of the matrix is labeled "values," shorthand for the general character, functions, or attributes in faculty work that express central values of the academy and its constituencies and that permit collective expert judgments of quality. Because any particular example of faculty work can be

FIGURE 1
MATRIX MODEL (GRID) OF FACULTY WORK

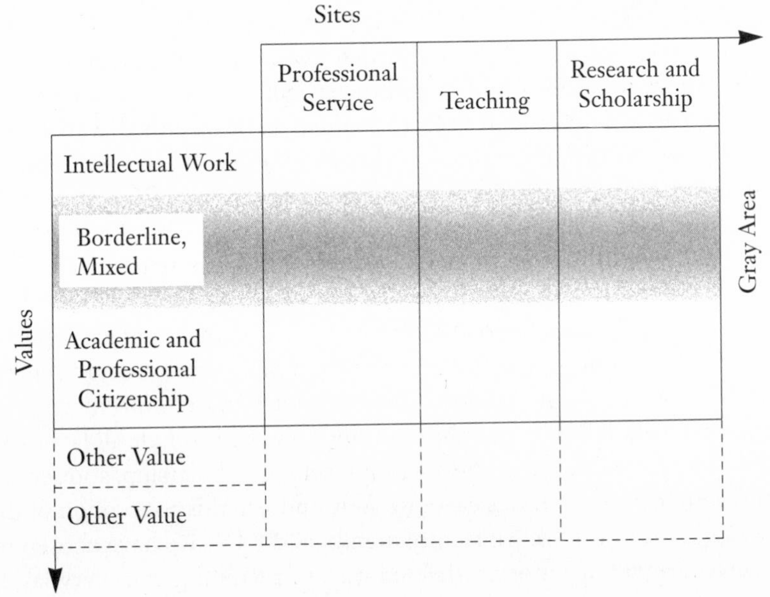

mixed in its character, we sometimes call these categories "dimensions" of faculty performance.

The commission initially identified for the grid two such types of contribution, or values: intellectual work and academic and professional citizenship. We chose these because they are broadly accepted as fundamental to the academy. We assume that there are other candidates for common or universal academic values, and certainly there are others that are crucial to the missions of particular disciplines or institutions. (Some of these other possibilities are explored in section 3, p. 204.) In addition, evaluation and reward must, as they become more sophisticated, take into account values that are specific to one or another site, like teaching, or its particular activities.

The two values named in the matrix stand in a special relation of complementarity. Intellectual work contributing to the development and use of knowledge is primary in the academic value system: it is the defining character of faculty work in an institution of higher learning and a prerequisite for its highest rewards. But there are many faculty tasks and responsibilities that do not constitute or demand substantive intellectual contributions by the individual faculty member, yet they are useful, even essential, and they require the application of professionally based skills and cultivated knowledge as well as time and effort. Academic and professional citizenship is a faculty obligation to carry out such work in the different sites of the academy in order to create, maintain, and improve the infrastructure that maintains the academy as a societal institution. These often invisible contributions to the academic community by its citizens demand respect and a more informed appreciation.

We use the terms *intellectual work* and *academic and professional citizenship*, then, to distinguish and so clarify an important range of values. But two comments are perhaps in order. First, *intellectual work*, especially if considered separate from the illustrations we offer and the specifications of meaning we try to develop, can all too easily lend itself to evaluative judgments that make vague, rather than more exact and exacting, the perception and interpretation of the highest activities faculty members undertake. For that reason, we take pains to locate its precise meaning in examples and case studies. Second, we should also note the ambiguities of *citizenship*. One significant meaning of the term would stress the relation between faculty work and the most important intellectual contributions to the social good that individual academics and academic communities make. In this sense of the term, *academic citizenship* could refer to all aspects of professional lives, expressing a crucial and comprehensive social function of the work faculty members do, and so would include all faculty work, including intellectual work, in the areas of teaching, scholarship, and service. As the following discussion makes clear, we fully endorse this conception of the social consequences of the work faculty members do. But we have chosen to use the term *citizenship* in a more restricted way, to recognize the everyday, often underappreciated professional and collegial responsibilities and activities—the faculty contributions that are crucial to intellectual work as we define it but, for our particular purposes, usefully distinguishable from that work.

These faculty functions may coincide in one activity, or cluster of activities, in different proportions. Indeed, often the difference is not in the task but in the individual's choice: it is possible to carry out a particular activity (editing, for example, or chairing a department) at different levels of intellectual investment, so that for one faculty member it becomes incorporated into his or her ongoing intellectual work while for another it is a relatively routine and discrete professional obligation. Reading up the grid from the work of academic and professional citizenship to predominantly intellectual work, one moves from professionally useful activities with a low requirement or opportunity for intellectual effort, through a gray area where the ratio of intellectual work to citizenship activities varies, into strongly ideational work that meets other criteria for significant, fertile intellectual work.

These two kinds of contributions (as well as many other values) play out across the various sites and occasions of faculty work, placed on the horizontal axis of the grid.

1. Intellectual work

Faculty responsibilities for teaching, research and scholarship, and professional service all reflect the historic commitment of American colleges and universities to enrich human knowledge and to make it widely available for personal and social use. The conception of knowledge as a cumulative societal resource, however, has undergone a subtle shift late in the twentieth century to emphasize not simply the value of knowledge produced but also the dynamic spirit of inquiry and processes of higher learning as common elements of academic practices and goals. Faculty members, higher education professionals, and students all participate in the processes of inquiry, discovery, invention, critical examination, enactment, and rhetorical communication by which knowledge is continually created, revised, disseminated, and integrated to enlarge human understanding and improve society.

Intellectual work, as defined here, refers to the various ways faculty members can contribute individually and jointly to the collective projects and enterprises of knowledge and learning undertaken to implement broad academic missions. Ways of engaging in such intellectual enterprises include, for example,

- creating new questions, problems, information, interpretations, designs, products, frameworks of understanding, and so on through inquiry (e.g., empirical, textual, historical, theoretical, technological, artistic, practical);
- clarifying, critically examining, weighing, and revising the knowledge claims, beliefs, or understanding of others and oneself;

- connecting knowledge to other knowledge;
- preserving, restoring, and reinterpreting past knowledge;
- applying aesthetic, political, and ethical values to make judgments about knowledge and its uses;
- arguing knowledge claims in order to invite criticism and revision;
- making specialized knowledge broadly accessible and usable, for example, to young learners, to nonspecialists in other disciplines, to the public;
- helping new generations to become active knowers themselves, preparing them for lifelong learning and discovery;
- applying knowledge to practical problems in significant or innovative ways;
- creating insight and communicating forms of experience through artistic works or performance.

For the purposes of faculty rewards, significant intellectual work should be recognizably an outgrowth of faculty members' professional expertise, rather than simply of their general knowledge and skills as educated, intelligent people, and should contribute in some way to the knowledge-related enterprises in which the faculty member is engaged *as* a faculty member. Intellectual work as understood in the academic setting is not simply any intelligent behavior or activities and accomplishments that demonstrate a certain degree of professional skill and knowledge. Even the application of disciplinary knowledge (as, for example, when a department chair leads a search or manages a curriculum initiative) does not itself define work as a substantive intellectual project. Intellectual work, in the academic context, must explicitly invoke ideas and explore their consequences, either in the world of concepts or in the world of action or both. One meaning of the requirement that intellectual work in the academy have a public dimension is that it be made explicitly available for assessment, evaluation, and modification by a critically informed group of peers as well as by those benefited or served by the work.

In fact, a crucial expectation of intellectual work in the academy is that it should point beyond itself and its immediate context in its meanings and benefits. We expect faculty members to situate their activity and its results within a collective intellectual enterprise of higher education and to make their work relevant and responsibile to the goals and standards of that community. That enterprise need not be accumulation of research knowledge, nor must the domain of responsibility and effectivity, along with the audience and judges, be defined only in disciplinary terms. The relevant referent could be the learning of students, the work world, a teaching community and its strategies, the audience affected aesthetically by a creative work, or a social problem and the effects of analysis or invervention.

Defining faculty activities as intellectual does not determine their quality. The work is simply presented as a function of ideas, their mode of production or application, and their consequences in the context of public, critical examination. Members of the relevant community have a responsibility both to evaluate intellectual work and to invite evaluation in these terms.

Intellectual work in a postsecondary setting may excel in various ways. Although not an exhaustive list, the following may distinguish respected intellectual work in any category of faculty effort: skill, care, rigor, and intellectual honesty; a heuristic passion for knowledge; originality; relevance and aptness; coherence, consistency, and development within a body of work; diversity and versatility of contribution; thorough knowledge and constructive use of important work by others; the habit of self-critical examination and openness to criticism and revision; sustained productivity over time; high impact and value to a local academic community like the department; relevance and significance to societal issues and problems; effective communication and dissemination. The potential for making substantive contributions that qualify as excellent intellectual work exists in all the arenas of faculty activity; intellectual work is not restricted to research and scholarship.

The commission believes that, in defining and judging the work of faculty members, institutions and professional organizations should recognize a wide range of possible achievements and audiences of intellectual work, which range from the esoteric, specialized, or local to the occasional breadth of a "public intellectual." Institutions should note particularly a distinction between the way intellectual work disseminates in scholarship and in teaching. Whereas scholarship reaches a specialized public outside the college or university immediately and directly, the impact of achievement in teaching and curricular work is indirect and more gradual. The products of teaching are a curriculum or successful program or institutional project, on the one hand, and, on the other, students, their work, and their intellectual development. This kind of intellectual work may be harder to observe, demonstrate, or evaluate, and its time frame for fruition may be far longer than that of scholarship or some forms of professional service. It is nevertheless valuable to the college or university and to society. The profession should work to establish the structures and processes for evaluating and rewarding such long-term investments and accomplishments.

2. Academic and professional citizenship

As we mapped the second value of our matrix, academic and professional citizenship, onto sites of faculty work, we changed (as noted above) the meaning of *research*, *teaching*, and *service*. They are now "sites" of faculty work, not a priori indicators of value; they serve to clarify the relation between specific faculty work and institutional and disciplinary needs (thereby assisting the development of appropriate reward schemes). Just as research in the model is no longer the exclusive site of intellectual work, so is service no longer the exclusive site of academic and professional citizenship. It can also entail substantive intellectual labor. Service is just one of the sites where intellectual work and academic and professional citizenship can be located.

The explicitly or purely intellectual element of faculty work is, more than we admit, surrounded by a penumbra of professional tasks that are quietly vital to sustaining intellectual work and the academy itself. This type of work or component in academic tasks and activities, for which we have no convenient separate term, is like intellectual work in being grounded in professional expertise and in being directed toward the health and maintenance of academic communities and institutions. The worthiness and necessity of such work led us to identify doing it with academic and professional *citizenship*. Just as intellectual work is not simply any work requiring intelligence and knowledge, worthy professional work done as an academic or professional citizen is not just any minor task done for academic purposes.

Like intellectual work, the professional work of citizenship can be found in any category or site of faculty effort. One purpose of the matrix is to make more visible this dimension of citizenship in research and scholarship and in teaching, where it has been largely ignored. The model requires us to approach each instance of any activity with an open mind, asking what ratio of intellectual work to citizenship it has required or elicited or how a faculty member has chosen to reconfigure that ratio from what is typically expected. Likely opportunities for citizenship in each site might include

Research and scholarship: participating in promotion and tenure reviews, reviewing manuscripts, working on committees in professional organizations, serving on task forces and commissions in one's field or interdisciplinary areas, editing, mentoring junior colleagues, serving as departmental advisor on library acquisitions, collecting and distributing information through electronic forums;

Teaching: recruiting, working on institutional retention programs, advising general lower-division or major students, participating in summer orientation programs for incoming students, performing routine committee work on curricular and general education issues, acting as occasional consultant to other faculty members or administrators in an area of teaching expertise, advising field-specific student organizations or projects;

Service: working on committees for one's institution or professional organizations; doing development work (raising institutional funds) as a faculty member; representing the institution or field on external task forces, boards, commissions; being interviewed as a professional on subjects of public interest; advising campus organizations and clubs; participating in the faculty role in educational policy debates on and off campus (e.g., free speech vs. speech codes); participating in parents' or alumni events; serving in the senate or on faculty councils.

Many of what used to be called service functions have been treated here as substrates of professional tasks (citizenship) in each area of faculty life, while service itself has been sharply redefined (see below) as a genre of work seen in terms of its purpose and audience, which can range in principle from citizenship to work that is primarily intellectual. We stress again that the degree of intellectual work is not in some predictable way intrinsic to the task or activity but is a function of both circumstance and choice. As time and effort increase, or as responsibility for decision making increases, the opportunity or necessity for intellectual investment increases. We have shown this in the grid as an ambiguous gray area in which many activities, including the examples listed above, might fall, with variable investments in generative intellectual work.

There is an important difference in the kind of credit and, therefore, reward that accrues to work done primarily as citizenship. We expect the citizen to be responsible and dedicated; we regard faculty members as having obligations in this regard that they meet more or less thoroughly, collegially, productively, and skillfully. The following may distinguish respected academic and professional citizenship in any category of faculty effort: care and commitment, honesty, punctuality and reliability; knowledge of the institution and of professional organizations; interpersonal skills; thoroughness and perseverance; availability; willingness to inform oneself about educational policy and practices and to keep abreast of changes; organizational skills.

This kind of professional contribution is expected as a sine qua non of faculty citizenship, necessary but not sufficient for professional achievement and the most significant academic rewards (rank, tenure, professional status, salary, the admiration of peers, the personal sense of accomplishment). In this sense the relation between knowledge accessed and the communities and enterprises to which professional citizenship is directed is more predictable and less transformative than in the case of intellectual work. Just as the evaluative measures and credit awarded for each are different, so must be the types of rewards available.

By asking us to map values against sites, the new model compels us to seek out and name the true intellectual work in service and teaching and to evaluate its distinction for purposes of the highest academic rewards—equivalent to those for intellectual work in research and scholarship. It also requires us to appreciate and evaluate the component of citizenship in teaching and research, often far larger than we realize, and to treat it consistently with the same kinds of contribution in service roles. Across categories, citizenship deserves more honor, more broadly shared faculty commitment, and appropriate rewards for its vital role in sustaining the academy as a communal enterprise.

B. Redefining Faculty Roles and Exploring the Sites of Faculty Work

The model proposed here treats the traditional sites of research, teaching, and service as useful heuristics, as long as we understand them to be conventional distinctions built around familiar, sometimes outdated prototypes. Such classifications have important ethical and political dimensions and material consequences. The process of trying to refine and broaden concepts of teaching, research and scholarship, and service and to describe and situate actual examples of faculty work in these categories was highly instructive in itself. It exemplifies the kind of work we need to do as a profession to account for recent changes in faculty work, to reveal and question prevailing values, and to test emerging premises and recommendations. Intellectual work, citizenship, and other values can be examined and evaluated regardless of site. These values should be made explicit, subjected to debate, and weighed against one another in applying them to cases, so long as one recognizes that classification in one category or another is somewhat arbitrary, since it depends on local custom and nomenclature, and that personal and collective intellectual projects often manifest themselves in several sites or are integrated across them.

At present, identification of work as service instead of teaching, or teaching instead of research and scholarship, carries a powerful charge of attributed positive or negative value, with enormous consequence for academic success, recognition, and reward. Our definitions are designed to change, or at least severely question, those assumptions. We affirm, as a major conclusion of this report, that the quality, significance, and impact of work on knowledge enterprises or in support of institutions are more important than its label as teaching, service, or research and scholarship. If intellectual work is valued wherever it is done and if other values are commensurately appreciated and rewarded wherever they appear, the classification of a particular activity or accomplishment as teaching, service, research and scholarship, or more than one of these will become increasingly less crucial and perhaps even irrelevant for individual faculty reward. These categories are more likely, however, to retain their significance for distinguishing, prioritizing, and balancing departmental, disciplinary, and institutional missions and negotiating faculty members' differential commitments to them according to individual talents, departmental or institutional need, career stage, and so on.

Although the categories have no set order in our new model (left to right in the matrix [fig. 1]), we begin with research and scholarship as the best-understood category and move to professional service, the category most in need of more discriminating attention and better definition.

1. Research and scholarship

We define research and scholarship here as a site for intellectual and professional work that is produced and legitimated in accordance with the standards of one or more disciplinary and professional communities that are cosmopolitan rather than local or institution-bound.[2] It is thus typically a virtual, transinstitutional site as well as a material one and, as locale, unpredictable compared with the classic classroom or committee or off-campus places of other missions. It is made public, that is, published or disseminated, typically in written (or now, electronic) form in some kind of linguistic record that makes information and argument available to that primary, peer audience for criticism, evaluation, and use. Scholarship as formal inquiry claims a place within a framework of current knowledge making and has its own traditions and standards of inquiry.

Scholarship can be exemplified in the following modes and forms, among others:

- products of original research: monographs, articles, chapters in books, review articles, edited volumes introducing new topics or ideas;
- creative professional work that is directly relevant to the faculty member's professional expertise: for example, literature, computer software;
- published work gathering, integrating, translating, and disseminating the original work of others, enriching it through interpretive, preservative, recuperative, or critical functions: for example, editing of journals and journal issues, research volumes, concordances, or editions of a historical work; book reviews, textbooks, and bibliographical essays; translations of works by others;
- external documents with scholarly content: for example, grant proposals, consulting reports;
- other forms of scholarly communication: conferences, workshops, literacy projects, participation in electronic lists.

Notice that we define scholarship here primarily by its interactive relation to a dynamic scholarly enterprise and participation in its community. Scholarship must be made public and open to peer criticism, but it need not be published or disseminated in traditional forums.

2. Teaching

Teaching can be broadly interpreted in the context of faculty roles as a contribution to the educational knowledge mission that originates in an institution of higher learning (but does not necessarily take place there) and serves whoever it defines as students. That is to say, institutions generally regard as "teaching" only those educational services (promoting and facilitating learning) that they directly sponsor and authorize for their own designated "student" populations. Much other faculty work that meets commonsense definitions of teaching (e.g., lecturing, running workshops, tutoring or mentoring learners) is treated by default as professional service because it is not budgeted and accounted for administratively as instruction or is addressed to learners not treated by the institution as its "students."

In listing possible instantiations of the intellectual work of teaching, we should point out that, just like service (and even research), teaching can legitimately be practiced at higher or lower levels of intellectual investment. Because teaching can be competently executed and acceptable without necessarily becoming for that teacher a substantive intellectual project, teaching that is truly inquiry-based and has other significant features of fresh, new intellectual work must be distinguished and rewarded. In addition to the more common areas of pedagogy (classroom effectiveness, developing curricula and assignments, etc.), the opportunities for serious intellectual work in teaching might include studying and monitoring the learning of one's students, translating scholarly knowledge into modes meaningful and accessible to learners at different stages, designing new forms of assessment, adapting pedagogical modes to different or "nontraditional" learners, and participating in interdisciplinary teaching projects requiring new learning.

Although commonly treated as an autonomous personal performance, the work of teaching is best seen in a broader way, as the equivalent of a team effort. Individual teaching activities are ideally embedded in the project of developing and sustaining a teaching community, in part through extensive oral, written, and electronic exchanges and documents. This community is a counterpart to the research community that is created through journals, correspondence, conventions, and professional organizations, and it can serve a similar function in peer review of teaching. To varying degrees in different fields and subfields of language and literature, local teaching communities have been extended regionally and nationally to share and test teaching knowledge and practices in ways that parallel those of the national research community and to facilitate interaction between the two communities. Creating and sustaining such a teaching network and such interactions are important forms of professional work that should be rewarded. The profession should encourage and facilitate the formation and spread of such teaching communities and it should encourage institutions to provide support and recognition of teaching as more than individual classroom performance.

Recognition and reward for teaching, not to mention efforts to prepare future professors and improve teaching performance, have been severely hampered in the academy at large by a restricted conception of teaching, which focuses heavily on classroom events and other direct student contacts along with only the most immediate tasks of preparing for or supplementing these events (e.g., writing a syllabus, grading). This conception needs to be expanded by taking into account activities that enrich student learning or enable better teaching, ranging from nontraditional teaching modes (outside classrooms or credit-bearing classes) to teachers' professional development as teachers and their activities in forming and sustaining teaching communities.

Sample activities under the heading of teaching include

- running a writing center or language lab;
- preparing for or improving one's teaching, by designing courses, reading material in one's field, participating in teaching groups, or attending teaching workshops and conferences;
- coteaching with others;
- conducting classroom research projects;
- advising majors or other students on matters significantly related to one's own academic expertise;
- arranging and supervising internships;
- serving on graduate examination and thesis, dossier, or dissertation committees;
- mentoring other teachers;
- developing courses and curriculum sequences;
- administering a multisection course or teaching program;
- developing multimedia software or teaching strategies for lab-based language instruction;
- designing and implementing the professional development of teaching assistants and professional instructors;
- offering faculty or student workshops in areas of one's professional expertise;
- participating in school-college partnerships to connect and improve learning across educational sectors.

Evaluation processes and criteria must account carefully for nontraditional teaching modes, including, for example, distance learning, teaching with computers, collaborative teaching, and involvement in interdisciplinary teaching ventures. Some forms of teaching by faculty members in these fields fall outside the traditional semester-long undergraduate or graduate course. Some teaching takes nontraditional forms such as tutoring, offering workshops or minicourses, or giving instruction in writing or language centers, activities for which participants may or may not earn credits. Providing professional development for others is a form of teaching, including offering workshops or individual consultations for faculty colleagues, their teaching assistants, or their students. This peer education can also be described under service as "internal outreach," and it often exemplifies administration or leadership—of a language or writing program, curricular diversity initiative, or the like. As with other ambiguous or integrated activities, it is often severely underestimated in its intellectual dimension and as a teaching effort.

As we attempt to redefine teaching as a site of faculty work, we need to keep in mind that it does not matter where an activity appears across the diagram. What matters for assessing and rewarding faculty work is whether it is viewed as intellectual work or professional citizenship on the vertical dimension.

3. *Professional service*

Service has functioned in the past as a kind of grab bag for all professional work that was not clearly classroom teaching, research, or scholarship. As a result, recent efforts to define it more precisely (as "professional service") have tended to select out one subset of these activities and have failed to account for all the clearly professional work previously lumped together under this rubric (see Elman and Smock; Lynton and Elman).[3] We were particularly dissatisfied with the failure of such conceptions to provide for the possibility of intellectual work in various forms of service to institutions, professional organizations, and higher education organizations. Yet it is hard to come up with a principled definition based on common features or family resemblances among all these activities and to avoid confusions with the concept of citizenship. Recently these difficulties have been exacerbated by changing expectations of faculty members: the introduction of qualitatively new faculty responsibilities, for example, those related to learning and using new technologies; and the increase in societal demands for applied knowledge and for a greater involvement of faculty members in public service as problem solvers, resources, and partners with other sectors of the society. To help clarify the concept of professional service, we distinguish between applied work (usually within contexts of professional, not institutional, missions) and institutional or organizational service.

a. *Applied work*

In some respects applied work involves or incorporates activities very similar to those called, in other contexts, teaching and research or scholarship, but in a different, typically external site where academic knowledge is made available for, and intersects with, practical affairs and problem solving. The beneficiaries might be government, industry, law or medicine, other educational sectors, business, the arts, and charities, among others, as well as, reflexively, academic knowledge itself. (Applied work is not a simple translation or transmission of academic knowledge to nonacademic users, any more than teaching is to students.) Other activities of applied work are more distinctive to external public contexts.

Examples of applied work in the fields encompassed by the MLA might include

- serving on a local, regional, or national humanities council;
- helping a local school system to revamp its curriculum or pedagogy in a language or literature field;
- working on a project to establish new standards for learning at different levels of education in a language or literature field;
- establishing or working on a community literacy project;
- acting as a technical consultant in communications for business, law, or other professions;
- working as a board member for a local (non-university- or college-affiliated) arts magazine;
- writing scripts for public television;
- consulting on expert testimony for Congress;
- testifying in court as an expert on academic issues like language varieties, second-language learning, or multicultural curricula.

A misleading and elitist presumption in many articulations of applied work is sometimes expressed by such terms as *technology transfer, dissemination*, and *application of knowledge*. The term *applied research* suggests more accurately that applied work in service, like teaching (also an applied or practical art), is not a mechanical or even an inventive transmission or application of specialized knowledge *by* faculty members *to* uninformed groups or publics. Rather, applied work involves the intersection of academic knowledge enterprises with practical activity that itself has creative and critical elements. Practical activity not only tests and refines academic ideas and predictions but also produces its own knowledge and skills—that is, it can itself be or incorporate intellectual enterprises. In *application*, rightly understood, the two interpret, stimulate, modify, and critique each other, and academics are partners with practitioners or with other beneficiaries of a joint knowledge enterprise. Together, they make knowledge usable, and they inform the ongoing teaching and research enterprises of higher education in the process.

The concept of applied work can be particularly confusing when the expertise developed or used for social benefit is knowledge about teaching and learning as an aspect of the intellectual work of one's field. Here, research, teaching, and service merge. This is true, for example, in the teaching of literature, writing, and languages when outreach activities involve demonstrating, training, and applying knowledge about educational practice in such external contexts as the public schools or for colleagues in other fields at one's institution.

b. Institutional and organizational service

Institutional and organizational service encompasses activities that dynamically create and sustain institutions and enable them to pursue global academic goals. Through such service, faculty members directly maintain and advance the functioning of departments, divisions, colleges, universities, and disciplinary and professional organizations that undergird all other forms of faculty work.

Within institutional and organizational service, we distinguish *governance* from other kinds of tasks in support of an institution's or organization's health and growth. Governance refers to participation in the decision-making roles of the institution or professional organization. Governance roles of particular salience and centrality in faculty life include chairing a department, serving in an active faculty senate, or directing a major program. The "other tasks" necessary for order, daily work, sustenance, and the advancement of institutions and organizations have grown most rapidly, often through the return of responsibility for what used to be administrators' tasks to faculty members. We consider these varied activities simply institutional "support." Examples gathered by the commission include

- recruiting students;
- participating in institutional development (fund-raising);
- negotiating in collective bargaining sessions;
- arranging for training or action on legal matters;
- serving on committees of a senate or faculty council;
- organizing events and conferences;
- performing special service on the basis of racial, gender, ethnic, cultural, linguistic, or sexual difference.

Many of these tasks have insufficient conceptual demands to qualify as intellectual work, although they may be labor- and time-intensive. Others (e.g., labor negotiations) may require the acquisition and exercise of technical and conceptual knowledge that falls outside the faculty member's academic role, no matter how broadly defined. As in every other site, however, they can present some significant opportunities for academic intellectual work, typically when faculty members take on leadership roles and especially in times of change or in service of educational reform. For example, a faculty member who takes on a leadership role in strategic planning for the future of an institution may undertake a major initiative that creates, interprets, researches, integrates, and communicates knowledge: indirectly for the sake of student learners, a discipline, or the community but directly for the institution's own health and development.

One special consideration in defining and evaluating service in the fields of language and literature involves minority as well as women faculty members on some campuses who have borne a special burden in service as result of administration and faculty initiatives to implement agendas in multiculturalism, diversity, affirmative action, and other such efforts. In addition, minority and women faculty members have proactively pursued their own agendas for change, often in leadership capacities. These efforts have usually proved to be thankless in the context of consideration for promotion and tenure and other rewards. The commission believes these problems need to be addressed throughout the reward system. Such work can be valued in either dimension or both as citizenship and as intellectual work, if appropriately analyzed and documented. At present there is an ethically unacceptable gap between stated or implicit expectations and actual rewards.

In reviewing these rather distinct roles and activities in the area of professional service, the common element, it appears to us, is the relation they forge between knowledge, learning, and practical action with real-world consequences. Professional service is distinguished from other sites of faculty work in that it is integrally active or related to practical action; if intellectual work, it has to do with ideas in action—problem definition and problem solving, interpretations of theory in practice and production (and vice versa), invention or design of activities, leadership or major responsibility for enactment of ideas, administration involving responsibilities for the actions and welfare of other people. As practical action, these activities invariably have social meaning and implications and raise often complex ethical and political questions. For the faculty member who is engaged in organizational or institutional service, it is the institution or organization, situated in relation to multiple and complex, interacting social systems, that constitutes a practical context, no less real and worldly than the business, government, or community groups benefited by applied work in outreach enterprises. For certain fields (e.g., composition and rhetoric, applied linguistics) whose scholarship is itself permeated with action or defined in relation to practical and productive knowledge, it is hard to separate the service and scholarly missions in practice. Rather, one can distinguish the service mission from the scholarly one within the same, integrated intellectual enterprise (e.g., a project in the public schools)—sometimes also including an extended teaching mission as well.

In figure 2, we have mapped some sample faculty activities onto the grid as an example of how it might be used for description and interpretation. The mapping is simply illustrative, since it is impossible to map activities definitively in the abstract. Placement will vary individually, according to the intent and achievement of the unique example being described, and contextually, according to local nomenclature, institutional missions, and purpose in using the grid. The grid itself is simply an idea that can be specified differently with respect to values or sites. The commission offers this model in the hopes that it will spark thoughtful debate and constructive change in the profession through a variety of possible uses, including experiments in applying it to faculty work as well as revision of its choices to fit specific institutions, disciplines and specialties in language and literature, and needs.

C. Negotiating Balance

We turn, finally, to reconsider the issue of balance from the different perspective created by the new model, which no longer simplifies it as a zero-sum game. As noted, early efforts to reform the roles and rewards system grew out of calls for "rebalancing" the time and value given to different faculty roles. As these efforts progressed, it became evident that great gulfs separated the rhetoric of promotion and tenure guidelines or faculty handbooks from the realities of faculty activities and responsibilities and institutional needs; that these realities were also changing rapidly; and that the value system was in need of urgent reform to correspond both to these circumstances and to the need for higher education to redraft its compact with society. All these factors urged institutions to strike new, more flexible and socially responsible balances in the work of faculty members and of departments.

The commission believes that faculty members must have a great deal of freedom to negotiate the ratios among different kinds of faculty work commitments at any given time and to change this balance from time to time in their career development. Such negotiations will involve mediating among goals and priorities that will be only partly convergent: those of the faculty member; those of the profession or discipline; the missions of departments, programs, and institutions; the demands of society; and the desires or needs of multiple constituents. In some cases, institutions are beginning to allocate faculty rewards to units rather than individuals, leaving the unit to create individualized profiles in faculty roles, along with commensurate rewards, among its members. We urge that such negotiations be as explicit as possible, starting in the hiring process and continuing throughout faculty members' careers, and that they guide not only administrators but also faculty peers and promotion and tenure committees. At the same time, faculty colleagues should have a voice in developing such understandings with all constituents as they affect departmental or programmatic missions in which they participate.

Less obviously, balances must be struck among the values we have identified (and others specific to situations and institutions), which have not up to now been explicit in schemes for analyzing and judging faculty work. While intellectual work is clearly for most academics the primary value in any role, academic professions are under increasing pressure from society to consider carefully

FIGURE 2
MAPPING FACULTY ACTIVITY ONTO THE GRID

Sites

Gray Area

| | Professional Service | | | Academic Missions | |
| | Institutional and Organizational Work | | Applied Work (Outreach) | Teaching | Research and Scholarship |
Values	Governance	Support			
Intellectual Work	Lead strategic planning group / Negotiate in collective bargaining / Chair department / Serve on college promotion and tenure committee	Create new advising system / Revise major policy / Implement diversity initiative / Participate in alumni activities / Raise funds	Work as consultant (in government, business, schools, etc.) / Develop action projects in community / Participate in school-college partnership / Advise local government / Give community lecture	Create or lead new teaching program / Develop new assessment plan / Direct writing across the curriculum / Teach classes / Write textbooks / Serve on curriculum committee / Train TAs	Engage in scholarly inquiry or publication / Do creative work or performance / Edit volume / Translate work / Give keynote speech / Edit journal / Run electronic list / Serve on commission or task force on scholarly issues
Academic and Professional Citizenship	Serve as member of faculty senate / Serve on department salary committee / Serve on search committee in another department	Talk to trustees / Advise campus groups / Make recruiting trips	Give expert testimony / Give interview as expert / Serve on community board	Participate in peer evaluations / Work on retention project / Do general advising / Review textbooks / Recruit students into major / Participate in summer orientation program	Put on conference / Participate in promotion and tenure reviews / Review manuscripts / Conduct external reviews of departments and programs / Serve as outsider on PhD defense / Serve on editorial board / Write recommendations
Other Value					
Other Value					

both the importance of other values (for example, the facilitation of student learning through direct contact and engagement or the direct benefit to society through local or regional involvement in solving problems) and the interaction among different values, as well as the beneficiaries of each. These kinds of ambiguous issues come up as we move beyond the critiques and defenses of the past system and find ourselves with a new, or newly visible, set of problems. We hope to draw out such questions in the fictionalized case studies in section 2 and to explore some of these questions more fully in section 3.

SECTION 2. CASE STUDIES IN THE PERCEPTION, INTERPRETATION, AND ASSESSMENT OF FACULTY WORK

The model developed in section 1 proposes to guide the complex process by which faculty work, in its multiple sites and dimensions, can be more clearly perceived, its meaning more carefully interpreted, and its effectiveness more justly assessed. The model's complexity is necessary, we believe, to provide the kind of clarity in perception, interpretation, and evaluation that is critical if we are to achieve a fair representation and analysis of faculty work.

Our commission was asked to focus on one aspect of faculty work—what is now called professional service—to help clarify what it is, how it relates to other work faculty members do, why it is valuable, and how it can be accurately represented and appropriately valued. To that end, we focus in this section on this arena of faculty responsibilities. And because our aim is to improve the representation and analysis of specific activities, we proceed somewhat inductively, looking at a number of cases that occasion reflection on central issues in our understanding and appraisal of professional service. In the course of these case studies, the following purposes guide our rethinking of the processes of defining faculty roles and establishing fair rewards.

1. We challenge the reductive understanding of the category of "service," as it is ordinarily understood, and the consignment of certain activities exclusively to that category. Instead, we highlight in these cases dimensions of intellectual engagement and professional contribution that legitimately fall into all three of the sites of faculty work discussed in the previous section: professional service (including both institutional service and applied work), research and scholarship, and teaching.

2. Across these three sites or domains, we distinguish dimensions of a faculty member's labor that range from intellectual engagement to the performance of the essential duties of good citizenship, thereby examining the variety of, and connections among, faculty activities and obligations.

3. Finally, we argue that the *quality* of all kinds of work—work involving both intellectual engagement and good citizenship demonstrated across the

sites—can be assessed more adequately within the categories we provide. The process of assessment becomes more complex and at the same time proceeds with greater clarity once we situate faculty work within this configuration. We have in mind a model that envisions assessment along axes of importance and execution: (A) the work's importance allows us to posit, according to widely accepted academic standards, that intellectual work would be given more credit than citizenship, even as both are respected; and (B) the work's execution entails rigorous assessment of the quality of each dimension.

The test of our model is its usefulness in the perception, interpretation, and assessment of individual cases. Our model should present a configuration of faculty responsibilities that enables more accurate perception and interpretation of faculty members' work and a more appropriate reward for it, in conjunction with basic principles of fairness and, of course, always in accord with the mission of a particular institution.

I. Perceiving and Interpreting Faculty Work

In our first example, we examine a hypothetical case of faculty work that has been customarily consigned to the category of service. Our analysis is meant partly to question that consignment and partly to offer a way of understanding this work that is at once less reductive, more accurate, and more just.

Assistant Professor Eric LeBeau has taught in the English department at Eastern State University (ESU) for five years. He is about to be reviewed for tenure and promotion. Like other universities, ESU values excellence in teaching, scholarship, and service and expects individual faculty members to perform well in all three areas. LeBeau's teaching evaluations place him in the upper third of the faculty, his department and university service is at least at the level expected of an assistant professor, and his scholarly productivity (three articles, two reviews), while below average, is respectable. Ten years ago, on this evidence alone, he would probably have received tenure. But now, tenure is possible though not probable.

In public statements about the mission of the university (though not in any official documents relating to tenure and promotion), senior ESU administrators frequently mention the importance of ESU's long-standing ties to the local and regional community. Partly in response to this sense of mission, LeBeau has created and administered an outreach program to local schools, working collaboratively with teachers in middle schools and high schools to develop writing-intensive curricula and courses. The project involves a seminar, facilitated by LeBeau and held alternately at ESU and one of the schools, designed to explore ways of improving the teaching of writing. Funded initially by an NEH Elementary and Secondary Education Grant, the program asks participants to read current theory in rhetoric and composition and discuss its applicability to their teaching. Several of LeBeau's colleagues from ESU have attended the seminar to talk about new developments in their specialized fields as they relate to the practice and politics of teaching reading and writing. The project is based on the principle that teachers can rethink their practices only within an ongoing mentoring process that engages them in reflective teaching, regular discussions with their colleagues, and frequent writing about their work assembled in portfolios that are shared with other participants. Because it requires of participating teachers a complete rethinking of the models they use in conceptualizing both language and learning, the program runs throughout the year, includes a great deal of reading and writing, and finds LeBeau regularly visiting each of the teachers' classrooms and meeting with students and other teachers who are not directly involved in the project. He has also sponsored annual meetings of the principals of the participating schools, to familiarize them with the aims of the project and listen to their concerns. Pedagogy and curricula at local schools have changed as a result.

This case concerns a particular kind of work that would seem to be almost universally admired, although not all that commonly rewarded, across the range of higher education institutions. The case thus poses problems that confront both faculty members and administrators as they contemplate work that does not readily fit the prevailing model of faculty roles and rewards.

Because the model we propose will of course need to be adjusted to the missions of particular institutions, our discussion of the case is designed primarily to clarify the categories of analysis and the process of review we recommend. Our first observation about the case would be this: The mission statement of any college or university needs to be articulated in specific relation to the institution's system of faculty obligations and rewards, so that faculty work supporting that mission can be accurately perceived and adequately recognized. Such specification would be an important step in establishing rigorous standards that would encourage work of high quality. It would also serve to clarify in a comprehensive way the role of intellectuals and their work in the various undertakings of higher education.

A. Clarifying the Sites of Faculty Work

1. Scholarly dimensions of the project

In this particular case, what might seem to be simply "service" also falls within the category of scholarship and provides perhaps the best evidence of LeBeau's continuing commitment as a scholar. It supports his application for tenure even more powerfully than do his published articles alone, in part because of the integral connections between the publications and this work, as we argue below. With respect to its scholarly aspects, his work with local colleagues derives from, and through this practice contributes to, the professional conversation concerning the study and teaching of writing. The project itself, developed as a truly collaborative program with teachers at local schools, reflects the best scholarship in rhetoric and composition and theories of professional development. More than that, LeBeau's work, in fostering cooperation among educators to analyze and develop curricula that make students' experiences coherent across their years of schooling, contributes to the field-wide effort to study and construct effective ways of bridging gaps between different educational levels. The project's involvement of a wide range of faculty members from ESU as well as the schools, working together in a collaborative examination of teaching, enables the production of new forms of knowledge about pedagogy that are sharable in the larger educational community and so contribute in important ways to the work of the discipline. The particular effort to consider how new developments in English studies have an impact on "the practice and politics of teaching reading and writing" offers the opportunity for a serious rethinking of the discipline in its differences and its possibilities for integration. Both the NEH grant proposal that shaped the program and the reports generated and new curricula developed and tested in the schools constitute a form of publication, subject to peer critique and revision and readily available for dissemination.

2. Teaching dimensions of the project

By representing the work of teaching in more comprehensive and refined ways, our model suggests how LeBeau's project can be understood as an aspect of his work as a teacher. His project, after all, is devoted to the design of curricula and courses. It engages both the participating teachers and LeBeau himself in reflective considerations of their students' learning. It requires of LeBeau the imaginative translation of scholarly knowledge to the different realms of schooling at the precollege level, including the possibility of shaping pedagogy to more diverse student populations with far more varied career interests than he usually finds at ESU. It is in important ways a project in mentoring teachers, involving presentations and workshops on new developments in pedagogy and the establishment and cultivation of what we have called a teaching network. It is thus a significant undertaking in the domain of teaching, and in addition to offering local educators very useful assistance, it challenges LeBeau to become more reflective not only about the larger professional issue of the teaching and learning of language and literature but also about the curriculum and pedagogy at ESU. Its manifold contributions to the teaching mission of his own university should not, therefore, be overlooked. Indeed, they are ignored only at some peril to the effectiveness of the education ESU can offer its undergraduates.

3. Professional service dimensions of the project

With a better grasp of LeBeau's work as scholarship and teaching, we can arrive at a more accurate understanding of the distinctive ways it counts as professional service. What emerges more clearly, now, is the kind of intellectual engagement the administration of such a program requires. By achieving a sophisticated, "scholarly" conception of the program's aims and intended interventions and by creating and sustaining a community of teachers devoted to reflecting critically on pedagogy, LeBeau's "service" as program director constitutes a form of intellectual and academic leadership that has the potential not only to influence the participating institutions but also to shape the possibilities for similar collaboration, on a national level, in both school-college programs and other intersections between the university and the world outside.

B. Clarifying the Dimensions and Values of Faculty Work

In the usual methods of scrutinizing and assessing LeBeau's project, what are immediately visible and most likely to be noticed are his generous time on task, the personal and social "worthiness" of the undertaking, and his excellent rapport with the participants. These are, of course, important dimensions of his work, corresponding to values legitimately associated with "good citizenship" (efficient administration, congenial and collegial attitudes, etc.). We could add a long list of similar duties effectively handled by LeBeau on which the success of the project depends: for example, scheduling, recruiting, timely reporting, organizing meetings, managing the budget, and maintaining contact with school administrators and others integral to the program's operation and impact.

But the tendency to interpret the entire project in terms of these features misses the more significant dimension of the work itself. That is, our customary focus on the effective execution of its "citizenship" features blinds us to LeBeau's intellectual aspirations and achievements. These intellectual dimensions have been sketched above in our clarification of the sites of his work. In insisting on the need to discriminate between the more intellectual and the more routine aspects of the project, we aim both to clarify the range of activities and skills involved and to foreground those dimensions of truly intellectual work, across the domains of service, scholarship, and teaching, that make LeBeau's project one with work more usually revered and rewarded in the academy. The principle underlying this analysis is one we believe to be widely shared in higher education but not so widely or fairly realized in current mechanisms for recognizing and supporting the full range of faculty work.

The model we propose is intended, then, to destabilize the routinized ways faculty members are currently regarded and to offer, in place of this routine, an interpretive and evaluative framework that is in fact more in keeping with generally accepted principles and assumptions than current models are. LeBeau's work, we believe, merits the same considerations as the best work in any one of the sites, or across the sites, where faculty members do their jobs.

II. Assessing and Rewarding Faculty Work

What the model provides is a systematic way of identifying and analyzing the significant components of LeBeau's project so that the work itself can be evaluated in relation to established professional standards and to the mission of the institution. But clarifying the nature of the work involved in relation to other faculty work is only part of the process. The other part includes the development of rigorous measures and methods of assessment. LeBeau's project, one can argue, entails important intellectual work. But the question remains, Is it any good? Can its quality be documented and appropriately rewarded?

With respect to possible ways of documenting and refereeing professional service, LeBeau's case is quite suggestive. The NEH grant proposal for his project, which has already gone through a peer-review process, can be made available; along with the proposal, the project's mandated annual evaluation and the curricular materials developed by participants can be reviewed by tenured colleagues and even by anonymous outside evaluators. Several colleagues have attended his seminar, so they could assess it. ESU could invite a distinguished scholar-teacher at another university to come to campus to review and evaluate the project—on the model of departmental and program evaluations customarily required by the university. Participants have already evaluated the quality of LeBeau's work as a scholar, teacher, and colleague and might be invited to expand on their evaluations. School principals could discuss the impact of his work on the discipline—if we assume that affecting the work of teachers and the learning of thousands of students might be characterized as "an impact on the discipline." There would seem, then, to be ample documentation, some of it quite conventional (e.g., the grant proposal) but some of it not (e.g., the new curricula and the evaluations of participants).

Ironically, while the participants are positioned to offer the most compelling analysis and assessment, their "authority" to do so may in fact be questioned. A reauthorization of evaluation itself is needed, a recognition that within the widely various missions of a particular institution, a wider range of voices needs to be involved in assessment. And LeBeau deserves to have a say as well. Not just the grant proposal, NEH peer reviews, annual reports, and participant evaluations but also LeBeau's reflections on the nature and quality of the work and its place in a national context should be included in the materials considered during the tenure review.

As mentioned above, we consider both the intellectual and the citizenship dimensions of LeBeau's work in our assessment of it. While we give more weight to the intellectual dimension, because it is substantially more important to the work of faculty members and the missions of their institutions, we also consider the citizenship dimensions as an indispensable part of the project's effectiveness. The quality of the work, its execution in its many dimensions, is important in determining its merit.

III. Further Elaborations and Applications of the Model

A. Institutional Service

While assisting in the interpretation and assessment of work like LeBeau's is one important purpose of this report, the model we are proposing is in no way restricted to such cases and is meant to apply generally to intellectual and citizenship work across the full range of faculty responsibilities. In that regard, and to illuminate the implications of such increased attention to the quality of such work, we will also consider a "service" that generally holds some prestige. Let us take, for example, the position of the director of graduate studies, one usually assigned to a tenured scholar who holds the admiration of his or her colleagues. This case, we believe, in some ways constitutes a minimal test of academia's willingness to reconsider its reward system to encourage distinguished service and to hold such service to rigorous standards.

Ordinarily falling into the current category of service, the position of the graduate director is imagined usually to mean little. In the way we normally see the job, the graduate director recruits and admits applicants, awards fellowships, keeps accurate records, maintains relations with the graduate school and the undergraduate program, and advises students about courses, requirements, examinations, and eventually job placement. Focusing on these features, we tend to perceive and interpret this work as responsible, and often honorable, citizenship, but citizenship nevertheless, marked by attention to managerial details and interpersonal skills.

But given the consequences for colleges and universities, for scholarship and teaching in our field and related fields, and for the morale of the future professoriat, the effective exercise of a graduate director's duties can clearly involve significant intellectual work. This work is particularly urgent now that so many departments in language and literature are undertaking curricular revision to integrate traditional approaches with new theoretical ones in literature, textual studies, and cultural studies. In such circumstances, the position of graduate director can, for example, require

- a knowledge of the field and the effective implementation of that knowledge in curricular planning and thoughtful leadership responsive to changes in the discipline;
- an ability to understand connections among the different intellectual interests of the graduate faculty, including new courses they are likely to teach and dissertations they are likely to inspire;

- familiarity with work in other fields that might complement each graduate student's department course work;
- serious attention to the role of graduate education in preparing new faculty members as scholars, teachers, and colleagues in a changing and increasingly diverse academic world.

Understood in this way, the "job" clearly entails intellectual work, and these features may constitute criteria for determining work of the highest quality. Doing the job can be, and often is, a site or opportunity for faculty members to do some of their most serious thinking, thereby enriching both their institutions and their disciplines. Because there is indeed a great deal at stake here and because of the potential for critically important intellectual interventions, we believe that their standards for evaluating such work should be as rigorous as the standards for publication and other work that generally receives our most conscientious scrutiny. To that end, the recommendations we offered above concerning the need for careful review and assessment apply here equally, and changes in customary practices are called for in at least two areas.

First, departments have to develop procedures for *documenting* such work. Documents in this case would include the graduate director's reports on individual graduate students; original or revised guidelines for graduate students planning their courses and preparing their dissertation prospectuses; original or revised guidelines for graduate faculty members, concerning their responsibilities as mentors and the role of particular graduate courses in the program; regular reports on the graduate program, not just noting but also analyzing enrollment patterns, attrition rates, graduation rates, and placement rates; proposals for changing curricula, requirements, or policies; and papers or other evidence of influential participation in national or regional conferences on graduate education.

Second, departments and graduate schools should establish procedures for rigorous *assessment*. For example,

- the director should submit annual self-evaluations of his or her own performance;
- graduate students, and even recent graduates of the program, should be asked to evaluate the director's guidance, helpfulness, and availability;
- members of the graduate faculty, especially the graduate committee, should review and comment on all pertinent documents;
- the department chair should annually assess the director's work;
- regular department self-studies and evaluations should take special care to assess the director's performance.

We realize that the documentation and assessment merely sketched here would require an extraordinary amount of labor; indeed, it will no doubt seem excessive, given the ordinary, supposedly "benign" neglect of such assessment. Moreover, assessing our own colleagues in such a way may seem intrusive, and particularly so because it is hard enough to get good people to do this work to begin with. So this combination of intensive labor and uncollegial surveillance makes such review unpleasant to consider, especially if the work itself does not seem to warrant it.

But, in the commission's view, the work clearly warrants it. It is in the vital interest of both particular institutions and the discipline itself to require and reward the highest quality of work in this position and positions of similar importance. Work that does not meet high standards should be viewed and documented as deficient and, in the worst cases, derelict. Excellent performance, as determined by rigorous assessment according to clear criteria and solid evidence, should be grounds for significant institutional reward, including promotion to full professor, significant merit increases in salary, and so on. The quality of the work, in its intellectual dimensions primarily but also in the dimensions of citizenship that include responsible administration and attention to the personal concerns of colleagues and students, requires our attention partly because it is fair to the merits of the faculty member involved and also because it is in our collective interest. Here is just another of the many sites of the faculty's intellectual work on which the life of the profession and of higher education itself depends, and it is perilous, at this time, to refuse to afford it the appropriate recognition.

B. Applied Work

The two cases considered thus far—coordinating a collaborative project with local schools and directing a graduate program—illustrate a common though by no means universal feature of what we are calling the intellectual dimension of faculty work in the domain of service. Work that emerges from a faculty member's substantial intellectual investment often manifests itself in leadership roles; the faculty member engages in the kind of shaping and transforming activity that gives direction to the work of others and that, through radical innovaton or the imaginative application of established professional practices, provides new directions for the field. Excellent work of this sort often influences other departments and programs, at home and at other institutions, and while there is no term in place right now to characterize it, we consider it "leadership," in the sense that we often think of certain scholars as "leaders" in their field.

What is ordinarily called applied work, in contrast to these perhaps more recognizable cases, involves faculty efforts that are usually solicited from outside the institution and so are more responsive to the needs and initiatives of others looking for someone with a particular expertise. Take the example of a faculty member in a rhetoric department who serves as a consultant on legislative testimony, offering workshops and individual guidance to those preparing to testify. This particular case, let us say, is pro bono, for the faculty member works primarily with representatives of community-based organizations (representing battered women's shelters, adult literacy programs, etc.) to familiarize them with the procedures of such testimony, to help draft position statements, and to take them through the process, the give-and-take, of such testimony.

How might a department and university most satisfactorily regard and assess such work? As noted frequently in this report, the weight given to the work would in part depend on the mission of the institution. It is conceivable, for example, that a college in a capital area, with established relations to federal or state legislatures and agencies, would attract some faculty members and students precisely because of those college-government connections. The value the institution is likely to assign to such work would differ from that assigned by a small, rural college having a different sense of its own mission and drawing faculty and students with different intellectual interests. We acknowledge the right of institutions to determine their priorities in this manner, though we remain concerned that these priorities be clearly articulated and that each faculty member have a clear sense of where his or her own work fits within this larger mission.

Whatever the weight or priority given a particular kind of work in relation to institutional mission, it is our view that the process by which that work is assessed should follow certain procedures and that the criteria by which it is judged should emerge from the best professional practice in the field. We emphasize that such work must be thoroughly scrutinized and assessed so that important work of high quality can be distinguished from routine work. With respect to the particular example under discussion, a strong case for the importance of the work involved and the quality of its execution might have these aspects:

- The faculty member's research and teaching interests center on political rhetoric and the unequal resources of various groups in society in finding a voice in policy discussions; thus the consulting work emerges from and enriches other kinds of intellectual work, and it can be seen as an essential aspect of the faculty member's continuing development.
- The consultations not only help the groups prepare testimony but also enable them to develop their own more forceful ways of continuing to represent their interests. In such a case, the quality of the work as teaching would, by commonly accepted standards, be considered higher, and so the work of consultation would be seen as more effective.
- The faculty member provides documentation so that others can determine the nature and quality of the work involved. This documentation could

take the form of actual testimony, letters from clients assessing the faculty member's help, and the faculty member's own description and analysis of his or her work.

In a relatively strong case like this, colleagues could find not just evidence of effective work but also clear indications that this work is a significant intellectual project for the faculty member and that it can in some way influence the standards for excellence governing other kinds of collaboration between faculty members and clients outside the academy.

In contrast, a weaker case would involve little or no direct connection between the consultation and the faculty member's intellectual work and growth in the domains of scholarship and teaching, would focus primarily on perfecting a particular piece of testimony without addressing the long-range needs of the client, and would provide no or only perfunctory documentation.

Again, the weight given to this work in part depends on where such an effort fits within the mission of the college or university, and we assume that advance negotiations among the administrators, chairs, and faculty members involved would clarify this matter (we return to this aspect in the next case study). The issue of most concern to the commission, however, has to do with the complex process of interpreting both the importance of the work (particularly the degree to which it entails intellectual work) and the quality of the work's execution.

IV. Holistic Evaluation, Faculty Mentoring, and Fitting the Model to the Institutional Mission

The case studies provided so far illustrate how reconceiving the boundaries of faculty work revises our understanding of the merits or deficiencies of faculty activities in the areas of research, teaching, and service. In each example, the traditional standards for assessment are not discarded but, rather, reexamined through the specifications in our model. These samples illustrate how institutions and scholars can enable their agendas to converge in a reward system. They suggest how both intellectual work and academic and professional citizenship can be acknowledged in ways that are equitable for and accountable to all publics served.

Convergence between responsibilities and rewards is crucial in rendering faculty work visible and establishing criteria for judging its merit. Responsibilities and rewards are created at the intersection between institutional and scholarly or professional interests, and so they must be consciously figured into assessment procedures used to evaluate faculty work. We therefore turn to yet another hypothetical case to illustrate the interplay between the generic categories proposed by our model and the local constraints imposed by particular institutions.

Professor Espana's department has recommended her, with two abstentions, for a tenure position in a large PhD-granting institution. She is one of four candidates this year in the Spanish department, one of the largest in the country. She has published one chapter from a manuscript volume in a leading journal in behavorial sciences (ten percent acceptance rate), and she is warmly supported in a letter by the editor of that journal. She has also published six refereed articles, two in widely recognized journals that specialize in literary scholarship and four in other specialties: computer applications, discourse analysis, and pedagogy.

Although Espana has not published as much as several colleagues at her rank have, she has produced software now used in computer laboratory sessions attended once a week by all first-year students of Spanish. Espana's teaching evaluations are in the good to very good category, but they are not exceptional when compared with institutional averages. The peer reviews of her work are extremely positive, but peer reviews for other candidates are equally enthusiastic. The result is that her file does not seem to stack up against the files of several other candidates from the same department.

In the traditional conception of research, teaching, and service there is no quality standard for Espana's major achievement, the creation and implementation of course software. Standards drawn either strictly from the discipline or solely from the institution's teaching evaluation structure render invisible the crucial line between the two. To assess Espana's work and the extent to which it represents significant intellectual work or academic and professional citizenship, one would have to ask whether her software development (1) creates or applies knowledge gained through research, (2) connects knowledge gained across disciplines and makes it available to the public, (3) connects knowledge gained through research and knowledge obtained through teaching, or (4) serves institutional and societal needs.

A. Institutional Specificity

To discuss the way our model can be useful in such a case, we must elaborate the case more fully, to take into account institutional specificity. Our hypothetical research institution has, in recent years, experienced an upsurge in enrollments in beginning Spanish, and Espana's work is clearly responsive to this development.

Faculty members in her department generally find such instruction onerous and do not share Espana's interest or training in language pedagogy. No one in the department is qualified to assess her expertise in current theory about using technology to teach foreign languages. In traditional practice, the institution would not have established the criteria for evaluating faculty work; published research would be the default standard for assessing intellectual work and faculty potential. Intellectual links between scholarship, teaching, and service, as illustrated in figure 2, are generally not explicitly addressed. Such time-consuming contributions to the institution as software development are viewed as "outside the discipline"; hence, peers are not in a position to assess it and are suspicious about the faculty member's qualifications to engage in such work.

More in keeping with the reconceptualized view of faculty work suggested in this report, Espana's institution has explicitly stated its criteria for weighing the intellectual work and the academic and professional citizenship of its faculty. The college dean and the Spanish department chair, recognizing that increasing numbers of beginning students were straining the department's capacity to co-ordinate and staff first-year programs, established a faculty committee to address the problem. Significantly, everyone involved understood that Espana's position was created to facilitate effective deployment of departmental resources in teaching beginning students. Accordingly, during her first year, Espana presented her software project as a way to alleviate staffing problems. The department subsequently made a projection for determining how that project would serve the institution. Goals and assessment criteria were developed.

Ultimately, when the time comes to put Espana's promotion file together, the chair or a designated committee will want to document the candidate's expertise in pedagogy and current theory as revealed in her relevant publications in refereed journals. Her supervisory skills, one aspect of her professional service, as well as her teaching capacities will be cross-referenced with her theoretical expertise attested to in journal publications. Furthermore, the department sees these enterprises as mutually informing pieces of the intellectual and professional work necessary to ensure success in reconfiguring the beginning Spanish program.

While the procedures in the case presented here would apply at any rank, we have chosen a tenure situation to illustrate the balance between institutional and individual responsibility suggested by our model. All too frequently in the tenure process, new faculty members may not "know the rules" at their institution; few venues exist for assisting them in professional development. Our model asks institutions to put all their cards on the table and entails a number of institutional obligations to the faculty member. In the hypothetical university discussed here, tenured faculty members would mentor new faculty members to help them develop a total professional profile and especially to establish which groups, professional meetings, and "how-to" publications in professional journals constitute peer evaluation in institutional professional service. Further, a faculty committee would advise Espana on maintaining a portfolio with sample syllabi, tests, remedial procedures, and documentation of links between research, teaching, and applied work or outreach (e.g., workshops, symposia, conferences, editing). On the committee's recommendation, candidate Espana would submit reviews of software from journals in applied linguistics and have experts in adjunct fields (e.g., a professor in educational technology from the school of education on campus) comment on the intellectual nature of her program.

Note that the role of the faculty mentor is not to judge the quality of this intellectual work but only to broaden the scope of a faculty member's perception of his or her work. A mentor has a difficult balance to maintain between an advocacy role and an informative one. This balance is all the more important because junior faculty members can easily confuse quantity with quality and the mentoring faculty member with a tenure advocate. Our main goal is to make junior faculty members aware of the broad range of values available in the various sites of faculty work. Without presuming the quality of the work accomplished, the mentor can help the junior faculty member to see the potential for serious intellectual work in sites not traditionally associated with intellectual work—for example, teaching, consulting, doing community projects—and to self-evaluate that work. How much of it is substantive new intellectual labor, and how much is academic and professional citizenship?

B. Negotiating Evaluation Criteria to Suit Institutional Mission

The example above reveals the proactive role that faculty members and institutions must assume in order to assess endeavors of their colleagues. It also reveals that this role varies according to the institution. At a small liberal arts college, Espana's portfolio might be viewed as displaying a preoccupation with research that reduces her availability for institutional support work or course development. At a technological institution that values "cutting edge" software development, her software program might be viewed as an example of "drill and kill" or as mechanically flawed, despite its evident success among students. At her own institution, the increased instructional capacities brought about by the use of her new software might outweigh its lack of genuine originality. The fair outcome of Espana's review depends on the clarity of purpose of the institution. For example, this candidate might not get tenure at a major PhD-granting institution that might find her intellectual work of insufficiently high quality. A small liberal arts college or a comprehensive university might, however, grant her tenure because they particularly value someone like Espana who is engaged in intellectually exciting "technology transfer" and who understands how to make connections among various sites of professional service, research, and teaching.

In either case, Espana's potential for intellectual growth can be assessed positively or negatively on the basis of *all* the intellectual effort she has committed to an institution. Her portfolio and reviews will clarify whether her current project represents a direction the institution wants to develop and whether the institution considers Espana the most appropriate person to pursue that direction. The assessment of how her research has informed her professional service will enable her reviewers to decide whether that service falls under the rubric "intellectual work" or "academic citizenship" and to assess its quality.

Whereas traditional practice has been to identify an institution's mission from its past appointments and tenure decisions, our model calls for defining this mission beforehand and then continually updating it, to account realistically for faculty members' changes in interest or intellectual development. The issue here is basic fairness and consistency throughout, involving both clear initial agreement and continual negotiations among faculty members, candidates, and administrators concerning how the individual case will be measured against the articulated standards of the institution. When standards appropriate to their institution have been articulated, fellow faculty members can decide about rewards on the basis of these standards.

What our model aims to make possible, then, is a more accurate perception of the range (across sites of teaching, scholarship, and service) of the work involved, the dimensions of both intellectual and citizenship work as they are evident in each of these sites, and the place of this work in the larger context of the faculty member's ongoing professional development. The model would also guide the assessment of this work, calling for thorough documentation and constant reference to a larger professional context—both the faculty member's other professional projects and the professional standards of particular disciplines. In diversifying the perception, interpretation, and evaluation of what has been achieved or not achieved, our model advances the larger effort of revealing more fully complex work and multiple responsibilities of the professoriat.

SECTION 3. QUESTIONS, PROBLEMS, ELABORATIONS, REFINEMENTS

I. Institutional Missions and Faculty Work: The Importance of Collaboration and Negotiation

In the previous section, all the case studies, but particularly the last of them, attempt to specify how a holistic conception of faculty responsibilities might be negotiated, documented, and evaluated. In the commission's view, a complete representation of faculty rights, roles, and responsibilities must include all contributions a faculty member makes to his or her academic institution and, through it, to society.

In other words, what academicians have to offer society is an *interrelated*, not an isolated, commitment to learning and education. In the profiles of individual faculty members, their roles and responsibilities emerge as a function of their being situated within a particular academic community, an institution that, through its mission, selects the set of goals its wishes to achieve vis-à-vis society. It must be understood that these missions (e.g., to provide a liberal arts education for students, to prepare them for major research efforts, or to train them for the professional world) represent the way colleges and universities agree to take on certain responsibilities toward society for which they and the faculty members within them are properly held accountable by the institution's constituencies.

That is to say, faculty members and institutions agree to take on reciprocal and mutually beneficial rights and responsibilities. Faculty members do not lay claim to rights in a vacuum, nor are they held to abstract "cosmopolitan" standards in a vacuum. Instead, both rights and responsibilities arise from, are mutually agreed on, and are cooperatively articulated by the members of the institution on the basis of its public commitments. Among other duties, professional organizations see to it that such commitments are spelled out, entered into freely, informed by models of effective practice in the field, and adhered to fairly in the conduct of the academy.

We believe that the MLA should use its prestige and stature to influence institutions and faculty members to consider the work faculty members do as a cooperative responsibility. Our profession needs to improve access for all faculty members, particularly those early in their careers, to the benefits of well-stated guidelines within which they can fruitfully conduct their lives and fulfill their multiple roles at any given time and place. With increasing emphasis on professional education, productivity, and outcomes, the very nature of a liberal education and its appropriate demands on and challenges for faculty members must be addressed by those of us in these fields, or we will have it addressed for us by outsiders. The only way to accomplish this task, arguably the heart of the humanities enterprise, is to have faculty members and administrators engage in intelligent collaboration to decide what kind of academic work can prove beneficial for all—the individual faculty member, the institution, and society at large.

II. Other Values Suggested for Inclusion in the Model

The commission recognizes that one appeal of the matrix model is the possibility for adding values or specifying them for particular disciplines or institutional settings. While not certain how to account for each of the following "values," the commission believes that it would be wise to incorporate them somehow into new conceptions of the faculty roles and reward system.

A. Faculty Growth and Development over a Career

Institutions must recognize that what constitutes appropriate practice in the weight accorded to teaching, scholarship, and service will fluctuate over an individual faculty member's career. Faculty members who have participated thoughtfully in evaluation of other faculty members for promotion, tenure, or annual reward are acutely aware that time is a crucial variable in evaluating a person holistically. The holistic judgment of the person, as distinct from the description and judgment of his or her work, is most clear here. Assessors are not merely making judgments about what has been accomplished, in what categories and with what quality, but also projecting what this faculty member is capable of and can be expected to do in the future.

Once these time factors become salient, it is obvious that there is a tacit value operating, or rather a set of them, concerning the development and growth of a faculty member's work over time and, by extension, the development and growth of the faculty member. Judges of faculty work expect that faculty members will grow and mature over time—progress, take up new ideas and interests, and enrich and deepen their understandings and skills. This expectation ensures that learning is as fundamental a value in the academy as knowledge achieved or produced and that faculty members should be learners throughout their careers, as evidenced in the development of their work over time. Examining faculty work from this perspective, one judges an individual's present achievements against past accomplishments and projects the direction and potential of a person's future work.

One reason for making the issue of time and the value of faculty growth and development explicit is that the commission wants to underline the need for institutions to provide flexibility for individuals in balancing their efforts and roles differently at different stages in their careers. Institutions need to be sensitive to the dynamic of faculty members' own self-reflective growth and learning. In addition, if faculty development itself is taken as an independent value that affects the health and vitality of institutions, then it should be encouraged and rewarded just as intellectual work is, with travel, fellowships, assigned time, honorary awards, and nonmaterial incentives.

B. Engagement and Interaction with Others

Teaching is, of course, a central function of faculty work. One dimension of value that everyone agrees is essential to quality in teaching is the teacher's personal, immediate engagement with students in interactions that inspire, facilitate, challenge, and in other ways enrich and enhance students' learning. The great teacher is often described as warm, caring, passionate, devoted to students, encouraging, demanding, and so on. Faculty members interpreting student evaluations of faculty teaching often emphasize the absence or presence of such personal attributes and effects on students. Most generally, these qualities may be thought of as the interpersonal skills by which faculty members actually accomplish their professional work and, more specifically, as the professional relationships through which they directly enhance the growth and achievement of others in higher learning and the uses of knowledge. Such relationships are relatively visible and valued in research teams, administrative leadership, school-college partnerships, committee work, advising, and external consultancies. Less obviously, faculty members advance the goals of the academy through their social-professional relationships and intellectual exchanges with peers, generating the stimulating and respectful environment called collegiality.

We think institutions should recognize the value of this ethical and interpersonal dimension and its role in evaluations, especially in holistic assessments of faculty members' effect on learners or, generally, on their academic environments and peers.

C. Effort

A certain credit in the assessment and reward of faculty work should go to sheer, conscientious labor. Effort—not only time but also intensity, or quality of attention and commitment—has a bearing on judgments about productivity: how much has been accomplished relative to the faculty member's investment in an activity or goal? Generally, extraordinary effort should be rewarded in professional tasks even when there is no expectation or achievement of intellectual work, although the rewards will necessarily be different ones. Finally, assignments, agreements, estimates, plans, and accounts of relative effort (e.g., the balancing of loads and assignments) are relevant to fair judgment of what can be expected and rewarded.

III. Disciplinary Knowledge and Faculty Achievement

Disciplines help to define the activities of faculty members as intellectual work by virtue of their connection with specific knowledge projects and learning enterprises. What disciplines offer is a way of understanding academic missions, and therefore a wide range of faculty work, as portable among institutions. But this function has been largely confined to research and scholarship. Understandably, in trying to acknowledge the potential for intellectual work in both teaching and service, professional organizations and policy advocates have tried to extend the model through analogy by defining intellectual work, or indeed professorial tasks of any kind, as necessarily discipline-based. The argument is that work suitable to be counted in the faculty roles and reward system can be recognized as professional only when it is an outgrowth of the faculty member's specialized training in an academic field.

We are uneasy with so narrow a conception of intellectual work, primarily because this constraint has the practical effect of eliminating much institutional service from consideration as intellectual work. We believe that a broader though carefully modulated concept is needed. Even with research and scholarship, one must qualify the disciplinary constraint by noting that faculty members' professional expertise is not fixed by their original training and disciplines but evolves through their professional growth, often in interdisciplinary or transdisciplinary transactions and projects. In addition, more and more knowledge projects are bursting the seams of single disciplines: in research, teaching, outreach, or institutional projects, faculty members may bring together multiple perspectives to study complex objects and events or to accomplish complex tasks. For the MLA fields, the claim of "disciplinarity" is becoming a significant intellectual problem as fields are internally reconfigured to incorporate, merge, or draw on other disciplines.

But teaching and service present other convincing reasons to enlarge the notion of intellectual work beyond the strict construction of "disciplinary knowledge." In teaching, important intellectual work occurs in curriculum design and pedagogical innovation concerning, for instance, relations between professional and liberal education; the roles, functions, content, and pedagogy of general education; or the varied learning needs of students (e.g., underprepared students, honors students, students of nontraditional age and purposes, ethnic and language minorities, disabled students, international students). Although often initiated by specialists and informed or driven by field-specific goals, for example in language education or cultural studies, such projects can develop and contribute to generalist, nondisciplinary knowledge enterprises that are increasingly important in reconceiving higher education.

Close examination of institutional and organizational service like working on a committee, chairing a department, or organizing a conference demonstrates that faculty members draw on at least two kinds of professional knowledge. The first is expert insider knowledge about such "disciplinary" matters as modes of inquiry, objects of study, teaching practices, and contexts of application, though we would not restrict the source of such knowledge to a single discipline. Less commonly recognized as professional knowledge is faculty-role expertise, which encompasses the generic skills and knowledge of faculty members, primarily acquired through experience and common to higher education contexts. Faculty-role expertise can range from basic knowledge of promotion and tenure rules and the duties of general advisors to the technical knowledge and political skills of administration. Faculty-role expertise, in institutional functions like governance or budgeting, is itself expanding and becoming increasingly professionalized like disciplinary knowledge.

The separation between the two kinds of professional faculty knowledge—the specialist base in disciplines or interdisciplinary formations versus faculty-role expertise—is not as sharp as might be expected. In most faculty work, the two sources of knowledge and exercise of expertise are blended and help to define the work as academic. In our view, however, faculty-role expertise alone is only rarely sufficient to qualify work as intellectual or to justify the highest academic rewards.

IV. Nontraditional Sites of Teaching and New Technologies

Teaching in the MLA fields often involves faculty members in teaching or consulting in settings outside the institutions in which they work. A substantial subset of such work involves teaching or supporting teaching in other sectors. Designating this work as teaching or service (outreach), or even in some cases as applied research, is often somewhat arbitrary, determined by local conventions. But the general rule is that it counts primarily as teaching when it is clearly sponsored by the faculty member's home institution as instruction (e.g., with course credit, listings in the catalog, credit toward instructional load). For example, like Professor LeBeau in our first case study, writing specialists work to connect the various settings for literacy practices and cultural instruction in writing and reading to one another and to higher education. Language specialists engage in similar activities. These activities may take faculty members as teachers, or in support of teaching, to a variety of settings: schools, prisons, nursing homes, workplaces, inner-city projects, legislative or legal contexts. Although these activities are primarily classified according to our scheme and most institutional practices as professional service (outreach), they should also count as teaching if they fit into a general pattern of intellectual or professional work on the teaching and learning of language or literature in nonuniversity settings.

Electronic media and new technologies for teaching are transforming pedagogy. (Professor Espana's efforts, described in our previous section, may be a case in point.) Part of the intellectual work of teaching now is the constant learning teachers must undertake to become conversant and skilled with these technologies and media and to put them to use for pedagogy. Using these evolving technologies requires teachers to develop substantive new technical, managerial, and intellectual skills and knowledge. In addition, they introduce significant conceptual, political, and ethical issues that need to be studied and connected to decision making and practices of teaching. Some teachers, as specialists, may become scholars in this area as well as pioneers in pedagogy, producers of new teaching materials, teachers of colleagues, disseminators of information and strategies on other campuses and at conventions, and communicators on electronic networks. In accord with institutional mission, the reward system should reflect these changing circumstances and new projects of the faculty.

V. Administration, Leadership, and the Managerial Component of Faculty Work

One possible refinement of our model concerns the place of faculty leadership in higher education and the concomitant managerial skills required. As with the case of the director of graduate studies discussed above, it is important for institutions to understand administration and other forms of faculty leadership more accurately as blending many different forms of knowledge, skills, and intellectual work across the various sites.

Responsibilities that we might call technical or managerial are an unacknowledged component within all faculty roles, requiring a range of organizational and often highly technical skills. Undoubtedly, the managerial element in scholarship (e.g., grant management, some kinds of editing) and in teaching (e.g., classroom management, overseeing student internships) has long been underappreciated, just as the intellectual component in service and teaching has been ignored. This element of faculty work is expanding alarmingly, however, for a variety of reasons. Among the most important are increasing federal and state regulations, greater vulnerability to lawsuits connected to these regulations, increasing demands for assessment in teaching and learning, and drastically curtailed budgets for administration and support staff. Department chairs and program directors are asked to do more and more with less and less support. Although some of the tasks required have an academic side (e.g., assessment), many are almost purely managerial. We believe it is incumbent on the profession to observe and document this increasing burden and to build it realistically into both faculty preparation and the reward system.

Administration, in institutional faculty roles like department chair or program director, is generally identified with the technical or managerial role when it has a distinct set of responsibilities, usually in a specific administrative appointment made by full-time administrators. We define it here as taking leadership responsibility that entails making important decisions, developing and articulating policy, coordinating or directing the tasks and responsibilities of others, reporting to and working closely with institutional or organizational administrators, and maintaining communications and good relationships among individuals and groups. *Leadership*, insofar as it is different from administration, involves simply the same type of responsibilities, in part or in whole, in a position that is not so clearly defined by the institution or organization as administrative: for example, as a senate member or chair of a task force. Both administration and leadership can be exercised within a professional organization (disciplinary or general higher education organization) as well as within one's home institution.

Faculty administration is more than simply "managerial." The increased responsibility and scope of action it involves open the door to intellectual work in the form of visions, plans, and the development and application of ideas in action with significant consequences. It presents major intellectual challenges and opportunities, and it should be evaluated for accomplishment in these terms. Strategic thinking as an administrator, certainly as a faculty administrator leading a program or unit, is focused by the teaching, research, and service missions of the unit; it may, for example, involve developing a new curriculum or revising one, developing a research center, fostering an intellectual community, and developing interdisciplinary projects and alliances. At its finest, when administration displays creativity and a strong intellectual dimension, the faculty leader's achievement merges all the faculty roles. It is important for the profession to analyze administrative performances, to recognize the scholarly and teaching as well as the service dimensions in them, and to make judgments about the quality of the intellectual work and other values that administrators pursue and demonstrate.

If higher education is to grow and nurture faculty leaders, the reward system (and their colleagues) must permit them to both lead and remain faculty members. Realistic responses to this problem may entail working out flexible patterns for faculty careers that involve moving in and out of heavier leadership responsibilities, including major administrative roles, while preserving faculty status.

VI. The Challenge of Assessing the Quality of Faculty Work in the Area of Service

We are well aware that colleges and universities do not necessarily reward, or even feel obliged to encourage, everything that their faculty members consider important. Traditionally, supporting and improving the quality of work in sites ordinarily associated with scholarship and teaching have been seen as the primary obligations. If work in the area of professional service is to enter the arena of rigorous evaluation and real rewards, the basis for its entry will be, at least in some measure, as follows: not only that a college or university deems professional service to include significant dimensions of intellectual work but also that guaranteeing the quality of such work is sufficiently relevant to the institution's mission to require the application of rigorous standards in a thoroughgoing and time-consuming process of assessment.

In this regard, our case studies may be instructive for yet one final reason. In addition to calling attention to the criteria and methods for discriminating and evaluating this sort of intellectual and citizenship work, the cases raise questions about the desirability of treating such work in the same way that scholarship and teaching are ordinarily treated. These questions involve both institutions and individual faculty members.

First, colleges and universities and individual departments within them will have to care that such work is more than simply "good citizenship," that it constitutes important faculty work. They will also have to decide that assessing and enabling the quality of such work, in all its aspects and especially in its intellectual dimensions, fall within the institution's responsibilities to its own traditional purposes, its students, and society.

Second, we do not assume that everyone engaged in such work would welcome its "elevation" to the level of more traditional scholarship and teaching. If it is to count more, it will be held more accountable. Simply doing it will no longer count, just as simply writing an article or simply teaching a course does not really count. Such work will have to be demonstrably excellent work, work that is marked as superior and that will expand the boundaries of knowledge and/or reshape pedagogical practice. Work like this, that at the present time might in itself earn modest regard and reward (if only because of the moral claim it makes on colleagues' gratitude) could, when assessed according to rigorous standards, *harm* one's claims on tenure or salary increase. There is no way of avoiding the possibility that, in raising the stakes, one increases the risk, a consequence that is in our judgment both inevitable and desirable if the full range of faculty work is to be recognized.

As we have suggested in our introduction, determining the quality of such work is now a subject of much discussion in learned societies and higher education associations. The prevailing view concerning assessment holds that documentation must be provided, norms established, and authorities identified to undertake the evaluations. Although we invoke these categories (documentation, criteria, referees) to make the evaluation of professional service parallel to the evaluation of traditional scholarship and teaching, we recognize that equivalency is far from being established. There is not at this time the same system of peer review in place for evaluating work in the area of professional service, nor is there a tradition of critical judgment informing our assessment of such efforts, nor is there, yet, a corps of established referees who possess the recognized authority to undertake such assessment. That is to say, a great deal of work remains to be done, first in establishing policies and procedures that can claim strong faculty, administration, and public support and then in integrating these policies and procedures with other practices currently in place. It is as a step toward achieving this comprehensive goal that we have proposed our model and explored some of its applications.

CONCLUSION

Our intent throughout this report has been to suggest ways that we might rethink the contexts of faculty work. Although our charge was to focus on faculty service, we saw from the beginning that such a focus was impossible without considering the entire range of faculty activity. In reflecting on this activity, we discovered that we often misidentify what we value. Frequently, in fact, faculty work is invisible because it is not well understood. Our basic argument has been that the conventional categories used to characterize faculty work— teaching, research, and service—often fail to represent adequately what faculty members do. Because faculty work takes its meaning now—and so becomes visible or invisible, respected or disdained, supported or neglected—from the status of the institutional sites where it happens, our report's purpose, in part, is to expand the range of sites that secure visibility, respect, and support.

The model we have proposed, therefore, emphasizes seeing and interpreting things in different and more complicated ways. Our case studies illustrate that understanding faculty work is a complex interpretive practice, and the model we propose for rethinking this process, while it does not abandon the traditional categories, seeks to clarify the nature and value of faculty work in new ways. In our view, faculty members serve higher education in a wide variety of institutional locations—the journal, the classroom, the faculty meeting room. Serious intellectual work of the kind and quality crucial to the mission of higher learning can find a public expression in activities as diverse as publishing an article or developing a curriculum or directing a graduate program or conducting a collaborative program with local school teachers. As a consequence, we strongly recommend that institutions and professional organizations recognize a wide range of possibilities for types of achievement and for the audience of intellectual work.

We believe that all institutions should analyze and reflect on the issues our report has raised. Reflective analysis and conversation are central to the study of language and literature, and our report is, among other things, a call for faculty members themselves to enter the conversation. Our report parallels the national discussion about faculty responsibilities, and it is not unrelated, of course, to the debate about the institution of tenure. Failure to engage in these dialogues will doubtless mean that others will define our roles for us and determine their worth. Part of the larger debate centers on the assessment of faculty work, and one of the obvious implications of the model we propose is that higher education will be called on to rethink the evaluation and rewarding of faculty activity.

If the interpretation of faculty work is, as we argue, more complex than the conventional, tripartite model assumes, the assessment and rewarding of that work are no less complex. Our report maintains that assessment and reward should be related directly to intellectual work and citizenship activities that are professionally significant, and the case studies suggest how faculty work that falls outside the conventional model can be documented, interpreted, and evaluated.

The means of assessing faculty work will tend to be what they have always been: peer review; written and oral testimony from administrative superiors, colleagues, students, and alumni; scores from standardized tests; portfolios; self-evaluations; data from citation indexes; public response; and the like. Similarly, the criteria for judging the value and excellence of faculty work in all three sites can be established. The model we propose, however, calls for the involvement of more constituencies (e.g., legislators, other policy makers, trustees, students, employers, and higher education associations) than evaluation has required in the past. Furthermore, we believe that the entire assessment process should take account of the changing nature of higher education. Documenting, interpreting, and judging the quality of faculty work is, of course, time consuming and difficult. The application of the model can assist institutions in classifying activities, but the model will not generate anything automatically, which is why we stress that its schematic representation is a heuristic device, intended to promote different ways of thinking.

Models for reconceiving faculty work and for developing new contexts for assessment and reward must be, we think, dynamic, flexible, and negotiable. They will have to recognize different institutional missions and changing needs. They will have to see assessment and reward as a negotiated process, one that makes more explicit the dialogue among faculty members, chairs, deans, and experts in the field and that is broadened to include the interests of the constituencies noted above. As institutions develop their own means of assessment, they should consider the wide range of activities that require faculty members' professional expertise. These would include, in addition to activities more traditionally recognized, inter- and cross-disciplinary projects, teaching that occurs outside the traditional classroom, acquisition of the knowledge and skills required by new information technologies, practical action as a context for analyzing and evaluating intellectual work, and activities that require collective and collaborative knowledge and the dissemination of learning to communities not only inside but also outside the academy.

Institutions should recognize that intellectual work and citizenship activities change over the course of a faculty member's career and that faculty roles change over time—that faculty members are called on at different stages of their careers to perform different tasks. In this regard, the commission believes that faculty members must have the freedom to negotiate the balance among different kinds of faculty work commitments at any given time and to change this balance in their career development. In particular, we believe that faculty members, especially junior faculty members, have a continuing right to help formulate clear guidelines within which they can effectively pursue their intellectual projects and develop their professional careers.

In the final meeting of our commission we observed that a large part of our work had centered, without any conscious intent, on the metaphor of sight, suggesting no doubt our desire to see things in a new way—to revise. We also reminded ourselves that much of our discussion had focused on discussion itself, reflecting our desire to foster a profession-wide conversation about the issues raised in our report. We now offer this report to our colleagues in the fields encompassed by the MLA as part of the continuing dialogue about our work in language and literature and with the invitation to those colleagues to join us in rethinking what we do and how we value it.

NOTES

[1]The general model of faculty work proposed in this document adapts and extends concepts and terms first developed in Phelps.

[2]*Research* and *scholarship* are sometimes used in disciplines of language and literature to distinguish between empirical studies (research) and textual and theoretical inquiry (scholarship), but this distinction is not maintained across disciplines. Institutional promotion and tenure documents generally treat the two as synonyms for disciplinary and professional inquiry in general, as well as for the production or performance of creative works. By combining the terms, we leave their interpretation open to either synonymous or contrastive usage. We do not, however, employ the Boyer-Rice redefinition of *scholarship*, which conceptualizes the term as roughly equivalent to our "intellectual work"—that is, the intellectual component of faculty work in all sites. In contrast to our decision to map this value against the traditional sites or missions of faculty work, Boyer, in *Scholarship Reconsidered*, attempts to disrupt these by introducing a new set of distinctions only partly equivalent to the old sites: the scholarship of discovery, integration, teaching, and application. Rice has elaborated these concepts.

[3]We use *professional service* inclusively, in contradistinction to the specialized use of it to mean "applied work" or "outreach," as in Elman and Smock, Lynton, and Lynton and Elman.

WORKS CITED AND CONSULTED

"ADE Statement of Good Practice: Teaching, Evaluation, and Scholarship." *ADE Bulletin* 113 (1996): 53–55.

ADFL. "Policy Statements on the Administration of Foreign Language Departments." *ADFL Bulletin* 25.3 (1994): 119–23.

American Historical Association Ad Hoc Committee on Redefining Scholarly Work. *Redefining Historical Scholarship*. Washington: AHA, 1993.

American Sociological Association Task Force. "Recognizing and Rewarding the Professional and Scholarly Work of Sociologists." Draft report. Amer. Sociological Assn., Washington. 1994.

Association of American Geographers Special Committee on Faculty Roles and Rewards. *Reconsidering Faculty Roles and Rewards in Geography*. Washington: AAG, 1994.

Booth, Wayne C. "The Idea of a University—as Seen by a Rhetorician." *The Vocation of a Teacher*. Chicago: U of Chicago P, 1988. 309–34.

Boyer, Ernest L. *Scholarship Reconsidered: Priorities of the Professoriate*. Princeton: Carnegie Foundation for the Advancement of Teaching, 1990.

Braskamp, Larry A., and John C. Ory. *Assessing Faculty Work: Enhancing Individual and Institutional Performance*. San Francisco: Jossey-Bass, 1994.

Diamond, Robert M., and Bronwyn E. Adam, eds. *The Disciplines Speak: Rewarding the Scholarly, Professional, and Creative Work of Faculty*. Washington: Amer. Assn. for Higher Education, 1995.

———, eds. *Recognizing Faculty Work: Reward Systems for the Year 2000*. New Directions for Higher Education 81. San Francisco: Jossey-Bass, 1993.

Edgerton, Russell, Patricia Hutchings, and Kathleen Quinlan. *The Teaching Portfolio: Capturing the Scholarship in Teaching*. Washington: Amer. Assn. for Higher Education, 1991.

Elling, Barbara. "Review and Evaluation of Faculty at the State University of New York, Stony Brook." *ADFL Bulletin* 16.1 (1984): 18–22.

Elman, Sandra E., and Sue M. Smock. *Professional Service and Faculty Rewards: Toward an Integrated Structure*. Washington: Natl. Assn. of State Universities and Land-Grant Colleges, 1985.

Joint Policy Board for Mathematics. *Recognition and Rewards in the Mathematical Sciences*. Washington: Amer. Mathematical Soc., 1994.

Lynton, Ernest. *Making the Case for Professional Service*. Washington: Amer. Assn. for Higher Education, 1995.

Lynton, Ernest A., and Sandra E. Elman. *New Priorities for the University*. San Francisco: Jossey-Bass, 1987.

Massey, William F., Andrea K. Wilger, and Carol Colbeck. "Overcoming 'Hollowed Collegiality.'" *Change* July-Aug. 1994: 11–20.

MLA Committee on Academic Freedom and Professional Rights and Responsibilities. "Advice to Search Committee Members and Job Seekers on Faculty Recruitment and Hiring." New York: MLA, 1993.

"MLA Statement of Professional Ethics." *Profession 92*. New York: MLA, 1992. 75–78.

Park, Shelley M. "Research, Teaching, and Service: Why Shouldn't Women's Work Count?" *Journal of Higher Education* Jan.-Feb. 1996: 46–84.

Phelps, Louise Wetherbee. *Writing Program Promotion and Tenure Guidelines*. Syracuse: Writing Program, Coll. of Arts and Sciences, Syracuse U, 1989.

"Report of the Commission on the Future of the Profession, Spring 1982." *PMLA* 97 (1982): 940–58.

Rice, Eugene. "The New American Scholar: Scholarship and the Purposes of the University." *Metropolitan Universities Journal* 1 (1991): 7–18.

"The Work of Arts Faculties in Higher Education." Draft report. Natl. Office for Arts Accreditation in Higher Education, Reston; Natl. Architectural Accrediting Board, Washington; Landscape Architectural Accrediting Board, Washington. 1993.

Guidelines for Evaluating Computer-Related Work in the Modern Languages

MLA COMMITTEE ON COMPUTERS AND EMERGING TECHNOLOGIES IN TEACHING AND RESEARCH

The Statement on Computer Support, adopted by the Modern Language Association in 1993, highlights the importance of new electronic technologies for the humanities and provides the basis for departmental and institutional support of modern language faculty members who use such technologies and integrate them into their work. As the statement notes, "Generating, gathering, and analyzing texts electronically is becoming a necessity for all education, especially for the contributions made by the humanities." As a supplement to the 1993 statement, the following guidelines address means of evaluating the scholarship, teaching, and service of faculty members who study, develop, and use electronic technologies in their work.

Because the role of computer technologies in the study of language, literature, and writing is evolving, departments wishing to hire and retain faculty members centrally concerned with the application of these emerging technologies to the humanities need to consider the tasks, support, and evaluative procedures involved. And faculty members who pursue computer-related work as part of their formal assignments should be prepared to make explicit the results, theoretical basis, and intellectual rigor of their work, as well as its relevance to the discipline. The following guidelines, which deal with both the hiring and the promotion processes, are designed to help departments and faculty members build productive working relations, effective evaluation procedures, and means of disseminating the results of computer-related work.

217

Guidelines for Search Committees and Job Candidates

When departments seek candidates with computer expertise or when candidates wish to have such work considered an important part of their positions, there should be an initial understanding of the recognition given to computer-related work and of what electronic facilities are available or planned.

Departments should ensure that computer-related work can be evaluated within their tenure and promotion procedures. In particular, search committees should be prepared to discuss the following with all candidates:

- how the department evaluates research and publication in computers and the humanities,
- what importance is attached to the development of new software and what criteria are used to evaluate such software,
- what credit is given for the integration of electronic technologies into courses,
- what recognition is given to professional activities relating to computing, and
- what criteria are used to evaluate faculty members who provide computing support to colleagues, staff, and students.

As candidates discuss the teaching, scholarship, and service responsibilities of an academic position, it is important that they ask questions, such as the following, about the role of electronic technologies in the department and the university: Are technical support staff members available to the department's faculty members and students? Does the department plan to undertake initiatives in the use of electronic technologies? What access do faculty members and students have to computer facilities and resources?

Guidelines for Reappointment, Tenure, and Promotion Reviews

Computer-related work, like other forms of scholarship, teaching, and service, should be evaluated as an integral part of a faculty member's dossier, as specified in an institution's guidelines for reappointment, promotion, and tenure. Faculty members are responsible for making a case for the value of their projects, articulating the intellectual assumptions underlying their work, and documenting their time and effort. In particular, faculty members expecting recognition for computer-related work should ensure that their projects remain compatible with departmental needs, as well as with criteria for reappointment, tenure, and promotion. Periodic reviews provide an opportunity to assess the match between a faculty member's scholarly and pedagogical development and the department's needs and expectations.

Because appropriate roles for computer technology in the study of language, literature, and writing are still emerging, faculty members should be prepared to explain

- what theory informs their work,
- why their work is useful to the discipline, and
- the evidence of rigor and intellectual content in their work.

Documentation of projects might include internal or external funding, awards and professional recognition, and reviews and citations of work either in print or in electronic journals.

For subsequent evaluation of professional service, faculty members should maintain a record of the duties involved in activities such as organizing and managing a lab facility, increasing the meaningful use of electronic media in instruction, training student aides or faculty colleagues, and moderating an electronic discussion group.

Pedagogy and scholarship involving technology often entail collaborative or interdisciplinary work. Departments need to find appropriate ways to evaluate the faculty member's role in such work. This process may include finding evaluators with expertise in both specific disciplines and computer technology; these experts are best qualified to evaluate and translate accomplishments in a rapidly changing field. Sources that may help departments choose appropriate evaluators include the editorial boards of computer-related journals (e.g., *CALICO Journal, Computers and the Humanities, Computers and Composition, Hypermedia*), the committees focusing on electronic technologies in appropriate scholarly and professional organizations (e.g., the MLA, CCCC, ACTFL, the AATs, NCTE), the courseware review sections of modern language journals (e.g., *CALICO Journal, Computers and the Humanities, Computers and Composition, Foreign Language Annals, French Review, Hispania, IALL Journal, IDEAL: Issues and Developments in English and Applied Linguistics, Language Learning Journal, Literary and Linguistic Computing*, the Northeast Conference *Newsletter*, the Institute for Academic Technology's *Newsletter* and *Research Reports, TESOL Journal, Tongues Untied, Unterrichtspraxis*), *Humanities Computing Yearbook* (Oxford UP), and the latest edition of the *CALICO Resource Guide* (Durham: CALICO).

**Advocacy
in the
Classroom**

Problems and Possibilities

◆

Edited by
Patricia Meyer Spacks

◆

St. Martin's Press
1996 · xiii & 445 pp.
Paper ISBN 0-312-16127-1
$26.95 (MLA members $21.56)

"This well-organized, provocatively diverse collection should promote dialogue and discussion among academics."

PUBLISHERS WEEKLY

" *Teachers* have the power to change students' minds," writes Patricia Meyer Spacks in the introduction to *Advocacy in the Classroom*. In this collection of essays on classroom advocacy in theory and practice, educators from a range of disciplines and political persuasions explore the possibilities and limitations of the influence teachers have over students.

The thirty-nine essays in *Advocacy in the Classroom*, the product of a national conference sponsored by fifteen major academic organizations, define three broad areas of inquiry: the history of advocacy and of attitudes toward it, principles for separating appropriate from inappropriate advocacy, and classroom practice. Drawing on issues in different historical periods, the book analyzes a range of topics, from the threat of oppression implicit in the principle of political advocacy to the nature of "good" advocacy. Contributors also examine relevant legal decisions, the argument for "fight training" in high schools, the dilemmas of teaching in public schools, and the special responsibilities of guiding culturally diverse students. A final section offers responses to the preceding essays.

Contributors

Felicia Ackerman	Troy Duster	Tom Jehn	Michael A. Olivas	C. Jan Swearingen
Shawny Anderson	Judith Entes	Ray Linn	Julie A. Reuben	John O. Voll
Angela Anselmo	Ernestine Friedl	Andrea A. Lunsford	Michael Root	Jeffrey Wallen
Ernst Benjamin	Penny S. Gold	Peter Markie	Jayne E. Sbarboro	Michael D. Yates
Michael Bérubé	Gerald Graff	Janice McLane	Richard Seeburger	Lambert Zuidervaart
Myles Brand	Carolyn G. Heilbrun	Louis Menand	Peter M. Shane	
Samuel W. Calhoun	Hilde Hein	Helene Moglen	Mark C. Smith	
Martha Chamallas	Susan E. Henking	Keith Moxey	Geoffrey R. Stone	
Whitney Davis	Gertrude Himmelfarb	Richard Mulcahy	Nadine Strossen	

Published by St. Martin's Press and available from the

Modern Language Association

10 Astor Place ◆ New York, NY 10003-6981 ◆ Phone: 212 614-6382 ◆ Fax: 212 477-9863

The
MLA Guide
to the
Job Search

*A Handbook for
Departments and
for PhDs and
PhD Candidates
in English and
Foreign Languages*

The MLA Guide to the Job Search

**A Handbook for Departments
and for PhDs and PhD
Candidates in English
and Foreign Languages**

◆

English Showalter
Howard Figler
Lori G. Kletzer
Jack H. Schuster
Seth R. Katz

◆

1996 · c. 180 pp.
Paper ISBN 0-87352-682-1
$10.00 (MLA members $8.00)

or over two decades graduate students—more than 25,000 of them—have relied on the Modern Language Association's guide for job seekers in the academic market, *A Career Guide for PhDs and PhD Candidates in English and Foreign Languages.* Now retitled *The MLA Guide to the Job Search,* this widely used resource has been updated and greatly expanded.

The guide offers students preparing to enter the job market of the 1990s invaluable advice on seeking jobs at two- and four-year colleges and universities, as well as outside the academy. It suggests when to start looking, how to begin, where to apply, whom to ask for letters of reference, which materials to include in a dossier, and what to expect from interviews and campus visits.

A new chapter by Howard Figler explores the many career opportunities outside higher education for PhDs in the humanities. Figler discusses which academic skills are valued in the nonacademic job market, what strategies job seekers can use to research fields and find positions, and how graduate students can make the transition from the academy to other fields.

The guide also offers advice to department administrators, on how to recruit prospective teachers, screen likely candidates, conduct interviews, and ensure that applicants receive fair and courteous treatment. It specifies ways to prepare graduate students for their careers and reviews types of job-placement services that institutions can offer.

Other sections of the guide provide useful statistics about the academic and nonacademic job markets, speculate on future prospects for academics, reprint policy statements made by MLA committees, and suggest additional resources for applicants and employers.

The MLA Guide to the Job Search includes

- Advice on preparing for and conducting an academic job search, from graduate work to the job offer

- Information on seeking employment in two-year colleges, four-year colleges, and universities

- Discussion of the nonacademic job market: how it differs from the market in academia and how PhDs can apply their training to it

- Advice for departments on handling each stage of the hiring process effectively

- Essays examining the past, present, and future of the academic and professional labor markets

- MLA statements on recruitment, hiring, and employment practices

- Dos and don'ts for interviewers and interviewees

- Statistics on the employment of PhDs in languages and literatures

- Sources of further information

---

10 Astor Place ◆ New York, NY 10003-6981 ◆ Phone: 212 614-6382 ◆ Fax: 212 477-9863